Professional Review Guide for the CHP and CHS Examinations
2005 Edition

Nanette B. Sayles, Ed.D, RHIA, CCS, CHP

Patricia Schnering, RHIA, CCS

PRG Publishing, Inc.
Professional Review Guides, Inc.

Professional Review Guide for the CHP and CHS Examinations, 2005 Edition

Published by:

PRG Publishing, Inc.
Professional Review Guides
P. O. Box 528
St. Petersburg, Florida 33731
Phone: (727) 526-3163
FAX: (727) 526-4474
Toll Free: (888) 383-PRG1~or~(888) 383-7741
E-mail: PJSPRG@aol.com
Web Page: http//www.prgpublishing.com

ISBN: 1-932152-23-7

Printed in the United States of America

Author: Nanette Sayles, ED.D, RHIA, CCS, CHP
                Patricia Schnering, RHIA, CCS

Disclaimer of Warranty
It is the authors' sincerest hope that each examination candidate using this review guide will pass the national examination. The authors suggest that the candidates avail themselves of all resources possible including text books, class notes and materials obtained during their educational process, attendance at examination review sessions, participation in study groups and the use of other examination review books.

The information and material contained in the book and on the CD-ROM are provided "as is" without warranty of any kind, express or implied, including without limitation any warranty concerning the accuracy, adequacy or completeness of such information or material or the results to be obtained from using such information or material. Neither Professional Review Guides, Inc., PRG Publishing, Inc., nor the authors shall be responsible for any claim attributable to errors, omissions or other inaccuracies in the information or material contained in this book or the CD-ROM. And in no event shall Professional Review Guides, Inc., PRG Publishing, Inc. or the authors be liable for direct, indirect, special, incidental or consequential damages arising out of the use of such information or material. Professional Review Guides Inc. and PRG Publishing, Inc. assume no liability for the data contained herein.

About the Authors

Nanette B. Sayles, ED.D, RHIA, CCS, CHP

Nanette Sayles is a 1985 graduate of the University of Alabama at Birmingham Medical Record Administration (now Health Information Management) program. She earned her Masters of Science in Health Information Management (1995) and her Masters in Public Administration (1990) from the University of Alabama at Birmingham. She earned her doctorate in Adult Education from the University of Georgia (2003). She is currently the Program Director/Assistant Professor for the Health Information Management and Technology programs at Macon State College in Macon, Georgia. She has a wide range of Health Information Management experience in hospitals, consulting, system development/implementation and education. She is currently the President of Middle Georgia Health Information Management Association, on the Board of Directors for the Georgia Health Information Management Association and on the American Health Information Management Association's Research Committee.

Patricia J. Schnering, RHIA, CCS

Patricia Schnering is the founder of PRG Publishing, Inc. and Professional Review Guides, Inc. She is a self-employed entrepreneur, working as owner, author and publisher for Professional Review Guides, Inc. and PRG Publishing, Inc. Mrs. Schnering is a 1995 graduate of the Health Information Management program at St. Petersburg College in St. Petersburg, Florida. In 1998 she was certified as a CCS and in 1999 she received her RHIA certification. Her education includes a Baccalaureate degree from the University of South Florida in Tampa, Florida with a major in Business Administration. Since 1993, she has worked in Health Information Services supervisory positions, as a HIM consultant and as an adjunct HIM instructor at St. Petersburg College. She has been involved in her local, state and national association since 1992 and has served on various committees and as a director for FHIMA. She was the recipient of the FHIMA Literary Award in 2000. Patricia has been a member of AHIMA Assembly on Education since 1996.

Acknowledgments

First and foremost, I want to thank my husband, Mark, for his patience while I worked on this project. It has taken a lot of time – time that I could have spent with him. Next, I would like to thank my parents, George and Jeanette Burchfield, who taught me to work hard and the importance of education. Finally, I would be remiss not to thank Pat Schnering for editing this book as well as providing some of the questions that it contains. Without her hard work, this study guide would not exist.

Nanette B. Sayles, MSHIM, MPS, RHIS, CCS

<u>Acknowledgments</u>

I especially wish to express my gratitude to Nanette Sayles, the author, who was instrumental in creating this book. At the AOE meeting in 2002, educators were asking if PRG Publishing was going to do a review guide for the new CHP and CHS certifications. Nanette said she would love to do the book. I was ECSTATIC! Nanette is a seasoned professional who is the director for both a RHIA and RHIT program at Macon State College. She should be the poster child for AHIMA's culture of life long learning. Her level of energy and dedication to the profession is amazing. I have the utmost respect for her and admire her as a friend as well as a professional colleague

There are some very special people in my life who make the work possible.
- My husband, Bob, as always, continues to keep me grounded while I tend to spin off in space while I work on the books.
- My mother, Emma Miller, is my role model for perseverance leading to success. She embodies grace, courage, strength and endurance.
- A special thanks to my daughter, Holly Hiltz, for helping in a myriad of ways throughout the year – from manning the office, to helping in the editing process, to being a cheerleader on developing new projects.

My thanks would not be complete without acknowledging all the HIM/HIT professionals, educators and students who support our efforts by using PRG Publishing products and letting us know how we can improve the products. Thank you for the letters and words of encouragement.

My reward is knowing that the materials you study here may assist you in preparing for the challenge of the examination. Whichever credential you seek, I wish you the very best now and throughout your career.

Until we meet......

Patricia J. Schnering, RHIA, CCS

Table of Contents

Introduction

Introduction

With the advent of the Health Insurance Portability and Accountability Act (HIPAA), the American Health Information Management Association (AHIMA) and the Healthcare Information Management and Systems Society (HIMSS) have developed a certification program for healthcare privacy and security. Three new healthcare certifications were created. AHIMA sponsors the certification: *Certified in Healthcare Privacy* (CHP). HIMSS sponsors the certification: *Certified in Healthcare Security*. Together, AHIMA and HIMSS, jointly sponsor the combined certification: *Certified in Healthcare Privacy and Security* (CHPS). The examinations for the CHP and CHS are administered by AHIMA.

The Health Insurance Portability and Accountability Act (HIPAA) requires covered entities to name a privacy official and a security official. Many of the covered entities will have one person responsible for both privacy and security. The privacy and security officials have mandatory duties under the HIPAA privacy and information security regulations. Both the privacy and security officers are concerned with the development of policies and procedures protecting data from inappropriate use or disclosure as well as staff training as required by HIPPA.

The AHIMA Candidate Handbook describes the privacy and security officers as having the following duties and concerns:

The privacy officer is responsible for:
- development and implementation of privacy-related policies and procedures
- the flow of protected health information within and outside the covered entity

The security officer is responsible for:
- management and supervision of use of security measures to protect data
- conduct of personnel in relation to data protection
- identifying and securing information under the control of healthcare organizations

The AHIMA Candidate Handbook further describes the CHP, CHS and CHPS credentials as follows:

> The *Certified in Healthcare Privacy* (CHP) credential denotes advanced competency in designing, implementing and administering comprehensive privacy protection programs in all types of healthcare organizations.
>
> The *Certified in Healthcare Security* (CHS) credential denotes advanced competency in designing, implementing and administering comprehensive security protection programs in all types of healthcare organizations.
>
> The *Certified in Healthcare Privacy and Security* (CHPS) credential denotes advanced competency in designing, implementing and administering comprehensive privacy and security protection programs in all types of healthcare organizations.

There are competencies that are common to both the privacy and security roles. These "core" content tasks are applicable to both exams.

Core Tasks common to both the privacy and security roles
- laws and regulations and accreditation standards protecting data from unauthorized access
- staff training programs
- policy and procedure documentation
- risk assessments and gap analysis of policies, procedures and practices
- development, implementation and compliance of privacy and security programs
- business relationships and contracts

In addition, there are competencies that are specific to the privacy role for the CHP certification and to the security role for the CHS certification.

The CHPS exam is no longer available. In August of 2004, AHIMA and HIMSS decided to discontinue the CHPS Examination and the Complementary CHPS Examinations effective January 1, 2005. To obtain the designation of CHPS certification you must pass both the Certified in Healthcare Privacy (CHP) examination for the CHP certification as well as the Certified in Healthcare Security (CHS) examination.

Layout of the CHP and CHS Certification Examinations

To help in visualizing the layout of the two examinations, we have developed several tables for you beginning with a snapshot of each examination in Table 1.

Table 1
- Shows the break out of competencies that are common to both roles as well as those that are specific to each certification.
- Some questions on the examinations are not used in scoring. This table also shows the number of questions for each exam and the break out of questions that are scored and not scored.

In developing each of the examinations, some questions that were included on the test are "pretest items". These pretest questions are used for testing questions, test banks and for future examinations. These questions are not used for scoring the exam.

Table 1 CHP and CHS CERTIFICATIONS WITH QUESTION CONTENT BY TYPE OF QUESTIONS							
EXAM	CORE CONTENT QUESTIONS		PRIVACY QUESTIONS		SECURITY QUESTIONS		TOTAL Questions On Examinations
	Number Questions	Percentage Of Exam	Number Questions	Percentage Of Exam	Number Questions	Percentage Of Exam	
CHP	35	30%	85	70%			120 questions
	30 scored		70 scored				100 scored
	5 pretest		15 pretest				20 pretest
CHS	35	30%			85	70%	120 questions
	30 scored				70 scored		100 scored
	5 pretest				15 pretest		20 pretest

Weights for Domains by Percentage of Questions in the Domain

Weights for each Domain are assigned by the number of questions in the Domain. Thus, each weight correlates to the degree of emphasis, or importance, given to each Domain (with the corresponding task statements) as it relates to the profession.

The following tables and charts (Table 2 with Chart 1 and Table 3 with Chart 2) display the number of questions and the weights that were assigned in percentage of questions in each domain to the total number of questions.

Table 2 Shows the CHP Examination question content weight by scored questions.

Table 2 Certified In Healthcare Privacy Examination Question Content		
Competency by Domain	Number of Questions in Domain	Weight by Percentage of Questions in Domain
1. CHP Core Tasks	30	30%
2. Legal, Ethical and Accreditation Issues	15	15%
3. Business Relationships and Contracts	8	8%
4. Policies and Procedures	8	8%
5. Compliance, Program Management and Public Relations	6	6%
6. Security Technology	10	10%
7. Health Information Management	8	8%
8. Individual Rights	15	15%
Total Number of Questions Scored	100	100%

Chart 1 CHP Competencies by Percentage of Examination

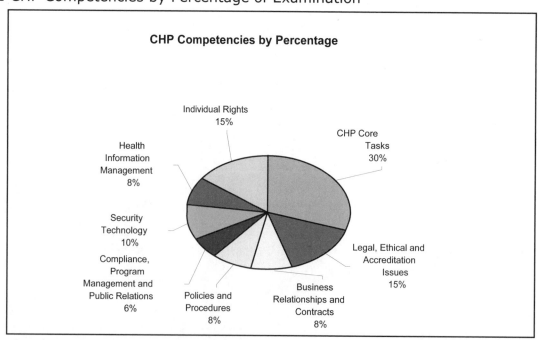

Table 3 shows the CHS Examination question content weight by scored questions.

Table 3 Certified In Healthcare Security Examination Question Content		
Competency by Domain	Number of Questions in Domain	Weight by Percentage of Questions in Domain
1. CHS Core Tasks	30	30%
2. Policies, Procedures and Guidelines	7	7%
3. Business Continuity	6	6%
4. Administrative Procedures	12	12%
5. Physical Safeguards	5	5%
6. Technical Security Services	11	11%
7. Networks, Operating Systems and Application Security	10	10%
8. Education and Training	5	5%
9. Law, Investigations and Ethics	7	7%
10. Privacy Requirements of Health Information	7	7%
Total Number of Questions Scored	100	100%

Chart 2 CHS Competencies by Percentage of Examination

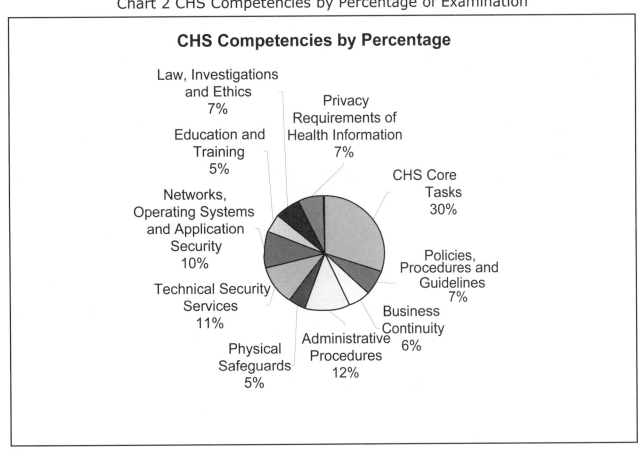

Cognitive Level of Questions

In addition to weights assigned to each of the Domains, cognitive levels were also assigned. Cognitive levels were not established for the individual task statements. The cognitive levels that are applied to the test questions on the certification exam are recall (knowledge), application and analysis. Each cognitive level relates to a corresponding ability to think and reason. A recall/knowledge question requires the lowest level of thinking. For example, when answering recall/knowledge questions, one simply needs to remember the needed information. An application level question expects you to recall the information and be able to work with it. On the other hand, an analysis question requires the highest level of thinking. To respond to an analysis question, one is required to recall the information and to compare, contrast and/or evaluate the information.

Recall/Knowledge questions involve the process of memorization. Memorization is committing information to the brain through repetition for recall at a later time. For this reason, these types of questions are frequently referred to as recall questions. Recall/knowledge questions require you to remember information that forms the basis of the competencies. Memorization can be facilitated by employing strategies that require your senses, such as reciting the information out loud, reviewing it in your mind or writing it down. To do well on these kinds of questions, you must be able to recall facts, definitions, descriptions, formulae, sequences, categories, classifications, theories etc.

Application questions challenge your ability to use information under new conditions. Before you can start the thinking process required to respond to application questions you must understand the information. You start with the facts and memorize them, but more importantly, you must translate and clarify them. If you can accomplish this, you have comprehended the information. You must take this thinking process one step further in order to respond to an application question. The process of applying information requires that you remember and comprehend concepts and apply them to specific situations. These concepts can be anything from theories of management to generalizations. It requires that you know, solve, modify, change, use or manipulate the information as it is applied to a "real" circumstance.

Analysis questions require your highest level of thinking. They are based on your ability to interpret the information, understand the likes and differences of the information and understand how all the information relates to the presented situation. Your ability to respond correctly to an analysis question is directly related to your ability to respond to recall and application questions. If you do not recall the information or you are unable to apply the information, you will have a very difficult time evaluating and interpreting the information and making a judgment or decision based on that evaluation. Analysis questions challenge your analytical abilities. These abilities are needed when making decisions, judgments or solving problems.

Table 4 provides a description of the three cognitive levels.

	Table 4 Cognitive Levels of Testing	
Cognitive Level	Purpose	Required for
RECALL Knowledge	Remembering previously learned material	Information recalled ranges from specific facts (i.e. a psychiatrist specializes in what type of medicine) to complex formulas such as those used in the Medicare Program for DRG payment. Verbs used in course objectives at the recall/knowledge level include: define, describe, identify, label, list, match, state, select etc.
APPLICATION	Ability to use new and learned information in a new and concrete situation	This cognitive level requires the application of rules, methods, concepts, principles, laws and theories. Verbs used in course objectives at the application level are: changes, computes, demonstrates, discovers, modifies, operates, predicts, prepares, produces, shows, solves, uses etc.
ANALYSIS	Ability to know, understand and apply new information appropriately by interpreting data and recognizing the interrelationships; breaking information into its component parts so that its organizational structure may be understood.	Information that is analyzed includes identification of parts, analysis of the relationship between the parts and recognition of the organizational principle involved. Analysis requires an understanding of both the content and structural form of the material. Verbs used in course objectives at the analysis level are break down, diagram, differentiate, illustrate, infer, relate, select and separate.

Table 5 shows the breakdown of questions by cognitive level in each domain for the CHP Examination. You can see that Table 5 shows that 78% of the questions will be either analytical or at least at the application level of cognitive level of testing.

DOMAIN NUMBER	DOMAIN NAME	Cognitive Level of Questions			NUMBER OF QUESTIONS
		*RE	*AP	*AN	
1	CHP Core Tasks	6	6	18	30
2	Legal, Ethical and Accreditation Issues	3	3	9	15
3	Business Relationships and Contracts	3	5	0	8
4	Policies and Procedures	2	5	1	8
5	Compliance, Program Management and Public Relations	1	4	1	6
6	Security Technology	2	6	2	10
7	Health Information Management	2	1	5	8
8	Individual Rights	3	3	9	15
	Totals	22	33	45	100

Table 5
Questions by Cognitive Level for the 2004 CHP EXAMINATION

*RE = RECALL   *AP = APPLICATION   *AN = ANALYSIS

Table 6 shows the breakdown of questions by cognitive level in each domain for the CHS Examination. You can see that Table 6 shows that 77% of the questions will be either analytical or at least at the application level of cognitive level of testing.

DOMAIN NUMBER	DOMAIN NAME	Cognitive Level of Questions			NUMBER OF QUESTIONS
		*RE	*AP	*AN	
1	CHS Core Tasks	6	6	18	30
2	Policies, Procedures and Guidelines	2	3	2	7
3	Business Continuity	1	4	1	6
4	Administrative Procedures	2	7	3	12
5	Physical Safeguards	2	3	0	5
6	Technical Security Devices	2	5	4	11
7	Networks, Operating Systems and Application Security	2	6	2	10
8	Education and Training	2	3	0	5
9	Law, Investigations and Ethics	1	4	2	7
10	Privacy Requirements of Health Information	3	4	0	7
	Totals	23	45	32	100

TABLE 6
Questions by Cognitive Level for The 2004 CHS EXAMINATION

*RE = RECALL   *AP = APPLICATION   *AN = ANALYSIS

Examination Content and Insights

You will need to review the specific Competency Task Statements in the 2005 Candidate Handbook provided by AHIMA for each certification. The candidate handbook has tables showing the number of questions asked in each of the major topic categories. These categories are documented using competency categories known as Domains and Task Competency Statements. These Domains and Task Competency Statements reflect the entry-level competencies necessary for practice. Consequently, you can expect that the examination results will be reported using this format.

The certification examinations are computerized. You will be given a brief period to familiarize yourself with the testing system. While taking the test, you will be able to return to previously answered questions to check your answers before you close the exam file on the computer.

Questions subjects on the examinations are scrambled and change topics from question to question. Therefore, you may have a legal question, followed by a policy and procedure question, followed by a compliance question, etc. Be prepared to shift gears quickly throughout the exam.

Because this is an advanced certification examination, the questions are skewed toward application and analysis rather than recall level of question difficulty.

This Review Guide Book is organized by Certification.

The questions in this review guide are divided into sections by domains.

The first part of the book has questions related to the CHP Examination.
>   Part 1.   Certified in Healthcare Privacy Examination (CHP)
>   Core Content Tasks
>   Privacy issues for the CHP

The second part of the book has questions related to the CHS Examination.
>   Part 2.   Certified in Healthcare Security Examination (CHS)
>   Core Content Tasks
>   Security issues for the CHS

Our major focus is on covering the critical concepts and entry level competencies in the body of knowledge for the certification examinations. Questions on the actual examination may combine several concepts into one question which may increase the level of difficulty in the question.

Questions in this book are tied to the competencies as accurately as could be judged. Most questions have the competencies the question relates to listed after the question. The candidate studying for the exam can gauge his/her proficiency in individual competencies as he/she studies. A detailed copy of the entry level competencies you are responsible for is provided in the Candidate Handbook from AHIMA.

We have carefully selected questions that are generic enough to cover the broad topic categories. Researching the questions as you study should expand your knowledge such that, when you encounter similar but different questions, you can arrive at the correct answer. We believe this review material will jog your memory and serve to help you build on information you have already gained through your examination preparation. Since we have no way of knowing exactly what will be on the examination, the authors tried to cover a broad base of healthcare privacy and security concepts.

REFERENCE MATERIALS
At the end of each section, there is a reference list of AHIMA articles and practice briefs, documents from federal web sites and books that were used as references for the questions.

Additional resources have been gathered from federal web sites and are provided on a Reference CD-ROM. The files are either MSWord or in PDF format.
Materials on the CD-ROM include the following files for your convenience:
1 Combined Regulation Text for the Privacy and Security Rules
2 HHS Fact Sheet: Protecting the privacy of patient's health information
3 HHS Fact Sheet: Modifications to the standards for privacy of individually identifiable health information – final rule
4 Frequently asked questions about the HIPAA privacy rule
5 Final Privacy Rule
6 Final Security Rule
7 minimum necessary
8 Sample Business Associate Contract.doc
9 HIPAA Guidance all sections
10 Guidance Introduction
11 Covered Entity
12 Covered Entity Flowcharts
13 Incidental Uses
14 Acronym List.doc
15 Glossary.doc
16 Sample Business Associate Contract
17 CDC Privacy Guidance
18 Complaint (How to file a privacy complaint with the OCR)

Study Strategies And Resources

Study Strategies and Resources

FORMAT OF THE EXAMINATION

As stated in the introduction to this book, the questions developed for the examinations are based on specifications currently referred to as Domains Subdomains and tasks. A complete copy of these entry level specifications is provided in the AHIMA Candidate Handbook for the CHP and CHS Examinations.

The general format of the exams is primarily designed to engage your problem solving and critical thinking skills. These types of questions require that you translate what you have learned and apply it to a situation. The introduction to this book has information on the cognitive levels of testing. The Candidate Handbook also provides sample questions that illustrate this point.

EXAMINATION STRATEGIES

Build Your Endurance: Preparing for a major exam is similar to preparing for a marathon athletic event. The time allotted for the CHP and CHS examinations is 3 hours.

One suggestion is to use your study process to slowly build up your concentration time until you can focus your energy for the appropriate period of time. This is like the runner who begins jogging for 30 minutes and builds up to one hour, then one and a half hours, etc., and gradually increases the endurance time to meet the demands of the race. Try this strategy; it could work for you!

Study Style/Study Groups: Everyone has his/her own particular study style. Some people prefer to study alone while others work best in a group. Regardless of your preference, we strongly recommend that you take advantage of group study at least some of the time. Studying with others can prove very helpful when working through your weakest areas. Each member of the study team will bring strengths and weaknesses to the table and all can benefit from the collaboration. So, even if you are a solitary learner, you may occasionally want to work with a group for those topics you find more challenging.

Effective and Systematic Review: Theoretically, material known thoroughly after one learning will fade predictably with time. After one day, the average person retains only 80% of what was learned; ultimately he/she will remember about 30% of it. That is why you are now relearning information you acquired over a period of years. Your aim is to achieve maximum recall through effective review. Make your study process a systematic review of all topic categories followed by achieving mastery of strategically selected subjects within the topic categories.

To facilitate this effort, we recommend that you design a ten-week study program. You should plan on spending an average of 10 to 12 hours per week studying. The idea is to study smart, not to bulldoze through tons of material in a haphazard way.

Organize a Study Program: First, you must get organized. You have to be deliberate about making sure that you develop and stick to a regular study routine. Find a place where you can study, either at home or at the library.

How you schedule your study time during the week is an individual decision. However, we recommend that you avoid all-nighters and other unreasonably long study sessions. The last thing you want to do is burn yourself out by working too long and too hard at one time. Try to do a little bit at a time and maintain a steady pace that is manageable for you.

Develop your individual study program. You could use the list of competencies to write the topics and subjects in a list. Reference the competencies to information from the list of references available on the AHIMA web site from a search for HIPAA articles. Write the topics and subjects in a list. Outline the sections in the HIPAA Rule. Pause at each section outline and recall basic points. Do you draw a blank, recall them more or less or do you feel comfortable with your recall? Pinpoint your weakest subjects. By using this approach, you can see where you stand.

Weigh the importance of each subject. How are the topics emphasized in the HIPAA Rule, in your research notes and the weights assigned to the competencies in the examination contents? Try to pick out concepts that would make good exam questions.

Make a list of the topics in the order that you plan to study them. Avoid trying to make a head-on attack by giving equal time and attention to all topics. Use your list to identify your weakest topics. Determine which ones you believe will require a significant amount of study time and which will only require a brief review.

Your list will give you a clear mental picture of what you need to do and will keep you on track. There are three additional advantages to a list. One, it builds your morale as you steadily cross off items that you have completed, and you can monitor your progress. Two, glancing back at the list from time to time serves to reassure you that you are on target. And three, you can readily see that you are applying your time and effort where they are most needed.

Keep the list conspicuously in view. Carefully plan your pre-exam study time and stick to your plan. Go to the exam like a trained and disciplined runner going to a marathon event!

A SUMMARY OF TIPS FOR ORGANIZING YOUR TIME AND MATERIALS

1) **Read the HIPAA Rule:** It is imperative that you read and review the content covered in the HIPAA Rule. We suggest that you start by reading the comments before the text of the rule. The comments help in understanding why and how the rule was conceived and built. The comments also have many examples of how the rule would work and what would and would not be included.

2) **Organize and review all of the following items:**
   a. the HIPAA Rule and preceding comments
   b. AHIMA Practice Briefs (go to WWW.AHIMA.ORG for information)
   c. any seminar notes (for example, the Getting Practical with Privacy Resource Book is an excellent resource for the CHP exam)
   d. sample test questions from continuing education quizzes in the Journal of AHIMA
   e. textbooks and other books on health information privacy and confidentiality and information systems
   f. articles from various professional journals
   g. information obtained from internet resources

3) **Review the major topic categories.** Determine what your areas of strength are and what areas are in need of improvement.

4) **Set up a realistic study schedule.** Customize the sample schedule provided in this book to best meet your needs.

5) **Concentrate on your weaknesses.** Spend more time and energy studying your areas of weakness, especially if these categories had a significant number of questions associated with them or are listed as analysis type questions on the exam. Remember, every question counts toward that passing score!

6) **Take practice tests.** One of the best ways to study for a test is to take tests. Practice answering questions and working problems as much as possible. Work with your watch in front of you. Time yourself so that you become accustomed to taking only 1 to 1-1/2 minutes per question.

7) **Carefully read the CANDIDATE HANDBOOK from AHIMA.**
   If anything in the Candidate Handbook is unclear, seek assistance from AHIMA. You are held accountable for the important information, deadlines and instructions addressed in this material. Review the information on applying for the exam. It takes some time to get the application to AHIMA and time for them to process it and notify you of approval for testing. Then, you have a window of dates in which to take the exam so you will have to set up an appointment to take the test.

SAMPLE STUDY SCHEDULE for the CHP Examination

Week 1   Read HIPAA Privacy Rule and Comments

Week 2   Read the HIPAA Security Rule and comments

Week 3   Review AHIMA Practice Briefs regarding HIPAA issues
- Legal ethical and accreditation issue of Privacy and Security
- Standards of accreditation agencies
- Applicable state and federal laws and regulations related to privacy and security
- Organization privacy and security training (evaluating effectiveness, reliability and validity of)
- Health information systems
- Risk assessments and Gap analysis
- Privacy compliance

Week 4   Review AHIMA articles on HIPAA Issues
- Policies and procedures (creating, updating and accessibility of)
- Notice of Privacy Practices
- Business associate contracts
- Minimum necessary
- Access restrictions
- Individual rights

Week 5   Review HIMSS information on
- HIPAA issues
- Information security
- Systems security

Week 6   Focus on Core Tasks

Week 7   Focus on CHP or CHS specific competencies

Week 8   Focus on CHP or CHS specific competencies

Week 9   Focus on CHP or CHS specific competencies

Week 10   Final Review of the HIPAA Rule with Comments and AHIMA Practice briefs

This is just a sample. You will want to customize your own study schedule. Obviously, for the CHS examination, you would want to focus more on information and systems security issues and spend less time on privacy.

STUDY RESOURCES

If your studies become stagnant, do not sit and grind yourself down. If what you are reading is not making the subject clear for you, don't spend time trying to memorize something you do not understand. The main issue is to understand the materials so you can use the knowledge in a practical way. Search for additional information that will help make the subject clear to you. There are four basic sources of information: books and periodical literature, people, educational program/college and, of course, the internet/web resources.

Books: Books and other written resources may use another style of presentation that you are more receptive to. A different textbook may be all you need to gain a better insight into the subject. It can offer a fresh point of view, provide relief from boredom and encourage critical thinking in the process of comparing the texts.

Periodical literature: in the health field provides well written articles that may open up the subject to you and turn study into an adventure in learning. AHIMA publishes authoritative and insightful information on every aspect of HIPAA and health information privacy and security. Sometimes an article can help put the text material into practical perspective and pull it together so that you gain a deeper understanding. With the rapidly changing healthcare world, HIM Journals and magazines have the most current information and are frequently used as references for test questions. HIMSS has extensive materials regarding healthcare information privacy and security.

Take advantage of your local library by requesting help in researching a concept you need additional information on for your study purposes.

People: Professional contacts in your HIM community can also be helpful in your study effort. Most people in our field are eager to share their knowledge and are flattered by appeals for information.

Collaborating with other exam candidates may reveal fresh viewpoints, stimulate thought by disagreement or at least let you see that you are not alone in your quest. Organize study groups and set aside specific times to work together. This interaction can be truly beneficial in keeping you motivated and on task.

Classes, workshops, and seminars: present opportunities to learn and review the subject matter in a new light. Take advantage of any HIPAA or Privacy and Security sessions available in your area. Talking to those who have recently taken the exam about tips for taking the exam can also be of great assistance in pointing the way to prepare for the exam.

AHIMA also provides educational opportunities through seminars, audio seminars and online classes for step by step guides to HIPAA implementation, compliance and management guidelines.

Internet/Web Sites: In this dynamic changing environment, the latest up-to-date materials may not be available in a book. Don't overlook the power of AHIMA's web site and the online library services for articles and practice briefs. The AHIMA Resources are extensive and quite easy to access. In addition, the Communities of Practice (CoP) which are available to members of AHIMA are a phenomenal source of contact with HIM professionals who are Privacy and Security Officers. The CoPs have extensive communities on all areas of HIPAA, privacy and security issues. AHIMA's web site: www.ahima.org

A wealth of information may be obtained through the Healthcare Information and Management Systems Society (HIMSS). Web site: www.HIMSS.org

Of course there are other important web sites to get information from such as Centers for Medicare and Medicaid (CMS), Office of Civil Rights (OCR), and Health and Human services (HHS) just to name a few. Take some time and look around on the internet and you will be surprised at the abundance of information available.

In summary, some of the study resources available to you include:

1) The HIPAA Rule and comments preceding the rule (see the Reference CD-ROM provided with this book)

2) AHIMA Practice Briefs and AHIMA Journal articles (many of them are available on AHIMA's web site)

3) General HIM Related Text Books
    Health Information: Management of a Strategic Resource 2nd Edition,
        Edited by Abdelhak, Grostick, Hanken, and Jacobs. Published 2001
        Published by W.B. Saunders
    Health information Management Technology An applied Approach,
        Edited by Merida L. Johns, PhD, RHIA, Published. 2002
        American Health Information Management Association AHIMA
    Health Information Management: Concepts Principles and Practice
        Edited by Latour, K. M. and Eichenwald, S,. Published 2002
        American Health Information Management Association (AHIMA)

4) HIPAA / Privacy / Security Educational Sessions

5) Study groups/partners

6) For the latest information go to various internet sites such as:
    AHIMA at: www.ahima.org
    HMSS at: www.HIMSS.org
    CMS at: www.cms.gov
    HHS at: www.hhs.gov
    OCR at: www.hhs.gov/ocr

THE DAY BEFORE AND THE MORNING OF THE EXAM

1) If necessary, spend the night before the examination in a hotel or motel near the exam test site if it is a great distance from home.

2) Avoid studying the night before the exam. Last minute studying tends to increase your anxiety level. However, you may want to allocate a small amount time to review any information that you feel you must memorize.

3) Organize in advance all the materials you need to take with you to the exam. Review the AHIMA Candidate Handbook carefully and be sure to have all the items required (especially the admission card and appropriate proof of identity).

4) Get a good night's sleep and have a healthy meal before exam.

5) Allow yourself plenty of time so that you may arrive at the test site early.

6) Dress comfortably and plan for possible variations in room temperature. Dressing in layers may prove helpful.

7) Verify that you are in the correct room for the examination you are to take. Examinations may be scheduled at the same time but held in separate rooms at the same testing site.

TAKING THE EXAMINATION

You have stuck to your study schedule and have conditioned yourself to be in the best physical and mental shape possible. Now comes the "moment of truth": the examination pops on the screen before your eyes. Every paratrooper knows that in addition to having a parachute, one must know how to open it. You have mastered the major topics; you have the parachute. Now, you need to utilize good test taking techniques to apply the knowledge you have gained; open the parachute!

1) Prior to starting the exam, you will be given a chance to practice taking an examination on the computer. Ten minutes will be allotted for this practice test. However, you may quit the practice test and begin the actual exam when you are comfortable with the computerized testing process.

2) Read all directions and questions carefully. Try to avoid reading too much into the questions. Be sensible and practical in your interpretation. Read ALL of the possible answers, since the first one that looks good may not be the best one.

3) Scan the computer screen quickly for general format of the questions. Like the marathon runner, pace yourself for the distance. A good rule of thumb is 1 to 1.5 minutes per question. You may wish to keep the timer displayed on the computer to check your schedule throughout the exam. For example, at question 31, about one half hour will have elapsed, etc.

4) Some people answer all of the questions that they are certain of first, and then go back through the exam a second time to answer any questions they were uncertain about. Others prefer not to skip questions, but to make their best choice for each question and go on. Both can be good approaches; choose the one that works best for you. You can also "mark" questions that you have left unanswered and/or those questions you may want to review. Before you sign off of the exam or run out of time, you have the ability to go back to those questions for a final review.

5) Answer all the questions. There are no penalties for guessing, but putting no answer is definitely a wrong answer.

6) Use deductive reasoning and the process of elimination to arrive at the most correct answer. Some questions will not have only one correct answer. You will be asked to select the "best" possible answer based on the information presented.

7) If the question is written in a scenario format, first identify the question being asked and then review the entire question for the information needed to determine the correct answer.

8) Use all the time available to recheck your answers. However, avoid changing your answers unless you are absolutely certain it is necessary. Second-guessing yourself often results in a wrong answer.

AFTER THE EXAM

Our advice is to reclaim your life and focus on your career. One good way to start is to plan a special reward for yourself at some point immediately following or shortly after the exam. Schedule a family vacation or a relaxing weekend get-away. Just find some way of being good to yourself. You certainly deserve it! You have worked hard, so relish your success.

REVIEW SECTION
FOR THE
CHP EXAMINATION

Core Questions
for the
CHP Examination

Core Questions
For the CHP Examination

1. You are looking at your policies, procedures, training program, etc. and comparing it to the HIPAA regulations. You are conducting a
   A) policy assessment
   B) risk assessment
   C) compliance audit
   D) gap analysis
   REFERENCE: OCR 164.308, 164.530
                    Amatayakul, et al., p 29-31
                    Pabrai, p 223-224, 336-337, 477-483
                    Johns (2002a), p 107
                    Hjort (2001), p 64A
   COMPETENCY: Core: 1K, 1M, 1U
                    Security: 4B

2. I am planning our new training program on privacy issues. I need to ensure that which of the following attends the training sessions?
   A) both current and new employees
   B) physicians
   C) volunteers
   D) all of the above
   REFERENCE: OCR 164.530
                    Amatayakul, et al., p 55-57
                    Pabrai, p 229, 327-328
                    Callahan-Dennis (2000), p 69-72, 74
   COMPETENCY: Core: 1D, 1E

3. As Chief Privacy Officer, you have been asked why you are conducting a risk assessment. Which reason would you give?
   A) get rid of problem staff
   B) change organizational culture
   C) prevent breach of confidentiality
   D) none of the above
   REFERENCE: OCR 164.308, 164.530
                    Pabrai, p 223-224, 336-337, 477-483
                    Callahan-Dennis (2000), p 31-32, 36
   COMPETENCY: Core: 1M, 1T

4. Florida Beach Hospital is reviewing the following new policy for approval and implementation. What problem with the policy do you have?

> Policy: Because of recent legislation, Florida Beach Hospital will track release of confidential patient identifiable information in the following circumstances as required by law:
> employers
> attorneys
> patient
> external researcher

A) tracking release to employers is exempted from legislation
B) tracking release to attorneys is exempted from legislation
C) tracking release to patient is exempted from legislation
D) tracking release to external researcher is exempted from legislation

REFERENCE: OCR 164.316, 164.528
    Amatayakul, et al., p 24-27
    Pabrai, p 146, 243-244
    Hartley & Jones, p 81
    Dougherty (2001), p 72E
COMPETENCY: Core: 1B, IT
    Privacy: 2B, 8C

5. Mark is in charge of the training department. While he does not conduct all of the training classes, he is responsible for maintaining documentation on the training provided. Which of the following documentation should he maintain?
A) attendance roster, content of course, handouts, announcements and quiz results
B) sign-in sheet and agenda only
C) content of course, handouts and transcript of questions asked by staff
D) handouts, attendance roster, content of course and list of people scheduled to attend but who did not show up.

REFERENCE: OCR 164.308, 164.530
    Amatayakul, et al., p 55-57
    Pabrai, p 229, 327-328
    Callahan-Dennis (2000), p 71-72
    Hjort (2002), p 60A
    Hartley & Jones, p 118
COMPETENCY: Core: 1D, 1E
    Privacy: 4A
    Security: 8C

6. You are on a task force that has the assignment of evaluating your privacy program. Which of the following should the task force do?
   A) evaluate policies and procedures
   B) ask the Chief Executive Officer to support your activities
   C) appoint a privacy officer
   D) all of the above
REFERENCE: OCR 164.308, 164.530
                Pabrai, p 330-332, 336-338, 477-483
                Johns (2002b), p 229-231
                Hjort (2001), p 64A
COMPETENCY: Core: 1I, 1J, 1K, 1L
                Privacy: 2A, 5A

7. Michaela tells Bob, the pharmacy tech, that only the HIM department is subject to privacy and security restrictions because they are responsible for the record. What should be Bob's response?
   A) I know. I am glad that I do not work in HIM.
   B) I disagree. Everyone who works in a covered entity is responsible for complying with privacy and security regulations.
   C) I disagree. Healthcare providers like physicians and nurses also have a responsibility to keep patient's confidential information private.
   D) none of the above
REFERENCE: Amatayakul, et al., p 55-57
                Pabrai, p 229
                Callahan-Dennis (2000), p17
                Hjort (2002), p 60A
                Hartley & Jones, p 24
COMPETENCY: Core: 1B, 1D, 1E
                Privacy: 2B, 4C

8. Employees should receive training on privacy at least
   A) upon hiring
   B) annually
   C) when something changes
   D) both A and C
REFERENCE: OCR 164.308, 164.530
                Amatayakul, et al., p 55-57
                Pabrai, p 229, 327-328
                Hjort (2002), p 60D
                Hartley & Jones, p 118
COMPETENCY: Core: 1D, 1E

9. You have been asked to define privacy. Which of the following definitions would you use?
   A) the patient has the right to control who reviews his or her medical record
   B) patients have rights regarding their individually identifiable health information
   C) access to medical record information has to be controlled by technical controls
   D) access to patient identifiable health information is available only to healthcare professionals

REFERENCE: LaTour and Eichenwald, p 233
               Amatayakul, et al., p 3-4
               Pabrai, p 15
               Cassidy, (2000), p 16A
COMPETENCY: Core: 1B, 1E, 1F

10. The agreement that you are looking at designates that all of the separate facilities that your organization owns are designated as a single covered entity. This must be a(n)
    A) affiliated covered entity
    B) organized healthcare arrangement
    C) traditional partner agreement
    D) data use agreement

REFERENCE: OCR 164.105
               Amatayakul, et al., p 20-22
               Amatayakul (2002d), p 24C
COMPETENCY: Core: 1I, 1J

11. HIPAA requires a healthcare facility to conduct privacy training at various points. These points include
    A) prior to the compliance date of HIPAA
    B) for new employees
    C) when new privacy policies impact employees
    D) all of the above

REFERENCE: OCR 164.308, 164.530
               Amatayakul, et al., p 55-57
               Pabrai, p 229, 327-328
COMPETENCY: Core: 1E, 1F

12. Sabrina is sorting through a large stack of old policies and procedures trying to determine which ones can be discarded. Which of the following policies could she retire?
  A) policy revised 2 years ago
  B) policy replaced 7 years ago
  C) policy implemented 5 years ago
  D) none of the above
REFERENCE: OCR 164.316
                Amatayakul, et al., p 24-26
                Pabrai, p 237-328, 243-244
                Dougherty (2002), p 64
COMPETENCY: Core: 1H, 1J
                Privacy: 2B, 4B

13. Thomas has identified a need to update a policy and procedure that is referred to on the notice of information practices. Which of the following is an appropriate step for him to take?
  A) change the policy whether or not the notice of information practices notifies the patient that the policy and procedure may be changed
  B) change policy if notice of information practice has a statement allowing change
  C) change policy whether or not the notice of information practice notifies the patient that the policy and procedure may be changed and then update the notice of information practice
  D) none of the above
REFERENCE: OCR 164.530
                Amatayakul, et al., p 24-27
                Pabrai, p146, 243-244
                Dougherty (2002), p 61
                Hartley & Jones, p 72
COMPETENCY: Core: 1H, 1J
                Privacy: 2A, 2B, 4A, 4B

14. Training is a key component of HIPAA. Which of the following types of training should be conducted?
  A) general privacy and security training
  B) job specific privacy and security training
  C) management specific privacy and security training
  D) all of the above
REFERENCE: OCR 164.308, 164.530
                Amatayakul, et al., p 55-57
                Pabrai, p 229, 327-328
                Amatayakul & Johns, p 16C
                Hartley & Jones, p 118
COMPETENCY: Core: 1D, 1E
                Security: 8A, 8B

15. Randy is developing the training plan for the privacy and security training. He should
    A) include policies and procedures
    B) consider using various training methods based on the audience
    C) provide core training for all staff
    D) do all of the above
    REFERENCE: OCR 164.308, 164.530
                    Amatayakul, et al., p 55-57
                    Pabrai, p 146, 229, 243-244, 327-328
                    LaTour and Eichenwald, p 581-592
                    Abdelhak, p 615-616
                    Johns (2002b), p 230
                    Amatayakul & Johns, p 16D, 16 E
    COMPETENCY: Core: 1D, 1E
                    Security: 2C

16. The agenda for the core privacy and security training has been established. Which of the following should be excluded from the agenda?
    A) definition of confidentiality
    B) definition of privacy
    C) patient right to his/her medical information
    D) copy of final privacy and security regulations
    REFERENCES: Amatayakul, et al., p 55-57
                    LaTour and Eichenwald, p 582-588
                    Pabrai, p 146, 229, 243-244, 327-328
                    Johns (2002b), p 171
                    Amatayakul & Johns, p 16D
    COMPETENCY: Core: 1D, 1E

17. Training is an important part of HIPAA privacy and security rules. Which of the following statements is a true statement regarding this training?
    A) the privacy and security rule mandates lecture training
    B) HIPAA mandates training and documentation requirements but not the method to be used
    C) requires training to be conducted upon hire and then on a semi-annual basis thereafter
    D) self directly learning is mandated
    REFERENCE: OCR, 164.308, 164.530
                    Amatayakul, et al., p 55-57
    COMPETENCY: Core: 1D, 1E

18. Janie is asked the difference between privacy and security. She explains it as
    A) privacy is the management of disclosures and security is controlling access from inappropriate disclosure
    B) security is the management of disclosures and privacy is controlling access from inappropriate disclosure
    C) privacy is protecting data from destruction and security determines who can have access to PHI
    D) security is protecting data from destruction and privacy determines who can have access to PHI
REFERENCE: LaTour and Eichenwald, p 223-224
              Amatayakul, et al., p 3, 9
              Pabrai, p 15
              Sullivan, p 92
COMPETENCY: Core: 1B, 1I

19. Violation of a patient's privacy may occur when using information in which of the following formats?
    A) paper
    B) verbal
    C) computer
    D) all of the above
REFERENCE: OCR 160.103
              Pabrai, p 2, 110-111, 119-121
              Amatayakul, et al., p 3-8
              Dougherty (2001), p 72E
              Hartley & Jones, p 241
              Davis, p 50
COMPETENCY: Core: 1I, 1K, 1Q

20. Dr. Thomas has a solo practice specializing in orthopedics. He does not file electronic claims. What is his status with regard to the privacy regulations?
    A) he must abide by the tenets of the privacy regulations since he is a healthcare provider
    B) he is not a covered entity since he does not transmit health claims electronically
    C) he is covered since he is a business associate
    D) none of the above
REFERENCE: OCR 160.102
              Amatayakul, et al., p 19
              Pabrai, p 190
              Choy, Pritts, & Goldman, p 35
              Hartley & Jones, p 5, 235
COMPETENCY: Core: 1B, 1I

21. The student clinic at the University of Macon treats students for a variety of services. The clinic provides free or low cost services and only accepts self-pay form of reimbursement. According to HIPAA, the student clinic is
   A) a covered entity because it is a health plan
   B) a covered entity because it is a clearinghouse
   C) not a covered entity
   D) a covered entity because it is a provider
REFERENCE: OCR 160.102, 164.104
               Amatayakul, et al., p 19
               Pabrai, p 190
               Choy, Pritts, & Goldman, p 34-35
               Hartley & Jones, p 5, 235
COMPETENCY: Core: 1B, 1I

22. Respond to the following comment. The VA Medical Center is not subject to HIPAA privacy requirements.
   A) This is wrong since governmental facilities are subject to HIPAA
   B) This is wrong since they submit electronic claims
   C) This is right since governmental facilities are not subject to HIPAA
   D) This is right since they do not submit electronic claims
REFERENCE: OCR 164.512
               Amatayakul, et al., p 18-19
               Pabrai, p 117, 185-186
COMPETENCY: Core: 1B, 1I

23. HIPAA's privacy rule was established by
   A) Department of Health and Human Services
   B) Congress
   C) CMS
   D) Centers for Disease Control
REFERENCE: Johns (2002b), p 673
               Pabrai, p 4-6
               Amatayakul (2000), p 34
               Doscher (2002), p 11
COMPETENCY: Core: 1B

24. Fred is responsible for privacy training and Bob is responsible for security training. Which of the following is true?
    A) they can work together since the training requirements are similar
    B) they must keep their efforts separate due to differences
    C) they must ensure that training is conducted by May
    D) none of the above
REFERENCE: OCR 164.308, 164.530
               Amatayakul, et al., p 9, 55-57
               Callahan-Dennis (2000), p 17, 67-76
               Pabrai, p 225-226, 474-475
               Hjort (2002), p 60B
COMPETENCY: Core: 1I
               Security: 10E

25. Mickey's job as a release of information coordinator just underwent substantial changes. He received privacy training 6 months ago. Which of the following is true?
    A) Mickey will not need to be trained again for 6 months
    B) Mickey should be given additional training on the changes
    C) Mickey should only receive training if he is a paid employee of the hospital
    D) Mickey should receive training only if he requests it
REFERENCE: OCR 164.308, 164.530
               Amatayakul, et al., p 55-57
               Pabrai, p 146, 229, 243-244, 327-328
               Hjort (2002), p 60D
COMPETENCY: Core: 1D, 1E

26. Greg is conducting a privacy training session. At the beginning of the course, he asks what role in the organization each participant has. He learns that there are people from environmental services, nursing, health information management and the business office. What problem does he have?
    A) he cannot proceed because of diverse group
    B) he should proceed with an extensive training program
    C) maybe none if he is conducting general awareness training
    D) none of the above
REFERENCE: OCR 164.308, 164.530
               Amatayakul, et al., p 55-57
               Pabrai, p 146, 229, 243-244, 327-328
               Johns (2002b), p 230,676
               LaTour and Eichenwald, p 586-588
               Hjort (2002), p 60B, 60D
               Hartley & Jones, p 118
COMPETENCY: Core: 1D, 1E

27. Michaela works at home for a covered entity. Because she does not work on the hospital campus, she is exempt from the training requirements. React to this comment.
    A) all employees must undergo training
    B) the training must be appropriate for her role
    C) she is exempt
    D) both A and B
REFERENCE: OCR 164.308, 164.530
               Amatayakul, et al., p 55-57
               Pabrai, p 146, 229, 243-244, 327-328
               LaTour and Eichenwald, p 586-588
               Johns (2002b), 230, 676
               Hjort (2002), p 60B
COMPETENCY: Core: 1D, 1E
               Privacy: 2B, 4A

28. If privacy training is divided into three levels of training (I, II and III) with level III being the most intense, at which level would you expect to find specifics on the disclosure of patient information?
    A) I – General
    B) II – Job specific
    C) III – Management specific
    D) Not included in any training
REFERENCE: OCR 164.308
               Amatayakul, et al., p 55-57
               Hjort (2002), p 60C
               LaTour and Eichenwald, p 581
COMPETENCY: Core: 1D, 1E

29. Which of the following formats could be used for HIPAA training?
    A) lecture
    B) computer based training
    C) handouts
    D) any of the above
REFERENCE: OCR 164.308, 164.530
               Amatayakul, et al., p 55-57
               LaTour and Eichenwald, p 590-592
               Pabrai, p 146, 243-244, 327-328
               Hjort (2002), p 60D
COMPETENCY: Core: 1D, 1E

30. At which level should the privacy officer operate?
    A) Vice president
    B) Department director
    C) Leadership
    D) None of the above
REFERENCE: OCR 164.530
               Pabrai, p 326, 330-331
               Johns (2002b), p 165-196, 229-230
               ·Hjort (2001), p 64A
COMPETENCY: Core: 1C, 1O, 1S

31. Madison Medical Center, which is owned by Hospital Corporation of California, is
    _____ bound by the Privacy Act of 1974.
    A) not
    B) absolutely
    C) partially
REFERENCE: Abdelhak, p 440
               Pabrai, p 188
               Callahan-Dennis (2000), p 12
               Hughes (2002c), p 64A
COMPETENCY: Core: 1B, 1I

32. Which law allows for patients to amend information?
    A) HIPAA
    B) Privacy Act of 1974
    C) Confidentiality of Alcohol and Drug Abuse Patient records
    D) Both A and B
REFERENCE: OCR 164.526
               Pabrai, p 145-146
               Abdelhak, p, 439-440, 443
               Johns (2002b), p 226-227
               Hughes (2002c), p 64A, 64B
COMPETENCY: Core: 1B, 1I

33. Ben and Jason have a difference of opinion. Ben says that the Confidentiality of
    Alcohol and Drug Abuse Patient Records rule supercedes HIPAA. Jason says it is
    the reversed. Who is right?
    A) Ben
    B) Jason
    C) both since neither law covers all of the clauses of the other
    D) neither since it depends on which part of the law is stricter
REFERENCE: OCR 160.201, 160.203
               Johns (2002b), p 209
               Hughes (2002c), p 64B
COMPETENCY: Core: 1B, 1I

34. The Confidentiality of Alcohol and Drug Abuse Patient Records rule includes all of the following except
    A) identity of patient
    B) diagnosis of patient
    C) treatment of patient
    D) payment of bill
REFERENCE: Callahan-Dennis (2000), p 70
               Johns (2002b), p 70
               Hughes (2002c), p 64B
COMPETENCY: Core: 1B, 1I

35. The Whitaker Clinic is an exclusive alcohol and drug treatment facility. They do not receive federal funds. Which of the following statements are true?
    A) They are not subject to the Confidentiality of Alcohol and Drug Abuse Patient Records rule since it is not a federally assisted program.
    B) They are subject to the Confidentiality of Alcohol and Drug Abuse Patient Records rule since they provide alcohol and drug abuse treatment.
    C) They are not subject to the Confidentiality of Alcohol and Drug Abuse Patient Records rule since they are privately owned.
    D) They are subject to the Confidentiality of Alcohol and Drug Abuse Patient Records rule since they are privately owned.
REFERENCE: Callahan-Dennis (2000), p12-14
               Johns (2002b), p 70-71
               Hughes (2002c), p 64B
COMPETENCY: Core: 1B, 1I

36. Laws and regulations that apply to confidentiality include
    A) HIPAA
    B) Privacy Act of 1974
    C) Medicare Conditions of Participation
    D) all of the above
REFERENCE: Callahan-Dennis (2000), p 12-14
               Hughes (2002c), p 64B
COMPETENCY: Core: 1B, 1I

37. The Conditions of Participation for _____ requires patient access to his/her medical records information within 24 hours.
    A) hospitals
    B) long term care
    C) home health
    D) hospice
REFERENCE: Hughes (2002c), p 64B
COMPETENCY: Core: 1B, 1I

38. The Joint Commission of Healthcare Organizations requires
   A) the maintenance of secure paper records
   B) the maintenance of secure computerized records
   C) the maintenance confidentiality, security and integrity of data and information
   D) protection of the patient's privacy
REFERENCE: LaTour and Eichenwald, p 187
               Johns (2002b), p 829-835
               Hughes (2002c), p 64B
COMPETENCY: Core: 1A

39. Reason(s) for conducting a privacy risk assessment is (are)
   A) HIPAA compliance
   B) reducing liability
   C) both A and B
   D) none of the above
REFERENCE: OCR 164.308, 164.530
               Amatayakul, et al., p 10, 29-31
               Pabrai, p 223-224, 336-337, 477-483
               LaTour and Eichenwald, p 188-189
               Johns (2002b), p 339-347
               Callahan-Dennis (2000), p 31-33
               Callahan-Dennis (2001a), p 2
COMPETENCY: Core: 1T, 1U

40. Bob has been asked to specify the difference between risk assessment and gap analysis. He should reply
   A) "Risk assessment is an evaluation of potential risks, gap analysis is comparing HIPAA requirements to actual practices."
   B) "Gap analysis is an evaluation of potential risks, risk assessment is comparing HIPAA requirements to actual practices."
   C) "Risk assessment requires computer software and security assessment does not."
   D) "Risk assessment is required for privacy regulations and gap analysis is required for privacy regulations."
REFERENCE: Johns (2002b), p 107, 339, 345-348
               Pabrai, p 338-339
               Callahan-Dennis (2000), p 31-33
               Callahan-Dennis (2001a), p 1
COMPETENCY: Core: 1L, 1M, 1T, 1U

41. The purpose of privacy risk assessment is to investigate
    A) the facility for HIPAA deficits
    B) the facility to identify privacy problems related to HIPAA only
    C) the facility to identify privacy deficits whether it is related to HIPAA or not
    D) the facility's policies and procedures
REFERENCE: OCR 164.308, 164.530
                Amatayakul, et al., p 10, 29-31
                Pabrai, p 223-224, 336-337, 447-483
                Johns (2002b), p 107, 339, 345-348
                Callahan-Dennis (2000), p 31-33
                Callahan-Dennis (2001a), p 1
COMPETENCY: Core: 1L, 1M, 1T, 1U

42. The Chief Privacy Officer's required role in training is
    A) conducting the training
    B) ensuring that the appropriate training policies and procedures are followed
    C) developing a training plan
    D) all of the above
REFERENCE: OCR 164.308, 164.530
                Amatayakul, et al., p 13, 46, 127-128
                Pabrai, p 229, 327-328
                Callahan-Dennis (2000), p 67-72
                Callahan-Dennis (2001b), p 35
COMPETENCY: Core: 1D, 1E

43. You have been asked by the administrator how successful the privacy program
    is. You can answer by giving him
    A) the number of breeches
    B) the number of complaints
    C) the rate of privacy training being conducted on time
    D) all of the above
REFERENCE: Callahan-Dennis (2000), p 67-76
                Amatayakul, et al., p 45-46, 58-60, 66
                Callahan-Dennis (2001b), p 37
COMPETENCY: Core: 1B, 1F, 1K, 1S

44. A healthcare facility is developing a policy on how to document privacy training. Which of the following should be included in the policy?
   A) biometrics to record attendance
   B) showing driver's license
   C) signing a statement that training has been received
   D) signing a statement that training has been received and that employee will honor policies and procedures
REFERENCE: OCR 164.308, 164.530
               Amatayakul, et al., p 55-57
               Pabrai, p 229, 327-328
               Callahan-Dennis (2000), p 67-76
               LaTour and Eichenwald, p 584-588
               Cassidy (2001), p 16A
COMPETENCY: Core: 1D, 1E

45. I have been given the assignment of evaluating the HIPAA training provided. Which of the examples below demonstrates an outcome that can indicates effectiveness?
   A) The admission clerk is able to answer patient's questions regarding the notice of practices
   B) The health information technician is able to document the disclosure of PHI as mandated.
   C) The nurse knows where to look up a policy and procedure on privacy as needed.
   D) all of the above
REFERENCE: OCR 164.308
               Amatayakul, et al., p A 55-57, 66
               LaTour and Eichenwald, p 599
COMPETENCY: Core: 1D, 1E

46. The new training policy identifies the frequency of retraining on privacy and security training. This retraining should occur
   A) when the recertification occurs
   B) when there is a substantial change in policies and procedures
   C) every six months
   D) none of the above
REFERENCE: OCR 164.308, 164.530
               Amatayakul, et al., p 55-57
               Pabrai, 229, 327-328
               Johns (2002b), p 230-231
               Cassidy (2001), p 16A
COMPETENCY: Core: 1D, 1E

47. Which of the following security training is not required by HIPAA?
    A) password management
    B) virus protection
    C) awareness training
    D) audit trails
REFERENCE: OCR 164.308
               Amatayakul, et al., p 55-57
               Pabrai, p 229
               Johns (2002b), p 676
               Cassidy (2001), p 16B
COMPETENCY: Core: 1C, 1D
               Security: 8A, 8B, 9B

48. The facility transmits health information. Which of the following is required by
    the security standard?
    A) assessment of risk
    B) using HL-7
    C) using ASTM standards
    D) encryption
REFERENCE: OCR 164.308
               Amatayakul, et al., p 10, 29-31
               Pabrai, p 223-224, 336-337, 477-483
               Johns (2002b), p 669
               Hartley & Jones, p 129
COMPETENCY: Core: 1A
               Security: 7A, 7D, 7E

49. Security awareness must be based on
    A) the employee's role in the organization
    B) policies and procedures
    C) HIPAA regulation
    D) past experiences with security violations
REFERENCE: OCR 164.308
               Amatayakul, et al., p 55-57
               Pabrai, p 229
               Johns (2002b), 366-337
               Hartley & Jones, p 144
COMPETENCY: Core: 1D, 1E
               Security: 2C, 8A

50. Law enacted by a legislative body is referred to as
    A) public law
    B) private law
    C) administrative law
    D) statute
REFERENCE: Johns (2002b), p 199
COMPETENCY: Core: 1B
               Privacy: 2B, 2E

51. There are laws that include a body of criminal law that bar conduct considered
    being harmful to society and set forth a system for punishment for bad acts.
    This type of law involves the government and its relationships with individuals or
    organizations and is referred to as
    A) administrative law
    B) public law
    C) tort law
    D) private law
REFERENCE: Johns (2002b), p 199
COMPETENCY: Core: 1B
               Privacy: 2B, 2E

52. The concept of preemption as used in the HIPAA privacy rule refers to
    A) stricter state statutes related to the confidentiality of healthcare information
       will take precedence over the provisions of the HIPAA privacy rule
    B) the mandate of a notice of privacy practice should include a statement that
       explains that individuals may complain to the secretary of the Department of
       Health and Human Services when they believe that their privacy rights have
       been violated
    C) the fact that Joint Commission on Accreditation of Healthcare Organizations
       sets the official record retention standards for hospitals and other healthcare
       facilities
    D) research projects in which new treatments and tests are investigated to
       determine whether they are safe and effective
REFERENCE: OCR 160.202, 160.203
               Amatayakul, et al., p 4
               Pabrai, p 9, 117
               Johns (2002b), p 209
               Hartley & Jones, p 112
COMPETENCY: Core: 1A, 1B

53. The leader of the HIPAA compliance team wants all of her team members to clearly understand the compliance process. Which of the following would be the best tool for accomplishing this objective?
    A) flowchart
    B) force-field analysis
    C) pareto chart
    D) scatter diagram
REFERENCE: Johns (2002b), p 736-737
COMPETENCY: Core: 1I, 1K, 1L, 1N

54. The primary functions of the Chief Privacy Officer are
    A) overseeing the development, implementation and enforcement of the healthcare organization's policies and processes for protecting patient-identifiable information from unauthorized access or disclosure
    B) overseeing the development, implementation and enforcement of the healthcare organization's policies and processes for complying with all federal, state and accreditation rules and regulations related to the confidentiality and privacy of health-related information
    C) assessing the healthcare organization's information needs, establishing information systems priorities and overseeing information systems implementation projects
    D) overseeing the healthcare organization's information resource management functions and leading the strategic information systems planning process
REFERENCE: OCR 164.530
               Pabrai, p 326, 330-331
               Johns (2002b), p 582, 826-827
COMPETENCY: Core: 1B, 1C, 1E, 1F, 1I, 1S

55. The training objectives for the privacy and security training
    A) should be what you expect to cover during the training session
    B) should be based on deficiencies that have been identified
    C) should be used during evaluation
    D) all of the above
REFERENCE: 164.308
               Amatayakul, et al., p 55-57
               LaTour and Eichenwald, p 599
COMPETENCY: Core: 1D, 1E

56. Which of the following is not true about a privacy gap analysis?
    A) A privacy gap analysis should be one of the first steps the privacy officer takes to prepare for HIPAA compliance.
    B) The privacy gap analysis compares where you are now with where you need to be.
    C) As part of beginning the privacy gap analysis, gather the existing policies and procedures and a copy of the HIPAA regulations.
    D) When your privacy gap analysis is completed, communicate your results to the Security Officer.
REFERENCE: Pabrai, p 336-339, 478-483
              Callahan-Dennis (2000), p 81-83
COMPETENCY: Core: 1L, 1M

57. Annualized Loss Expectancy (ALE) refers to
    A) the financial impact or loss to the organization should the system fail
    B) the calculated financial cost for an occurrence of a harmful event
    C) the calculated relative attractiveness of a target to the perpetrators (i.e. the attractiveness of hacking into a system)
    D) the probability of a harmful event happening
REFERENCE: OCR 164.308
              Miller & Gregory, p 119
              Johns (2002a), p 342
COMPETENCY: Core: 1P

58. The first step in conducting a risk analysis is to
    A) evaluate assets in terms of value to the organization
    B) identify the information assets
    C) calculate the risk based on types of intentional/unintentional occurrences
    D) calculate a risk measurement index
REFERENCE: OCR 164.308
              Amatayakul, et al., p 29-33
              Johns (2002a), p 345
              Pabrai, p 336-337, 477-483
              Hartley & Jones, p 130
COMPETENCY: Core: 1F, 1I, 1L, 1M, 1T, 1U
              Security: 4B

59. Which of the following statements is NOT true of methodologies of determining risk?
   A) a methodology may consider level of risk of unintentional occurrences happening based on probability of occurrence and cost impact
   B) methodology may consider level of risk of potential intentional occurrence based on attractiveness of system to a specific perpetrator and impact of success of the attack on the targeted system
   C) methodology may be based on specific, objective verifiable information in determining level of risk
   D) methodology may use historical statistical data or arbitrary measurements to determine level of risk
REFERENCE: Johns (2002a), p 344
COMPETENCY: Core: 1F, 1I, 1L, 1M, 1T, 1U
               Security: 4B

60. Coastal Hospital is a covered entity under HIPAA. In order to comply with the requirements they must train their workforce on Policies and Procedures with respect to Protected Health Information (PHI). Which of the following levels of the work force would be exempt from training?
   A) HIM staff because they have already received training in release of information
   B) Staff Physicians because they have taken the Hippocratic Oath
   C) Administrative Staff because they do not perform hands on care
   D) None of the above would be exempt from training.
REFERENCE: OCR 164.308, 164.530
               Pabrai, p 229, 327-328
               Callahan-Dennis (2000), p 1
               Hjort (2002), p 60C
COMPETENCY: Core: 1D
               Security: 8D

61. In determining how a person in a position in a department uses health information, the HIPAA Privacy and Security trainer would most certainly review the
   A) past performance evaluations of persons in the position
   B) job description
   C) facility policy on protecting health information
   D) facility policy and procedure on documenting training
REFERENCE: LaTour and Eichenwald, p 598-600
               Hjort (2002), p 60C
COMPETENCY: Core: 1D, 1E

62. The general New Employee Orientation training would most likely cover which of the following HIPAA components?
    A) marketing issues
    B) business associate agreements
    C) physical/workstation security
    D) Job specific training (example: patient right to amend record)
REFERENCE: OCR 164.308
              LaTour and Eichenwald, p 582-584
              Hjort (2002), p 60C
COMPETENCY: Core: 1D, 1E

63. The teaching method selected by an instructor influences the student's ability to understand the material. Instructor-led classrooms may work best when
    A) in-depth training and interaction is desired
    B) there are 3 shifts of employees to train
    C) you want to minimize cost for training
    D) employees from all departments must be trained
REFERENCE: OCR 164.308
              LaTour and Eichenwald, p 590-592
              Hjort (2002), p 60D
COMPETENCY: Core: 1N

64. To ensure consistency of coverage among trainers, you may want to develop
    A) training manuals
    B) meeting handouts and minutes
    C) signed confidentiality statements acknowledging receipt and understanding of any training attended
    D) ongoing training to keep the issues in front of the work force
REFERENCE: OCR 164.308
              LaTour and Eichenwald, p 598-600
              Hjort (2002), p 60D
COMPETENCY: Core: 1N

65. In developing a training "to do list", you would consider the staff and what general training and specialized training topics would be necessary. What tool would be most helpful in organizing this information?
    A) a GANTT chart to show who gets trained when
    B) a spreadsheet with grids identifying who needs what type of training
    C) a "Train-the-Trainers" training manual to help in consistency in training
    D) documentation of previous orientation training to see what has already been covered.
REFERENCE: OCR 164.308
              LaTour and Eichenwald, p 580-584
              Hjort (2002), p 60D
COMPETENCY: Core: 1N

Use the following information to answer questions 66-68.

The training staff in the Human Resources Department is proposing a computer based training program for 200 employees and needs to prepare a budget for the time and cost of the training.
- The training program will be 30 minutes in length.
- The employees may take the training on line at any time.
- There are 200 employees to be trained.
- The rate of pay for 50 of the employees is $15.50 per hour.
- The rate of pay for 50 of the employees is $12.00 per hour.
- The rate of pay for the other 100 employees is $18.00 per hour.

66. How many employee clock hours will be needed to complete the training?
   A) 200 hours
   B) 150 hours
   C) 100 hours
   D) 50 hours
REFERENCE: Basic math calculation
              Amatayakul, et al., p 133-135
COMPETENCY: Core: 1E, 1P

67. In submitting the cost of training, how much should the training staff request in the budget for doing the computer based training?
   A) $3,175.00
   B) $1,975.00
   C) $1,887.50
   D) $1,587.50
REFERENCE: Basic math calculation
COMPETENCY: Core: 1E, 1P

68. What would be the average cost for training an employee?
   A) $15.87
   B) $15.50
   C) $ 9.00
   D) $ 7.94
REFERENCE: Amatayakul, et al., p 133-135
COMPETENCY: Core: 1E, 1P

69. One of the greatest threats to the confidentiality of health data is
    A) when medical information is reviewed as a part of Quality Assurance activities
    B) re-disclosure of information for purposes not authorized in writing by the patient
    C) lack of written authorization by the patient
    D) when medical information is used for research or education
REFERENCE: Abdelhak, p 456-457
COMPETENCY: Core: 1C, 1I
                          Privacy: 2B, 2E

Case Study:
William is a 16-year-old male who lives at home with his parents and works part-time as a dishwasher at one of the local restaurants. While performing his duties William is severely scalded and rendered unconscious while emptying the dishwasher. He is taken to the emergency room of the local acute care hospital for emergency treatment.

70. Referring to the Case Study, in order to provide treatment to William, who should the health care provider receive consent from?
    A) the employer
    B) the parents
    C) the patient
    D) no consent is needed for emergency care
REFERENCE: Pozgar, p 331
                          Roach, W., p 76-77
COMPETENCY: Core: 1B

71. Referring again, to the Case Study, in order to release information to his employer, the hospital must receive
    A) a consent signed by the patient
    B) a court order
    C) no consent is needed
    D) a consent signed by the patient's parent
REFERENCE: Abdelhak, p 454-455
                          Pozgar, p 76-77
COMPETENCY: Core: 1G, 1H
                          Privacy: 4B, 8B

72. Which of the following is an example of the breach of confidentiality?
    A) a nurse speaking with the physician in the patient room
    B) staff members discussing patients in the elevator
    C) the admission clerk verifying over the phone that the patient is in house
    D) the hospital operator paging code blue in room 3 north
REFERENCE: Abdelhak, p 434
                      Amatayakul, et al., p 5-8
                      Pabrai, p 169
                      Pozgar, p 302
COMPETENCY: Core: 1K, 1L, 1M, 1Q
                      Privacy: 4A, 8B, 8C

73. HIPAA mandated the collection of information on healthcare fraud and abuse. As a result, what data bank was developed?
    A) the National Practitioner Data Bank
    B) the Healthcare Integrity and Protection Data Bank
    C) the National Health Provider Inventory
    D) the Nationwide False Claims Data Bank
REFERENCE: Johns, (2002b), p 152
COMPETENCY: Core: 1K, 1L
                      Privacy: 2B, 2C, 5B

74. The administrator needs to be notified of a privacy breech. Who would be the most likely person or group who would tell him?
    A) Chief Privacy Officer
    B) privacy oversight committee
    C) HIM director
    D) Chief Information Officer
REFERENCE: OCR 164.308, 164.530
                      Amatayakul, et al., p 46, 58-60
                      Pabrai, p 236, 330-331
                      Johns (2002b), p 230, 826-827
                      AHIMA, p 37
COMPETENCY: Core: 1K, 1L, 1Q, 1R, 1S

75. The Chief Privacy Officer feels overwhelmed. He has been trying to do everything by himself. What actions should he take?
    A) develop privacy oversight committee
    B) work with attorney
    C) work more hours
    D) both A and B
REFERENCE: Johns (2002b), p 195-196, 826-827
                      Pabrai, p 326, 330-331
                      AHIMA, p 37
COMPETENCY: Core: 1K, 1L, 1Q, 1R, 1S

76. An evaluation of the privacy and security training has determined that there is a deficit in the training program. What should be done?
    A) determine where problem occurred and make necessary change
    B) change instructor
    C) change teaching method
    D) change content
REFERENCE: OCR 164.308
               Amatayakul, et al., p 55-56, 66
               LaTour and Eichenwald, p 599
               Pabrai, p 229, 327-328
COMPETENCY: Core: 1D, 1E

77. I am describing what I expect from my Chief Privacy Officer. My expectations include all of the following except
    A) the CPO must be able to function at a high level within the organization
    B) the CPO must have a reputation as being credible
    C) the CPO must understand patient data
    D) the CPO must have a master's degree
REFERENCE: Johns (2002b), 195, 826-827
               Pabrai, p 326, 330-331
               Apple and Brandt, p 28
COMPETENCY: Core: 1I
             Privacy: 2D

78. I am looking for people to help with the risk assessment. What would I want these people to have a strong understanding of?
    A) HIPAA laws
    B) health information management
    C) flow of information
    D) data quality
REFERENCE: OCR 164.308
               Amatayakul, et al., p 31, 127-128
               Dennis-Callahan (2000), p 81-90
               Pabrai, p 223-224, 336-337, 477-483
               Apple and Brandt, p 28
COMPETENCY: Core: 1T
             Privacy: 7D

79. HIPAA requires which of the following to be a part of the risk assessment?
    A) follow the steps specified in the regulations
    B) develop policies and procedures that best suit the organization and meet the requirements of the rule
    C) use project management skills
    D) use technology
REFERENCE: OCR 164.308, 164.530
               Amatayakul, et al., p 24-27, 36-38, 108
               Pabrai, p 223-224, 336-337, 477-483
               Dennis-Callahan (2000), p 31-34, 81-90
               Apple and Brandt, p 28
COMPETENCY: Core: 1M, 1T, 1U

80. Risk assessment should look at
    A) organizational level risks
    B) departmental level risks
    C) both A and B
    D) none of the above
REFERENCE: OCR 164.308, 164.530
               Amatayakul, et al., p 34-38
               Pabrai, p 223-224, 336-337, 477-483
               Dennis-Callahan (2000), p 31-34, 81-90
               Apple and Brandt, p 30
COMPETENCY: Core: 1M, 1T, 1U

81. The covered entity should _____ risk assessment tools.
    A) ask each department director to develop
    B) develop uniform
    C) use tables as
    D) conduct training on
REFERENCE: Dennis-Callahan (2000), p 31-34, 81-90
               Pabrai, p 223-224, 336-337, 477-483
               Apple and Brandt, p 30
COMPETENCY: Core: 1M, 1N, 1T, 1U

82. Tools that could be used in mapping information flow include all of the following except
    A) data flow diagrams
    B) checklist
    C) project management software
    D) flow chart
REFERENCE: Johns (2002a), p 153-154
               Pabrai, p 332-335
COMPETENCY: Core: 1N
               Privacy: 7D

83. Twenty-five areas of concern were identified in the risk assessment. Which of the following is a good tool to identify which area needs to be addressed first?
A) assign weight to each of the issues based on seriousness of risk
B) handle in the order identified
C) patient care areas first
D) GANTT chart

REFERENCE: OCR 164.308
            Amatayakul, et al., p 38-41, 108
            Johns (2002b), 339, 344-347, 504-505
            Pabrai, p 223-224, 336-337, 477-483
            LaTour and Eichenwald, p 188-189
            Apple and Brandt, p 31
COMPETENCY: Core: 1F, 1M, 1T, 1U

84. I am concerned about the risks involved with using a business associate. I am specifically concerned with releasing large amounts of PHI. Which of the following would I most likely be concerned about?
A) collection agency
B) contract coder
C) hospital to which you refer patients
D) environmental services

REFERENCE: OCR 164.308, 164.530
            Amatayakul, et al., p 22, 66-68
            Pabrai, p 234, 152-155, 340-342
            Johns (2002b), p 222-223
            Apple and Brandt, p 32
COMPETENCY: Core: 1F
            Privacy: 3C

85. Risk assessment should include all of the following except
A) business associate agreements
B) policies and procedures
C) forms
D) hardware

REFERENCE: OCR 160.103, 164.308
            Amatayakul, et al., p 36-38, 108
            Pabrai, p 223-224, 336-337, 477-483
            LaTour and Eichenwald, p 188-189
            Apple and Brandt, p 32
COMPETENCY: Core: 1F, 1M, 1T, 1U
            Security: 8E

86. The outcome of the risk assessment currently being conducted should include all of the following except
    A) identifying business associates
    B) forms
    C) policies and procedures
    D) hardware inventory
REFERENCE: OCR 164.308
                     Amatayakul, et al., p 36-38, 108
                     Pabrai, p 223-224, 336-337, 477-483
                     LaTour and Eichenwald, p 188-189
                     Apple and Brandt, p 32
COMPETENCY: Core: 1M, 1T, 1U
                     Privacy: 3A, 3B, 4A, 4C
                     Security: 8E

87. Which of the following is not the purpose of risk assessment?
    A) educate administration on HIPAA regulations
    B) train staff on the HIPAA regulations
    C) it is the basis for planning for HIPAA compliance
    D) evaluate privacy policies and procedures
REFERENCE: OCR 164.304, 164.308
                     Amatayakul, et al., p 29-31, 108
                     Pabrai, p 223-224, 336-337, 477-483
                     LaTour and Eichenwald, p 188-189
                     Apple and Brandt, p 32
COMPETENCY: Core: 1M, 1S, 1T, 1U
                     Security: 8E

88. I have developed an inventory of privacy and security policies and procedures. This was primarily done
    A) to meet requirement of HIPAA
    B) as good management practice
    C) because I was asked to complete it by my supervisor
    D) because I did not have anything better to do
REFERENCE: OCR 164.304, 164.308, 164.316, 164.530
                     Amatayakul, et al., p 24-27, 131-132
                     Pabrai, p 243-244, 336-337, 477-483
                     Apple and Brandt, p 32
COMPETENCY: Core: 1H

89. The chief financial officer needs to develop a budget for implementation of HIPAA. Which of the following types of budgets would be the most appropriate for this type of project?
A) flexible budget
B) fixed budget
C) activity-based budget
D) zero-based budget
REFERENCE: LaTour and Eichenwald, p 622
              Amatayakul, et al., p 133-135
COMPETENCY: Core: 1P

90. Based on the risk assessment, Macon General Hospital identified a need to renovate nursing units in order to protect privacy. What type of budget should these expenses come under?
A) capital
B) operating
C) personnel
D) fixed
REFERENCE: LaTour and Eichenwald, p 618
              Amatayakul, et al., p 133-135
COMPETENCY: Core: 1P

91. The new policies and procedures required as part of the new HIPAA regulations have been written. What is the key to change implementation?
A) communication
B) type of training provided
C) policy format
D) all of the above
REFERENCE: OCR 164.308, 164.560
              Amatayakul, et al., p 127-128
              LaTour and Eichenwald, p 230, 656
              Pabrai, p 229, 327-328
COMPETENCY: Core: 1G

92. The project plan is being developed for changes resulting from the HIPAA requirements. The initial budget for the proposed changes should be
A) detailed
B) the same as the final budget
C) estimates
D) none of the above
REFERENCE: LaTour and Eichenwald, p 638
              Amatayakul, et al., p 133-135
COMPETENCY: Core: 1P

93. Marjorie has the responsibility of implementing the new policies and procedures. Upon which management skill will she be drawing?
A) controlling
B) planning
C) leadership
D) organizing
REFERENCE: LaTour and Eichenwald, p 499
               Amatayakul, et al., p 46, 128
COMPETENCY: Core: 1G

94. Thomas has just completed teaching a privacy and security awareness training program. Which of the following would not be an appropriate assessment of the results?
A) evaluation
B) feedback from participant's supervisor
C) follow-up in a week or two with the employee
D) input from supervisor
REFERENCE: OCR 164.308
               LaTour and Eichenwald, p 588
               Amatayakul, et al., p 55-57
COMPETENCY: Core: 1D, 1E

95. The administrator wants to be kept apprised of the privacy and security issues. Which of the following communication tools could be used?
A) bulletin boards
B) daily contact with employees
C) weekly status report
D) quarterly reports
REFERENCE: LaTour and Eichenwald ,p 570
COMPETENCY: Core: 1O, 1S

96. JCAHO security requirements are
A) mandatory for everyone
B) voluntary for everyone
C) mandatory for those choosing to be JCAHO accredited
D) more stringent than HIPAA
REFERENCE: LaTour and Eichenwald, p 203
COMPETENCY: Core: 1A

97. The security rule specifically identifies two instructions to be included in the incidence response system. Which of the following is not an example of ways these instructions could be implemented?
    A) contact Chief Privacy Officer immediately
    B) interview appropriate staff
    C) document findings
    D) revise forms
REFERENCE: OCR 164.308
               Amatayakul, et al., p 58-60
               Pabrai, 203-231
COMPETENCY: Core: 1Q, 1R

98. An employee just was found to have violated a patient's privacy. The proper disciplinary step has been taken. Which of the following statements is the most likely to made by the Chief Privacy Officer to the administrator?
    A) there may still be financial ramifications to the healthcare facility
    B) the problem has been resolved
    C) the employee is the only one that has any risk from legal action
    D) none of the above
REFERENCE: OCR 164.308
               Amatayakul, et al., p 58-60
               Pabrai, p 224-225, 230-231
COMPETENCY: Core: 1P

99. Randall is reading a privacy manual and watching a video. These are examples of
    A) self-directed learning
    B) formal training
    C) seminar
    D) traditional methods
REFERENCE: LaTour and Eichenwald, p 590
COMPETENCY: Core: 1D

100. Which of the following steps are REQUIRED by the HIPAA requirements?
    A) documentation of an incident response process
    B) documentation of a damage mitigation system
    C) notification of OCR of incident
    D) both A and B
REFERENCE: OCR 160.308, 164.530
               Amatayakul, et al., p 58-60
               Pabrai, p 230-231, 328-329
               Ruano, p 68
COMPETENCY: Core: 1K, 1Q, 1U

Answer Key Core Questions

1. B

2. D Although physicians are not technically under the control of the facility, they still need to be included in the HIPAA training program.

3. C

4. C

5. A

6. D

7. B

8. D

9. A

10. A

11. D

12. B

13. B

14. D

15. D

16. D

17. B

18. A

19. D There is not a restriction in the format used, only that the information is released.

20. B The physician does not meet the definition of a covered entity since he/she does not file claims electronically.

21. C

22. A

23. A

24. A

25. B

26. C

27. D

28. B

29. D

30. C

31. A

32. D

33. D

34. D

35. A Confidentiality of alcohol and drug abuse patient record regulation only applies to federally assisted programs.

36. D

37. B

38. C

39. C

40. A

41. C

42. B

43. D

44. D

45. D

46. B

47. D

48. A

49. A

50. D

51. B

52. A

53. A

54. B

55. D

56. D The privacy officer should be communicating with the security officer as well as others on a team formed to work through the gap analysis to avoid duplication of efforts. With a variety in staff team members, each member will have special perspectives and insights to help in detecting potential risks.

57. A ALE is usually defined as the financial impact or loss to the organizations should the system fail. It is typically calculated by multiplying the financial cost per each occurrence of a harmful event times the number of times the event is expected to happen in one year.

58. B The first step in conducting a risk analysis is to know what constitutes the organizational information assets.

59. C Ultimately, the determination of risk is based on management judgment. The probability estimates can be based on historical statistical data or could be arbitrary measurements based on judgment and experience of the organizational security team.

60. D

61. B

62. C

63. A

64.   A

65.   B

66.   C   Calculation: 200 employees X .5 hour for training=100 clock hours

67.   D   Calculation:
           50 employees X .5 hour X $15.50 per hour = $387.50
           50 employees X .5 hour X $12.00 per hour = $300.00
           100 employees X .5 hour X $18.00 per hour = $900.00
           387.50 + 300.00 + 900.00= $1587.50

68.   D   Calculation: $1587.50 divided by 200 employees = $7.94 per employee

69.   B

70.   D

71.   D

72.   B

73.   B

74.   A

75.   D

76.   A

77.   D

78.   C

79.   B

80.   C

81.   B

82.   B

83.   A

84.   B

85. D

86. D

87. B

88. A

89. C This type of budget is used for projects that affect many groups or departments.

90. A

91. A

92. C

93. C

94. D

95. C

96. C

97. D

98. D

99. A

100. D

CORE REFERENCES

Abdelhak, M., Grostick, S., Hanken, M., & Jacobs E. (Eds.) (2001). *Health information: Management of a strategic resource*. Philadelphia: W.B. Saunders Company.

AHIMA (2001). Help wanted: Privacy officer. *Journal of AHIMA, 72*(6), 37-39.

Amatayakul, M. (2000). Getting ready for HIPAA privacy rules. *Journal of AHIMA, 71*(4), 34-36.

Amatayakul, M. (2002d). HIPAA on the Job: United under HIPAA: A comparison of arrangements and agreements. *Journal of AHIMA, 73*(8), 24A-D.

Amatayakul, M., et al. (2004) *Handbook for HIPAA Security Implementation.* AMA Press.

Amatayakul, M., & Johns, M. L. (2002). HIPAA on the job series: Compliance in the crosshairs: Targeting your training. *Journal of AHIMA. 73*(10), 16A-F.

Apple, G. J., & Brandt, M. D. (2001). Ready, set, assess: An action plan for conducting a HIPAA privacy risk assessment. *Journal of AHIMA, 72*(6), 26-32.

Callahan-Dennis, J. (2000). Privacy and confidentiality of health information. San Francisco: Jossey-Bass.

Callahan-Dennis, J. (2001a) Leading the HIPAA privacy risk assessment. *AHIMA Convention Proceedings.* Retrieved January 16, 2003, from http://www.ahima.org.

Callahan-Dennis, J. (2001b). The new privacy officer's game plan. *Journal of AHIMA, 72*(2), 33-37.

Cassidy, B. S. (2000). HIPAA on the job: Understanding chain of trust and business partner agreements. *Journal of AHIMA, 71*(9), 16A-C.

Choy, A., Pritts, J., & Goldman, J. (2002). E-health: What's outside the privacy rule's jurisdiction? *Journal of AHIMA, 73*(5), 34-39.

Dougherty, M. (2001). Practice brief: Accounting and tracking disclosure of protected health information. *Journal of AHIMA, 72*(10), 72E-H.

Dougherty, M. (2002). It's time to finalize your privacy policies. *Journal of AHIMA 73*(10), 61-64.

Hjort, B. (2001). AHIMA practice brief: A HIPAA privacy checklist. *Journal of AHIMA 72*(6), 64A-C.

Hjort, B. (2002). Privacy and security training. *Journal of AHIMA, 73*(4), 60A-G.

CORE REFERENCES

Hughes, G. (2002c). AHIMA practice brief: Laws and regulations governing the disclosure of health information (Updated November, 2002). Retrieved February 1, 2003, from http://www.ahima.org

Johns, M. L. (2002a). *Information Management for Health Professions.* Albany, NY: Delmar Publishing.

Johns, M. L. (2002b). *Health information technology: An applied approach.* Chicago, IL: American Health Information Management Association.

LaTour, K. M., & Eichenwald, S. (2002). *Health information management: Concepts principles, and practice.* Chicago, IL: American Health Information Management Association.

Pozgar, G. D. (1999). *Legal aspects of healthcare administration (7th ed.).* Gaithersburg, MD: Aspen Publications.

Roach, Jr., W. (1998). *Medical records and the law* (3rd edition). Boston, MA: Jones and Bartlett Publishers.

Ruono, M. (2003). Moving toward a unified information security program. *Journal of AHIMA, 74*(1), 66, 68.

Sullivan, T. (2002). Mind your business associate access: Six steps. *Journal of AHIMA, 73*(9), 92, 94, 96.

U. S. Department of Health and Human Services (2003) HHS Fact Sheet: *Protecting The Privacy Of Patients' Health Information (*April 14, 2003) Retrieved January 15, 2004, from http://www.hhs.gov/news/facts/privacy.html

OCR
U.S. Department of Health and Human Services Office for Civil Rights (2003)
Standards for Privacy of Individually Identifiable Health Information
Security Standards for the Protection of Electronic Protected Health Information General Administrative Requirements Including, Civil Money Penalties: Procedures for Investigations, Imposition of Penalties, and Hearings Regulation Text (Unofficial Version) (45 CFR Parts 160 and 164)
December 28, 2000 as amended: May 31, 2002, August 14, 2002, February 20, 2003, and April 17, 2003
Retrieved November 5, 2004, from http://www.hhs.gov/ocr/combinedregtext.pdf

Privacy Questions for the CHP Examination

Privacy Questions
for the CHP Examination

1. You are the Chief Privacy Officer for Georgia Premier Medical Center. Which of the following are you NOT responsible for?
   A) privacy training
   B) developing the plan for reporting privacy complaints
   C) writing policies on how to deal with violations
   D) writing policies on encryption standards
   REFERENCE: Hjort (2001), p 64B
                 Johns (2002b), p 195-196
                 Pabrai, p 326, 330-331
   COMPETENCY: Core: 1S
                 Privacy: 2B, 4C

2. Which of the following situations violate a patient's privacy?
   A) The hospital sends patients who are scheduled for deliveries information on free childbirth classes.
   B) A physician on the quality improvement committee reviews the medical record for potential quality problems.
   C) The hospital provides patient names and addresses to a pharmaceutical company to be used in a mass mailing of free drug samples.
   D) The hospital uses aggregate data to determine whether or not to add a new operating room suite.
   REFERENCE: OCR 164.501, 164.508
                 Pabrai, p 126-133, 146-147, 173-175
                 Amatayakul (2001b), p 16B
                 Davis, p 142
   COMPETENCY: Privacy: 2B, 8C

3. Margaret has signed an authorization to release information regarding her ER visit for a fractured finger to her attorney. Specifically she says to release the ER history and physical, x-rays and any procedure note for finger fracture. Which of the following violates her privacy?
   A) release of facesheet used in ER as a history.
   B) release of x-ray of chest
   C) release of x-ray of finger
   D) documentation of setting finger
   REFERENCE: Hughes (2002a), p 56A
                 Pabrai, p 141-142, 146-147
   COMPETENCY: Privacy: 7A, 7C, 8C

4. I have just written a new policy on tracking release of patient identifiable information. Which of the following was included in the list of disclosures to track?
A) release for patient care
B) release to the patient
C) release to attorney
D) release made to law enforcement agencies
REFERENCE: OCR 164.528
                Dougherty (2001), p 72E
                Hartley & Jones, p 80-81
COMPETENCY: Privacy: 2B, 8C

5. You are walking around the facility to identify any privacy and security issues. You walk onto the 6W nursing unit and are able to watch the nurse entering confidential patient information. You make a note of this. What are you doing?
A) gap analysis
B) risk assessment
C) monitoring audit trail
D) none of the above
REFERENCE: Pabrai, p 206-208, 447
                Hjort (2001), P 64A
                Hartley & Jones, p 130
COMPETENCY: Core: 1M
                Privacy: 2B, 6A, 8B
                Security: 4B, 4C, 4E, 10A, 10B, 10C

6. You are walking around the facility to identify any privacy and security issues. You walk onto the 6W nursing unit and are able to watch the nurse entering confidential patient information. How can you best improve the privacy of the patients?
A) ask the nurse to type the data at another computer
B) turn the computer screen so that the public cannot see it.
C) give the nurse additional training
D) none of the above
REFERENCE: Pabrai, p 206-208, 447
                Amatayakul (2002a), p 16C
                Hartley & Jones, p 130
COMPETENCY: Privacy: 2B, 6A
                Security: 4B, 4C, 4E, 5C, 10A, 10B, 10C

7. I am conducting an environmental risk assessment. Which of the following would be excluded from my assessment?
   A) placement of water pipes in the facility
   B) verifying that virus checking software is in place
   C) status of fire protection
   D) presence of back-up power

REFERENCE: OCR 164.310
                Pabrai, p 235-238
                Callahan-Dennis (2000), p 18
COMPETENCY: Privacy: 6A, 8C
                Security: 3A, 3D, 4B, 5C

8. In preparing your regular new employee presentation on privacy, you realize that you have never added technology to the content. In updating the presentation to include privacy issues surrounding technology, which of the following would not be added?
   A) the need to back up data
   B) talking about patient while reviewing computer screen in public area
   C) the need to face monitors away from public area
   D) locking doors to computer rooms

REFERENCE: OCR 164.308, 164.312
                Pabrai, p 238-241
                Amatayakul (2002a), p 16A-16C
COMPETENCY: Privacy: 2B, 8B, 8C

9. You are writing policies and procedures on what is and what is not confidential information. Which of the following would you classify as not confidential information in most cases?
   A) diagnosis
   B) date of service
   C) allergy
   D) none of the above

REFERENCE: Callahan-Dennis (2000), p 10
                Pabrai, p 31-32
COMPETENCY: Privacy: 2B, 7A, 7C, 8C
                Security: 10A, 10F

10. Today is June 30, 2003. Barbara has received a written authorization from an attorney for records on John Marshall. The dates of service requested by the authorization is the admission of June 2, 2003 through June 8, 2003. The authorization is dated June 3, 2003. Which of the following is the appropriate response?
   A) release the records as requested
   B) return authorization and request one dated after June 8, 2003
   C) ask supervisor to process request
   D) none of the above

REFERENCE: OCR 164.508
               Pabrai, p 138-143
               Callahan-Dennis (2000), p 37
               LaTour and Eichenwald, p 205-206
COMPETENCY: Privacy: 8C
               Security: 10A

11. I have decided that the current method of tracking release of confidential information is just not working. I have decided to purchase a computerized tracking system. The administrator is supportive of the purchase, but has asked for a formal justification of the system. Which of the following is not a reason to purchase the system?
   A) Everyone in the facility who releases information can enter information into a common database.
   B) A report can be printed upon demand.
   C) The system restricts the release to the HIM department.
   D) Will no longer have to track down manual entries.

REFERENCE: Dougherty (2001), p 72F
               Abdelhak, p 704
COMPETENCY: Privacy: 8C

12. Brad Thomas is a former patient at Alabama General Hospital. He came to the HIM Department today and asked for a list of people who have requested his medical record over the past 10 years. He also wants to know what was released. Which is the appropriate response to Brad's request?
   A) give him what he requested
   B) give him the information on records released since the HIPAA privacy rule was implemented, not to exceed six years
   C) do not give him any information
   D) give him his medical record and let him find out who requested information for himself

REFERENCE: OCR 164.316, 164.528
               Pabrai, p 143, 243
               Dougherty (2001), p 72E
               Hartley & Jones, p 81
COMPETENCY: Privacy: 5C, 8B, 8C

13. The local newspaper has notified the hospital that they have received a computer listing of the names of patients receiving HIV treatment in your facility. What method(s) could be used to identify the source of this breach of confidentiality?
A) a review of computer audit trails to determine who may have accessed such information
B) identify where, when and by whom such data is originated and distributed
C) identify all employees whose passwords would permit access to such information
D) all of the above
REFERENCE: OCR 164.312
                           Abdelhak, p 678-680
                           Pabrai, p 110-114, 238-241
COMPETENCY: Privacy: 6A, 6B, 6E
                           Security: 4B, 4D, 4E, 4F, 4I

14. Nathaniel says that hand-written medical records are exempt from HIPAA privacy standards. Greg said that oral communication is exempt. Julia says that computerized records are exempt. Beverly says that all patient identifiable information is protected regardless of the form. Who is right?
A) Nathaniel
B) Greg
C) Julia
D) Beverly
REFERENCE: OCR 160.103, 164.502
                           Pabrai, p 2, 23, 121, 169-171
                           Davis, p 50
COMPETENCY: Privacy: 2B, 7A, 7C

15. Which of the following groups does not meet the definition of a business associate?
A) release of information company
B) food service provider
C) information systems vendor helping with installation
D) all of the above
REFERENCE: OCR 160.102
                           Johns (2002a), p 222, 674
                           Pabrai, p 192-193
COMPETENCY: Privacy: 3A

16. Which of the following statements demonstrate an inappropriate communication of protected health information?
   A) "Yes, Mr. Smith is in room 222. I will transfer your call."
   B) Physician's office staff calls centralized scheduling and says: "Dr. Smith wants to perform a bunionectomy on Mary Jones next Tuesday."
   C) "Mary, at work yesterday, I saw that Susan had a hysterectomy."
   D) Dr. Jones tells a nurse on the floor, "Ms. Brown may have Demerol for her pain."

REFERENCE: OCR 164.510
               Pabrai, p 169-171
               Roach, M., p 45
COMPETENCY: Privacy: 7A, 8B, 8C

17. Plans for a manual back-up system for locating patient records in the event the computer system is not operating would include:
   A) converting from terminal digit filing to alphabetic filing
   B) issuing all patients WORM smart cards indicating their medical record number
   C) using the same number for the patient account number and medical record number
   D) using an MPI card system or maintaining a paper/microfilm copy of an alphabetic MPI listing

REFERENCE: Abdelhak, p 188
COMPETENCY: Privacy: 6C
               Security: 3A, 3D

18. Ms. Thomas was a patient at your facility. She has been told that there are some records that she cannot have access to. These records are most likely
   A) psychotherapy notes
   B) alcohol and drug records
   C) AIDs records
   D) physical health assessment

REFERENCE: OCR 164.524
               Johns (2002b), p 69-70
               Hughes (2001a), p 90
COMPETENCY: Privacy: 2B, 7B, 8B, 8C

19. Ms. Hall has requested that Dr. Moore amend her medical record. He emphatically refused. What type of documentation is required, if any?
   A) no documentation is required
   B) document request and refusal
   C) document request
   D) none of the above

REFERENCE: OCR 164.526
               Pabrai, p 145-146
               Hartley & Davis, p 80
               Amatayakul (2001b), p 16C
COMPETENCY: Privacy: 2B, 4A, 7D, 8B, 8C

20. Which of the following is (are) policies that should be implemented regarding passwords?
    A) they should be changed periodically
    B) it should not be something that can be easily guessed like spouse's name
    C) passwords should not be repeated
    D) all of the above
    REFERENCE: Johns (2002a), p 356-357
                   Amatayakul & Walsh, p 16C
    COMPETENCY: Privacy: 6A, 6B, 8C
                   Security: 4D, 6A, 6C

21. On the day that a new employee is hired, he requests that no one in the department have access to his computerized record. You tell the employee that you will
    A) send a memo to everyone in the department informing them of his request for confidentiality
    B) increase the level of confidentiality on his record
    C) examine his record yourself and determine who else currently has access to it
    D) delete his record from the system
    REFERENCE: Pabrai, p 143-144
                   Abdelhak, p 679-680
    COMPETENCY: Privacy: 2B, 4A, 8A, 8C

22. Marjorie has filed a request asking to be notified before any of her medical records are released to anyone outside of the healthcare facility. You receive a request from an insurance company. There is a patient authorization attached. What do you do?
    A) release the chart because you want to get paid
    B) release the chart because the patient has consented
    C) notify patient and follow her instructions
    D) notify patient and release chart as per authorization
    REFERENCE: OCR 164.522
                   Amatayakul (2001b), p 16B
    COMPETENCY: Privacy: 8B, 8C

23. Which of the following would be the most appropriate means of protecting data being passed over the Internet?
    A) call back
    B) firewall
    C) encryption
    D) audit trail
    REFERENCE: Pabrai, p 210, 213, 240
                   Johns (2002b), p 679
    COMPETENCY: Privacy: 6A, 6B
                   Security: 6F, 7A, 7E

24. The notice of privacy practices says, "Your medical record may be used for quality reviews." The reason this statement is on the notice is that:
A) the verbiage is required by HIPAA
B) it is an example of healthcare operations
C) it is the purpose of the medical record
D) the covered entity cannot use the medical record unless this is specifically documented in the notice.

REFERENCE: OCR, 164.520
               Pabrai, p 133-138
               Hughes (2002A), p 64I
COMPETENCY: Privacy: 2B, 8C

25. You are an employee in the lab. You have been asked to run the culture and sensitivity on a urine sample. You pull the patient up in the lab system to do your work. While in the system, you see the patient's PSA is elevated and the RBC is normal. Are you violating a patient's privacy?
A) yes, because this is more than you "need to know" to do your job
B) no, because you are working in the lab and are running a lab test on the patient
C) yes, you should not be in the system at all
D) none of the above

REFERENCE: U.S. Department of Health and Human Services (2003), p 2
               OCR 164.508
COMPETENCY: Privacy: 2B, 4A, 8C

26. Marvin has trouble remembering his password. He is trying to come up with a solution that will help him remember. He reads the policies on passwords. Based on the policy, he eliminates all of his ideas except to
A) use the same password all of the time
B) use his children's names
C) write the password down and place the paper under his calendar
D) select a password that is based on something related to the time of the year.

REFERENCE: Amatayakul & Walsh, p 16C
               Johns, p 664
COMPETENCY: Privacy: 6A, 6B
               Security: 4D, 6A, 6C

27. Nicole is developing an agreement that will be used between the hospital and the healthcare clearinghouse. This agreement will require the two parties to protect the privacy of data exchanged. This is called a
A) business associate agreement
B) chain of trust partner agreement
C) trading partner agreement
D) none of the above
REFERENCE: OCR 160.103
                Pabrai, p 34, 152-155, 192-193, 234, 242
                Hartley & Jones, p 234
                Amatayakul, (2001a), p 16B
COMPETENCY: Privacy: 3B, 3C

28. You work for a 60 bed hospital in a rural community. You are conducting research on what you need to do to comply with HIPAA. You are afraid that you will have to implement all of the steps that your friend at a 900 bed teaching hospital is implementing at his facility. You continue reading and learn that you only have to implement what is prudent and reasonable for your facility. This is called
A) scalability
B) risk assessment
C) technology neutral
D) access control
REFERENCE: OCR 164.306, 164.502
                Pabrai, p 160-161, 166-167, 198, 218
                Dougherty (2002), p 61
COMPETENCY: Privacy: 2A, 2B

29. You have been working with your computer vendors to ensure that the systems that you are using are secure and will protect the patient's privacy. Which of the following can the vendor assist you with?
A) access restriction
B) monitoring activity
C) backing up data
D) all of the above
REFERENCE: LaTour and Eichenwald, p 189-190
                Brandt, p 2
COMPETENCY: Privacy: 2B, 3D, 6A, 6B

30. The coroner is requesting the medical record for Susan Brown because he is trying to identify a body. Which of the following is true?
    A) HIPAA requires release without authorization
    B) HIPAA allows release according to state law
    C) the coroner must have authorization
    D) none of the above
REFERENCE: OCR 164.512
               LaTour and Eichenwald, p 204-205
               Hughes (2002f), p 56A
COMPETENCY: Privacy: 2B, 4A, 7D, 8C

31. Mary sold confidential patient information on a celebrity to a tabloid. Mary has been given repeated privacy training by the hospital where she works. The hospital regularly monitors access. In fact, they reported Mary. Mary had never done anything like this before. Who should be awarded any penalty?
    A) Mary
    B) the healthcare facility where Mary works
    C) both Mary and the healthcare facility
    D) none of the above
REFERENCE: U.S. Department of Health and Human Services (2003), p 2
               OCR 160.506
               Pabrai, p 114-115
COMPETENCY: Privacy: 2B, 8B, 8C

32. You overheard a conversation between two nurses. They are discussing confidential personal information. You are a nurse who works on the same unit. The conversation is occurring in the office behind the nursing unit and the nurses are speaking in a low voice. You are not taking care of the patient. Are the two nurses violating patient privacy?
    A) yes because you are not involved in the care of the patient
    B) no because prudent actions are being taken
    C) not if you are the nurse manager
    D) none of the above
REFERENCE: U. S. Office of Civil Rights (2002b), p 11
               Pabrai, p 169-172
COMPETENCY: Privacy: 2B, 8B, 8C

33. I am writing policies on what is and what is not protected health information. Which of the following would not be protected?
    A) the list of drugs that a patient takes
    B) a flier on diagnosis and treatment of diabetes mellitus
    C) a note summarizing what the patient's wife said about the patient
    D) lab results
REFERENCE: U. S. Department of Health and Human Services (2002a), p 2
               Pabrai, p 32-33, 109
               Davis, p 50
COMPETENCY: Privacy: 2B, 7A, 7C, 8C

34. Dr. Smith is a psychiatrist. He has a file cabinet full of private notes that are not stored in the medical record. These notes include a number of documents. Which of the following notes are not subject to the psychotherapy restrictions?
A) analysis of group therapy
B) documentation of family therapy
C) counseling start and stop times
D) summary of private conversations with patient
REFERENCE: OCR 164.501, 164.508
                      Doscher, p 223
COMPETENCY: Privacy: 2B, 7B, 8B, 8C

35. A business associate agreement has been established between Tallahassee General Hospital and Metropolitan Billing Collection Company. Tallahassee has not been satisfied with the service provided by Metropolitan and is terminating the agreement. If the contract is written according to HIPAA requirements, what should be done with any protected information in the possession of Metropolitan?
A) return the information to Tallahassee General Hospital
B) destroy the information
C) keep the information for their documentation
D) either A or B
REFERENCE: OCR 164.504
                      Pabrai, p 347-348, 461-467
COMPETENCY: Privacy: 2B, 3B, 3C, 3D, 8C

36. Which situation would not require patient consent prior to the release of psychotherapy notes?
A) patient's attorney requests records
B) use by covered entity to defend itself in court
C) sending records to a new physician
D) patient review
REFERENCE: OCR 164.508
                      Pabrai, p 117
                      Hartley & Jones, p 111
COMPETENCY: Privacy: 2B, 7B, 8B, 8C

37. Jeffersonville Hospital is developing a new marketing strategy because of the HIPAA requirements. Which of the following would require patient consent?
    A) explaining the new program developed by the covered entity in a face-to-face meeting
    B) a gift of a pencil with the new program's name and phone number
    C) mailing a flier on a new diabetes management program offered by a business associate
    D) none of the above
REFERENCE: OCR 164.508
              Pabrai, p 175
              Johns (2002b), p 229
              Davis, p 143
COMPETENCY: Privacy: 2B, 8C

38. Today's date is March 25, 2003. Which one of the following authorization is invalid?
    A) Authorization contains core elements. The date signed is March 24, 2003. The signature does not match the one in the chart.
    B) Authorization contains information requested, who is authorized to release, who is to receive the information, purpose of information requested, an expiration date that has not passed, the signature of patient and date signed. It also contains the appropriate required statements.
    C) Authorization contains information requested, who is authorized to release, who is to receive the information, purpose of information requested, an expiration date that has not passed, the signature of patient and date signed. The authorization includes a statement allowing for the right to revoke, and exemptions to the right to revoke the authorization.
    D) Authorization includes core elements, required statements and is dated March 12, 2003. The authorization says that the authorization expires in 30 days.
REFERENCE: OCR 164.508
              Pabrai, p 138-141
              Johns (2002b), p 218-219
COMPETENCY: Privacy: 2B, 7C, 8B, 8C

39. A medical professional can use his or her medical judgment to use personally identifiable medical information to notify/contact family members of a patient's status in which of the following situations?
    A) locate family member in event of patient's incapacity
    B) notify family of patient's death
    C) notify family of patient's location
    D) notify family of patient's diagnosis
REFERENCE: OCR 164.512
COMPETENCY: Privacy: 2B, 2C, 2D, 8B, 8C

40. As Chief Privacy Officer, you are reviewing policies and procedures with regard to collecting and using information without patient consent. Which of the following would not be included in the policy under review?
    A) completing birth certificate and reporting it to the state
    B) reporting communicable diseases to public health authority
    C) notifying FDA of problem with medical equipment
    D) giving the patient medical record to police
REFERENCE: OCR 164.502
             Johns (2002b), p 223-226
COMPETENCY: Privacy: 2B, 4A, 7B, 7D, 8B, 8C

41. Birmingham General Hospital has requested copies of a patient record from the Alabama Medical Center. Which of the following steps is the appropriate action of the Alabama Medical Center?
    A) ask specific questions to ensure that only the minimal necessary information is being released
    B) provide the properly requested information since HIPAA requires covered entities to only request minimally necessary information
    C) request documentation to justify the request for the entire medical record
    D) both B and C
REFERENCE: OCR 164.502
             Amatayakul (2002b), p 96E
             Pabrai, p 164-166
             Johns (2002b), p 198-212-213
COMPETENCY: Privacy: 2B, 8B, 8C

42. A patient has complained that his privacy has been violated. What actions should the healthcare facility take?
    A) investigate if the patient is believable
    B) investigate the complaint
    C) investigate to see if there has been a trend of this type of complaint
    D) Both B and C
REFERENCE: Amatayakul (2002c), p 24A
             Hartley & Jones, p 82-83
COMPETENCY: Privacy: 5A, 5B, 5C

43. In developing the business associate agreement, which of the following would not be included?
   A) business associate must notify covered entity of inappropriate use of information
   B) regular monthly report of use of data to covered entity
   C) subcontractors must follow the agreement
   D) at termination of the agreement, the patient specific health information will be destroyed or returned
REFERENCE: OCR 164.314
               Pabrai, p 152, 156, 192-193, 234, 392, 461-467
               Amatayakul (2002d), p 24C
               Hartley & Jones, p 115
COMPETENCY: Privacy: 2B, 3B, 3C, 3D

44. Limiting access to data based on the need to know is an example of
   A) personnel security
   B) physical security
   C) hardware security
   D) communications security
REFERENCE: OCR 164.301
               Pabrai, p 158-159, 235-238
               Johns (2002a), p 341
COMPETENCY: Privacy: 2B, 4A, 5A, 8C
               Security: 2D, 4B, 4F, 4G, 6A, 6G

45. Sam suspects Brett of intentionally altering the amount that he owes the healthcare organization for a surgery that he had last year. Brett works in the Business Office, so he did have the capability of making the alteration. How can Sam prove this?
   A) ask Brett
   B) check the audit trail
   C) through access control
   D) through status message
REFERENCE: Johns (2002a), p 358
               Pabrai, p 211
COMPETENCY: Privacy: 6B
               Security: 4G, 5C

46. Martin has been given the responsibility to determine the physical security of the planned new computer center. Which of the following should be excluded from his deliberations of contents of the computer system?
    A) ensure that the computer center is not near any electromagnetic radiation
    B) fire detection and suppression systems
    C) encryption
    D) inventory of contents of computer system
REFERENCE: OCR 164.301
               Pabrai, p 235-238
               Johns (2002a), p 352-353
COMPETENCY: Privacy: 6B
               Security: 4G, 5C

47. Dr. Smith has a patient who just died. He has reason to suspect the death resulted from criminal activities. He should
    A) ignore it since reporting it would violate the patient's privacy
    B) report it to hospital administration
    C) report the death and suspicions to the police for investigation
    D) none of the above
REFERENCE: OCR 164.512
               Pabrai, p 115-116
COMPETENCY: Privacy: 2B, 2C, 2D, 8B, 8C

48. The HIM program at State University has requested copies of medical records for the health information courses. You have to decide how to respond to the request. The appropriate response would be
    A) to provide the records
    B) to not provide the records
    C) to provide the records after all identifying information has been removed
    D) none of the above
REFERENCE: OCR 164.514
               Pabrai, p 121-123, 456-459
COMPETENCY: Privacy: 2B, 8B, 8C

49. A group of researchers has asked Lincoln Hospital to provide some de-identified information that they need for research. The request includes a request for diagnoses, medical device identifiers, year of implant and gender of patient. How should the hospital respond?
    A) provide the information since none of it can identify the patient
    B) do not provide the patient information since it asked for the year of implant
    C) do not provide the information since it asked for the medical device identifier
    D) do not provide the information since it asked for the patient's gender
REFERENCE: OCR 164.514
               Pabrai, p 121-123, 456-459
COMPETENCY: Privacy: 4A, 7A, 8A, 8B, 8C

50. Mallory's medical record said that she was anxious. She disagrees. She formally requests an amendment to her medical record. The request was denied because the physician believes that the statement is true. The hospital then allowed Mallory to write a note describing her disagreement. This note was then filed in the medical record. The hospital is acting
A) appropriately, because the information is accurate
B) inappropriately, because the patient has control over the information in his/her chart
C) appropriately, because they are in control of the information
D) appropriately since the hospital followed the guidelines outlined in the privacy rule

REFERENCE: OCR 164.526
              Pabrai, p 145-146
              Johns (2002b), p 226-227
COMPETENCY: Privacy: 2B, 4A, 8B, 8C

51. Mercy Hospital has received a request to amend information in a medical record. The clerk is on maternity leave and will not return for 75 days. Which of the following is the most appropriate response to the request?
A) leave the request for the clerk to process upon her return
B) return the request and ask for it to be resubmitted in 75 days.
C) identify someone else to process the request since it has to be processed within 30 days of receipt
D) identify someone else to process the request since it has to be processed within 60 days of receipt

REFERENCE: OCR 164.526
              Pabrai, p 145-146
              Johns (2002b), 226-227
              LaTour and Eichenwald, p 211
COMPETENCY: Privacy: 2B, 4A, 7D, 8B, 8C

52. A patient has asked that a written a note of disagreement be filed in the medical record. The disagreement is regarding the diagnosis of anxiety. The hospital has received a request that would require releasing documents containing the diagnosis. What action should the hospital take?
A) release the information
B) do not release the information
C) release with information and include a copy of the statement of disagreement
D) release the information but obliterate all references to anxiety

REFERENCE: OCR 164.526
              Pabrai, p 145-146
              Johns (2002b) , p 226-227
COMPETENCY: Privacy: 8B, 8C

53. John Welch has requested a list of everyone who has had access to the medical record. The hospital has created this list. This list should include:
A) access for patient care
B) access provided to law enforcement in all cases
C) access by attorneys
D) none of the above
REFERENCE: OCR 164.528
                          Johns (2002b), p 228-229
COMPETENCY: Privacy: 2B, 4A, 4B, 5C, 6E, 8B, 8C

54. Sabrina has requested a list of everyone who has had access to her confidential information. The request specifies a timeframe of 2 years. What should the hospital's response be?
A) provide the information for the past 2 years since that is what is requested
B) provide the information for the past 6 years since HIPAA specifies 6 years
C) provide the information for the past year since HIPAA limits this type of request to 1 year
D) none of the above
REFERENCE: OCR 164.528
                          Pabrai, p 143-144
                          Johns (2002b), p 228-229
COMPETENCY: Privacy: 2B, 4A, 4B, 8B, 8C

55. Cleo received a request for an accounting of who has had access to a patient's record. When retrieving this information, she found that attorney Sam Talbot requested information on four separate occasions. How should she document this?
A) document that Sam Talbot received information
B) document that information was provided to Sam Talbot four times
C) document only the number of times information was released, the date of the last request, the date of the initial request and the information provided
D) document the number of times information was released, the date of the last request, the date of the initial request, the information provided and the purpose of the releases
REFERENCE: OCR 164.528
                          Johns (2002b), p 228-229
COMPETENCY: Privacy: 2B, 4A, 4B, 8B, 8C

56. Gretchen is being admitted as an inpatient at Butte Community Hospital. Gretchen receives a statement notifying her of her rights. Based on the HIPAA regulations, which of the following would not be a required part of this document?
    A) how the patient can complain about a privacy violation to the Department of Health and Human Services
    B) examples of how patient health information may be used for the payment and operations of the facility
    C) brief explanation of how the patient can exercise his/her rights
    D) list of official policies and procedures enforcing privacy issues

REFERENCE: OCR 164.52
               Pabrai, p 134-138
               Johns (2002b), p 212-214
               Hughes (2001c), p 64I
               Hartley & Jones, p 69
COMPETENCY: Privacy: 5B, 5C, 8B, 8C

57. Beth is the Chief Privacy Officer at Athens Hospital. She is explaining how patients should be notified of their rights. She must list all of the following except to
    A) provide copy of notice at the patient's first service date
    B) post notice in prominent location
    C) have notice available to give to patient
    D) place notice on website

REFERENCE: OCR 164.520
               Pabrai, p 134-138
               Johns (2002b), p 212-214
               Hughes (2001b), p 64J
               Hartley & Jones, p 70-71
COMPETENCY: Privacy: 2A, 2B, 4A, 5C, 8B, 8C

58. Which of the following formats is an acceptable format in which to provide the required confidentiality notice and acknowledgement?
    A) mail
    B) electronically
    C) email
    D) all of the above

REFERENCE: OCR 164.520
               Pabrai, p 134-138
               Hughes (2001b), p 64J
               Davis, p 177
COMPETENCY: Privacy: 2A, 2B, 4A

59.James is working on a policy where the hospital sends the confidentiality acknowledgement to the patient at home when one was not captured at the hospital due to an emergency. Which of the following should NOT be included in the policy and procedure?
A) make a good faith effort to contact the patient
B) follow-up with patient if acknowledgement is not received in 2 weeks
C) send to patient by mail
D) document the reason why acknowledgement was not obtained
REFERENCE: OCR 164.520
                        Pabrai, p 134-138
                        Hughes (2001b), p 64J
                        Hughes (2002b)
                        Davis, p 177-178
COMPETENCY: Privacy: 2A, 2B, 4A

60.Mary is comparing her Iowa state laws to the HIPAA regulations. In which of the following circumstances would Mary follow the state laws?
A) never because the HIPAA regulations supercede the state laws
B) when the state law is more stringent regarding confidentiality of PHI
C) when state law was passed after HIPAA implementation
D) when state law has been reviewed and approved as a substitute by DHHS
REFERENCE: OCR 160.202, 160.203
                        Johns (2002b), p 209
                        Hughes (2002c), p 64
                        Davis, p 83
COMPETENCY: Core: 1C
                        Privacy: 2B, 2E, 4A, 5A, 8C

61.Peter has requested that a copy of his medical record including the discharge summary, history and physical, operative note, pathology report, lab and graphic report be sent to a specific person. The HIM professional responding to the authorization should
A) process the request as it is since the patient authorization overrides the minimum necessary rule
B) refuse the authorization since the professional believes that more information than is minimally necessary may have been requested
C) send the request back to Peter and ask for clarification
D) refuse the request since patients do not have the right to access their medical record except under certain circumstances
REFERENCE: OCR 164.502
                        Pabrai, p 158-166
                        Rode (2002), p 16
COMPETENCY: Privacy: 2B, 4A, 8B, 8C

62. Amanda is developing an authorization form to be used when releasing information. Which of the following is not a required element?
   A) description of introduction to be used
   B) remuneration for marketing information
   C) signature and date
   D) who to report violations to
REFERENCE: OCR 164.508
               Pabrai, p 139-140
               Johns (2002b), 69-71
               LaTour and Eichenwald, p 205-206
               Hughes (2002d), p 65
COMPETENCY: Privacy: 2A, 2B, 4A, 8C

63. Charlotte Community Hospital, a 60 bed hospital, is reviewing the policies and procedures of Charlotte Medical Center, an 800 bed hospital. Charlotte Community Hospital wants to ensure that they follow the same rules as their larger sister hospital. This is
   A) not required since the policies and procedures should reflect the size and scope of the facility
   B) required for hospitals owned by the same organization
   C) not required since hospitals of different sizes have different rules
   D) required for all hospitals to follow the same policies and procedures.
REFERENCE: OCR 164.306, 164.502
               Pabrai, p 160-161, 166-167, 198, 218
               Dougherty (2002), p 61
COMPETENCY: Privacy: 2B, 2E, 8C

64. Dr. Smith is treating Joan Jackson in the ER at General Hospital for a fractured hip. He has requested a copy of all discharge summaries, operative reports, and history and physicals from Mercy Hospital. According to HIPAA, can these documents be released to Dr. Smith, even if the admissions are for childbirth and gastroenteritis which have no direct bearing on this case?
   A) yes, because requests by healthcare providers for treatment are exempted from minimum necessary rule
   B) no, because it is more than the minimum necessary
   C) yes, because physicians can get anything they want
   D) no, because Dr. Smith is not on our staff
REFERENCE: OCR 164.504
               Pabrai, p 158-166
               Johns (2002b), p 212-213
COMPETENCY: Privacy: 2B, 4A, 7A, 7C, 7D, 8B, 8C

65. Coders Extraordinaire is a contracted company who needs the medical record in order to carry out their coding duties. Which of the following is true?
   A) the medical record must be de-identified first since the coders will not be hospital employees
   B) Coders Extraordinaire can have access to the medical record if they provide adequate assurance to the hospital that they will protect data
   C) the medical record must de-identified because coding does not need to be connected back to the individual patient
   D) Coders Extraordinaire cannot have access to patient information since they are a business associate
REFERENCE: OCR 164.504
                Pabrai, p 126-127
                Johns (2002b), p 222-223
COMPETENCY: Privacy: 3A, 3B, 3C

66. Dr. Jones is writing an order for his patient to see an orthopedist. This activity is considered to be
   A) treatment
   B) marketing
   C) billing
   D) none of the above
REFERENCE: OCR 164.501
                Davis, p 143
                Pabrai, p 175
COMPETENCY: Privacy: 2B, 7D, 8C

67. Dallas Hospital wants to send prescription refill reminders to patients. With the privacy regulations, under what condition can this be done?
   A) they can send if not subsidized by a third party
   B) they can send if subsidized by a third party
   C) cannot ever send
   D) both A and B
REFERENCE: Davis, p 142
                Pabrai, p 175
COMPETENCY: Privacy: 2B, 2E, 8C

68. Houston County Hospital notifies patients via the privacy notice that gun shot wounds will be reported to the appropriate authorities. Why is this documented in the privacy notice?
   A) it is an example of using patient information for billing
   B) it is an example of using patient information for patient care
   C) it is an example of using patient information for healthcare operations
   D) it is required by HIPAA
REFERENCE: OCR 164.514
                Hughes (2002e), p 98
                Johns (2002b), p 213-214
COMPETENCY: Privacy: 2A, 2B, 8B, 8C

69. Sandra asks the Ashville General Hospital for a list of disclosed PHI. According to HIPAA, which of the following is included in the list she receives?
    A) information released for preadmission approval by insurance company
    B) lab receiving blood for testing
    C) reporting gunshot wound to authorities
    D) reporting infectious diseases to public health officials
    REFERENCE: Hughes (2002e), p 98
    COMPETENCY: Privacy: 2B, 7D, 8B, 8C

70. Ned describes the minimum necessary rule as
    A) policy and procedure limiting access to PHI to what is needed to perform the purpose of the request
    B) list of people who need information and what information they need
    C) both A and B
    D) access to PHI
    REFERENCE: OCR 164.502
                    Pabrai, p 160-168
                    Hughes (2002e), p 99
                    Hartley & Jones, p 5-6
    COMPETENCY: Privacy: 4A, 7A, 7B, 7C, 7D, 8B, 8C

71. The Georgia Public Health Department has asked for the entire medical record to investigate an anthrax case. What action should the hospital take?
    A) comply with request
    B) identify specific information needed
    C) apply minimum necessary standard
    D) none of the above
    REFERENCE: Pabrai, p 188
                    Hughes (2002e), p 98
                    Davis, p 152
    COMPETENCY: Privacy: 2B, 4A, 7D, 8B, 8C

72. Omaha Hospital has found a better way to maintain privacy. This will result in a policy change. Which of the following apply?
    A) the facility must wait a year before applying the new policy
    B) the facility must write the policy and procedure and wait 6 months before implementing new policies
    C) the facility should write the policy and procedure and apply to documents created both before and after implementation of the new policy
    D) the facility should update policy and apply to violations that occur after the implementation date
    REFERENCE: OCR 164.520
                    Pabrai, p 135
                    Hartley & Jones, p 72
    COMPETENCY: Privacy: 2A, 2B, 2C, 2D, 4A, 7D, 8B, 8C

73. Mary Hamilton filed a privacy complaint against Las Vegas Memorial Hospital. The hospital should do which of the following?
   A) bar Mary from being a patient at the facility again
   B) flag Mary's chart as a trouble maker
   C) charge Mary for the cost of investigating the complaint
   D) treat Mary as anyone else
REFERENCE: OCR 164.520
                Hartley & Jones, p 83
COMPETENCY: Privacy: 2B, 4A, 5B, 5C, 8B, 8C

74. James is writing the privacy notice required by HIPAA. He writes that hospitals will use PHI to report infectious diseases to public health officials. Why can he write this?
   A) it is an example of how PHI will be used for healthcare operations
   B) it is an example of how PHI can be used for treatment
   C) it is an example of how PHI will be used for payment
   D) it is a violation of HIPAA to release this information
REFERENCE: OCR 164.520
                Hughes (2002e), p 99
                Pabrai, p 133-138
COMPETENCY: Privacy: 2B, 4A, 8A, 8C

75. Craig is creating a database that will be used to establish the minimum necessary decisions. What data does he need?
   A) condition surrounding access
   B) role
   C) type of protected health information needed
   D) all of the above
REFERENCE: U. S. Office of Civil Rights (2002a), p 21
COMPETENCY: Privacy: 2A, 2B, 7A, 7C, 7D, 8B
                Security: 10A, 10F

76. Gabe is in charge of privacy and security policies and procedures. He should ensure that the policies are reviewed at least
   A) every 6 months
   B) periodically
   C) quarterly
   D) every 2 years
REFERENCE: OCR 164.316, 164.530
                Sullivan, p 96
COMPETENCY: Core:1G
                Privacy: 2A, 2B, 4A, 4B

77. Barbara has asked for a copy of her medical record. She is horrified that she is expected to pay for the copies. She complains to the Director. Which of the following would you expect the director to say?
A) we are allowed to charge reasonable, cost-based fees
B) we are allowed to charge cost-based fees which include chart retrieval
C) we are mandated by HIPAA to charge for copies of records
D) none of the above
REFERENCE: U. S. Office of Civil Rights (2002a), p 1
                          OCR 164.524
COMPETENCY: Privacy: 2B, 8C

78. Terry is concerned about the government database being created by HIPAA. He is afraid of how the information will be used. How will you calm his fears?
A) tell him that HIPAA also limits how the data can be used
B) explain to him that HIPAA does not create a government database
C) explain to him how important this type of database is to healthcare
D) none of the above
REFERENCE: U. S. Office of Civil Rights (2002a), p 2
                          Pabrai, p 186
COMPETENCY: Privacy: 2B, 2E, 7D

79. Dr. Steen's office has patients sign in. As a privacy consultant, you have been asked if this is a violation of the patient's privacy. How will you respond?
A) not as long as the information on the form is minimal
B) yes
C) no
D) none of the above
REFERENCE: U. S. Office of Civil Rights (2002a), p 3
                          OCR 164.528
                          Davis, p 97
                          Pabrai, p 170-171
COMPETENCY: Privacy: 2B, 2E, 4A, 7D, 8B, 8C

80. Dr. French is used to having his patient's charts in a box on the door to his office examination rooms. He is upset that he will have to stop this practice. What would you tell him?
A) that he will not have to stop this practice
B) that he will not have to stop this practice if reasonable steps are taken to protect the confidential information
C) that it will create more work on him, but it is important to protect the patient's privacy
D) he can put them in a box if the box locks
REFERENCE: U. S. Office of Civil Rights (2002a), p 3
                          OCR 164.528
                          Davis, p 97
                          Pabrai, p 170-171
COMPETENCY: Privacy: 2B, 2E, 7D, 8B, 8C

81. Patient names have always been placed outside their hospital room at McKenzie Memorial Hospital. As privacy consultant, what would you recommend to the hospital?
A) stop this practice immediately
B) continue to post names if there is a healthcare operational purpose
C) continue to post names
D) stop the practice by December 31, 2004
REFERENCE: U. S. Department of Health and Human Services (2002a), p 3
OCR 164.528
Davis, p 97
Pabrai, p 170-171
COMPETENCY: Privacy: 2B, 2E, 7D, 8C

82. Xavier Hospital is trying to collect payment from Fred for healthcare services provided. The hospital calls Fred's home and tells his wife that $250.00 is owed for services rendered on May 1, 2002. Is this a violation of Fred's privacy?
A) yes, because it is related to payment collection
B) no, because only a minimal amount of information is provided
C) yes, because protected information was released
D) none of the above
REFERENCE: U. S. Office of Civil Rights (2002a), p 5
COMPETENCY: Privacy: 2B, 3A, 3C

83. Warm Springs Hospital is planning on obtaining a signed business associate agreement from every physician on staff. What would you tell this hospital?
A) this must be accomplished by the compliance date
B) this would only be necessary for physicians who were providing services for the hospital such as case management
C) this is not generally necessary
D) there is no reason to obtain a business associate agreement from a physician
REFERENCE: U. S. Office of Civil Rights (2002a), p 5
OCR 160.103
COMPETENCY: Privacy: 2B, 2E, 5C, 8B, 8C

84. Thomaston Hospital plans to visit business associates at least annually. This is
A) not required by HIPAA
B) more stringent than the HIPAA requirement of bi-annual audits
C) required by HIPAA
D) not required, but a quarterly report is required
REFERENCE: U. S. Office of Civil Rights (2002a), p 5
OCR 164.504
COMPETENCY: Privacy: 2B, 3D

85. Quality Drugs just purchased Drug Market. Which of the following is the appropriate action that should be taken by Quality Drugs?
A) Quality Drugs can access PHI created by Drug Market
B) Quality Drugs cannot access PHI created by Drug Market
C) Quality Drugs has to destroy PHI created by Drug Market
D) Quality Drugs is required to combine the PHI between the two facilities
REFERENCE: OCR 164.501
COMPETENCY: Privacy: 2B, 8B, 8C

86. Dallas Memorial Hospital requires nurses to show proof of a TB test before hiring. This proof is filed in the Human Resources Department. This documentation
A) is protected health information
B) is required to be filed in the employee's patient record
C) is not protected health information
D) none of the above
REFERENCE: OCR 160.103
COMPETENCY: Privacy: 2A, 2B, 4A, 8C

87. Grant works for Talbotton General Hospital. He was admitted for an appendectomy last week. Which of the following actions is required?
A) treat Grant's medical record as human resource records
B) treat Grant's medical record as PHI
C) file the medical record in both human resources and medical records
D) lock Grant's record in a special cabinet to protect privacy
REFERENCE: OCR 160.103
COMPETENCY: Privacy: 2A, 2B, 4A, 8C

88. Bertha is a HIM clerk who is responsible for coding outpatient records. She reads a discharge summary from an inpatient record. Given this information, which of the following is true?
A) Bertha is acting appropriately because she desires a promotion to inpatient coder
B) Bertha is following the minimum necessary rule
C) Bertha is violating the minimum necessary rule
D) none of the above
REFERENCE: OCR 164.501
COMPETENCY: Privacy: 2B, 4A, 8C

89. Fred is a patient at a covered entity. Marjorie is a nurse at the facility. She walks over to Fred and, using a quiet voice, gives him the test result. Another patient overhears the test results.
    A) This is an obvious example of a violation of Fred's privacy.
    B) This is a serious problem that needs to be addressed by the covered entity.
    C) A reasonable effort was taken to protect his privacy so no privacy violation occurred.
    D) none of the above
REFERENCE: OCR 164.530
                        Pabrai, p 170-171
COMPETENCY: Privacy: 2B, 4A, 8B, 8C

90. Health Insurance of America's policy is that they will not pay a claim until the patient signs an authorization giving them access to psychotherapy notes. Carmen complains to the appropriate authorities. Which of the following would be the authority's ruling?
    A) Health Insurance of America has every right to know the contents before paying the bill.
    B) Uphold Carmen's claim of a privacy regulation complaint due to the fact that it violates the minimum necessary rule.
    C) Uphold Carmen's claim of a privacy regulation complaint due to the restriction of health plans from making payment conditional on being granted access to psychotherapy notes.
    D) none of the above
REFERENCE: OCR 164.508
                        Pabrai, p 117
COMPETENCY: Privacy: 2B, 2C, 2D, 2E, 4A, 5A, 8C

91. Mel is a coder at a covered entity. He is coding a difficult chart and needs to review the entire chart in order to understand the situation. The Coding Supervisor's response to his request is that
    A) the request is denied due to the fact that it is more than the minimum necessary to do his job
    B) the request is denied due to the fact that the record is not readily available
    C) the request is approved since the information is needed to code the chart for reimbursement
    D) the request is approved since the information is readily available
REFERENCE: OCR 164.506
COMPETENCY: Privacy: 2B, 8B, 8C

92. The Georgia law requires the release of PHI for worker's compensation claims. Using the HIPAA regulations as her guide, Wynona tells her staff which of the following?
    A) follow the Georgia law since it is a law and release the record
    B) follow the Georgia law since HIPAA allows a covered entity to release worker's compensation records if established by the law
    C) do not release the records since HIPAA does not specifically authorize
    D) obtain a patient consent before releasing the records
REFERENCE: OCR 164.512
COMPETENCY: Privacy: 2B, 4A, 8C

93. Sheriff Smith has orally requested that Mark Jones not be notified of the Sheriff's request for PHI for the next 6 months. What action should the covered entity take?
    A) release information as required by HIPAA
    B) temporarily suspend ability of Mark Jones to be notified of Sheriff's request for 60 days
    C) deny request unless made in writing
    D) none of the above
REFERENCE: OCR 164.528
               Dougherty, (2001), p 72E
COMPETENCY: Privacy: 2B, 7D, 8C

94. A covered entity has received a verbal request to suspend notifying patient of disclosure to police. This request can be honored for
    A) a maximum of 30 days
    B) up to 60 days
    C) a maximum of 30 days unless a written request is filed
    D) up to 90 days
REFERENCE: OCR 164.528
               Dougherty (2001), p 72E
COMPETENCY: Privacy: 2B, 2C, 2D, 4A, 5C, 8C

95. Warren has requested a copy of disclosures of his PHI. This is the second request that he made this year. Which of the following is true?
    A) the covered entity may charge a reasonable fee
    B) the covered entity must notify Warren about the fee and allow him to decide whether to pay the fee or reduce the fee.
    C) the covered entity should honor the request
    D) both A & B
REFERENCE: OCR 164.524
               Dougherty (2001), p 72G
COMPETENCY: Privacy: 2B, 7D, 8C

96. Timothy made a statement that said that he had received patient consent to release PHI to an attorney. His comment was
A) appropriate since a consent is required for this release
B) a misstatement since an authorization is the appropriate term for this action
C) inappropriate since patient does not have to O.K. this release
D) none of the above
REFERENCE: OCR 164.508
                         Pabrai, p 137, 212
                         Johns (2002b), p 219
                         Hughes (2001b), p 64E
COMPETENCY: Privacy: 2B, 8C

97. A request for PHI has been received. The request asks for notes documenting a private counseling session, medication prescriptions and counseling start/stop times. The employee responding to this request should
A) recognize that this is a request for psychotherapy notes and deny request
B) recognize that this as a request for psychotherapy notes and release only the medication prescriptions and the counseling start/stop time.
C) honor the request
D) contact supervisor for instructions
REFERENCE: OCR 164.501
                         Johns (2002b), 70
                         Nicholson, p 38
                         Pabrai, p 116
COMPETENCY: Privacy: 2B, 7B, 8C

98. Matt makes the statement that the privacy regulations pre-empt the federal confidentiality of alcohol and drug abuse records. Susan's appropriate response should be to
A) agree with Matt
B) disagree since HIPAA only pre-empts state laws
C) disagree
D) agree that it does pre-empt when the privacy law is stricter
REFERENCE: LaTour and Eichenwald, p 211-212
                         Nicholson, p 38
COMPETENCY: Privacy: 2B, 2E, 4A, 8C

99. Medical References International has a website that publishes medical information such as a medical dictionary. According to HIPAA, Medical References is
A) a covered entity because it is a health plan
B) a covered entity because it is a clearinghouse
C) not a covered entity
D) a covered entity because it is a provider
REFERENCE: OCR 160.103, 164.500
Pabrai, p 27, 109
LaTour and Eichenwald, p 173
Choy, Pritts, & Goldman, p 34-36
COMPETENCY: Privacy: 2B, 3A

100. Online Drugs.com provides prescriptions to patients. The company is paid by credit card and does not accept third party reimbursement. The transactions are always conducted electronically via the Internet. According to HIPAA, Online Drugs.com is
A) a covered entity because it is a health plan
B) a covered entity because it is a clearinghouse
C) not a covered entity
D) a covered entity because it is a provider
REFERENCE: OCR 160.103, 164.500
Pabrai, p 27, 109
LaTour and Eichenwald, p 173
Choy, Pritts, & Goldman, p 38
COMPETENCY: Privacy: 2B, 3A

101. Health Data is a company that allows patients to enter, store and access health information. The patient has control over the health information. According to HIPAA, Health Data is
A) a covered entity because it is a health plan
B) a covered entity because it is a clearinghouse
C) not a covered entity
D) a covered entity because it is a provider
REFERENCE: OCR, 160.103, 164.500
Pabrai, p 27, 109
LaTour and Eichenwald, p 173
Choy, Pritts, & Goldman, p 38
COMPETENCY: Privacy: 3A, 5C, 8B

102. My privacy was violated. The offense happened 65 days ago. I can file a complaint since the violation happened less than _____ days ago.
   A) 180
   B) 365
   C) 90
   D) 120
REFERENCE: OCR 160.306, 164.530
                Pabrai, p 21
                Rode (2001), p 32A
COMPETENCY: Core: 1Q, 1R
                Privacy: 2B, 4A, 5A, 5B, 8B, 8C

103. Healthcare Support is a business associate of Wallace General Hospital. Healthcare Support wants to use some information they are provided for fundraising. Which of the following is appropriate?
   A) Authorization from patient is required
   B) Authorization from patient is not required and they can use any information
   C) Authorization from patient is not required and they can only use certain information
   D) None of the above
REFERENCE: OCR 164.508, 164.520
                Johns (2002b), p 229
                Amatayakul (2001c), p 16C
COMPETENCY: Privacy: 2B, 3A, 3C, 3D

104. I just received a brochure from the hospital where I was treated asking for a donation to their foundation. I hate mail like this. How can I stop it?
   A) I cannot
   B) call the foundation
   C) write the foundation
   D) follow the instructions provided in the mailing that give you the option to excuse yourself from future mailings
REFERENCE: OCR 164.520
                Johns (2002b), p 229
                Amatayakul (2001c), p 16C
COMPETENCY: Privacy: 2B, 2C, 2D, 4A, 5B, 5C

105. Kyle, the HIM Director, has received a request to modify a patient's medical record. The appropriate action for him to take is to
   A) make the modification
   B) file the request in the chart
   C) route the request to the physician who wrote the note in question
   D) return the notice to the patient
REFERENCE: OCR, 164.526
                Thieleman, p 46
COMPETENCY: Privacy: 2B, 8C

106. Implementation of HIPAA is expected to be expensive. Why then is HIPAA said to be able to save money?
A) the experts are wrong
B) it streamlines processes and procedures
C) it provides more uniformity across the country
D) both B and C
REFERENCE: Pabrai, p 2-3, 6-9
                        Amatayakul (2000), p 34
COMPETENCY: Core: 1P
                        Privacy: 2B, 2E

107. How can the privacy and security officers work together?
A) they cannot since the roles are too different
B) they can jointly develop the policies and procedures
C) they can establish safeguards to protect patient identifiable health information
D) none of the above
REFERENCE: Pabrai, p 225, 244, 324-326
                        Amatayakul (2000), p 36
COMPETENCY: Privacy: 4A, 5A
                        Security: 4A, 4M, 4N

108. Which of the following would be the most appropriate way for home health agencies to fulfill the written notice of information practice requirement?
A) post the notice in a public area in the office
B) send email notice to the patient
C) mail notice to the new patient
D) post it on their website
REFERENCE: OCR 164.520
                        Pabrai, p 133-137
                        Abraham (2002), p 39
COMPETENCY: Privacy: 2A, 2B, 4A

109. A home health patient has asked the nurse for a copy of her medical record. How should she handle this request?
A) give the patient the copy
B) have the patient sign an authorization and give a copy to the patient
C) refer request to an expert
D) none of the above
REFERENCE: LaTour and Eichenwald, p 206-207, 222
                        Abraham (2002), p 40
COMPETENCY: Privacy: 2B, 4A, 8C

110. Atlanta State College offers a number of healthcare degrees including nursing and health information. The hospital where students perform their clinicals has asked the college to sign a business associate agreement. What should be the college's response?
   A) sign the agreement
   B) sign the agreement and the standard contract
   C) refuse to sign the agreement since the contract is the equivalent
   D) refuse to sign the agreement since the college does not meet the definition of a business associate

REFERENCE: OCR 160.103
               Cassidy (2000b), p 16B
               Roach, M., p 45
COMPETENCY: Privacy: 2B, 3A, 3B, 3C

111. Microfilm Corporation microfilms protected health information for Sparrow Hospital. The contract is not up for renewal until six months after the HIPAA compliance date. What action should the healthcare facility take?
   A) update all contracts including Microfilm corporation
   B) wait until the expiration date of the contract in order to renew it.
   C) cancel the contract
   D) update the contract with Microfilm Corporation and any other business associates

REFERENCE: OCR 160.103, 164.502
               Pabrai, p 154-155
               Roach, M., p 46
COMPETENCY: Privacy: 2B, 3B, 3C

112. Maine Hospital routinely refers patients to Portland General Hospital. What action should Maine Hospital take with regard to Portland and business associate agreements?
   A) ask Portland to sign a business associate agreement
   B) stop referrals
   C) none since a business associate agreement is not required for referrals
   D) ask Portland to sign a business associate agreement if other services are performed

REFERENCE: OCR 160.103
               Roach, M., p 46
COMPETENCY: Privacy: 2B, 3B, 3C, 3D

113. I work for a company that is a business associate of the local hospital. I just discovered that we had a breach of PHI provided by the hospital. What action should be taken according to the business associate agreement?
A) take the necessary steps to contain the problem
B) cover up the problem
C) notify the healthcare provider in the timeframe specified in the agreement
D) notify the healthcare provider within the next 2 weeks
REFERENCE: OCR 164.314, 164.502
                Pabrai, p 154-155, 234, 340-357
                Roach, M, p 47
COMPETENCY: Privacy: 2B, 3B, 3C, 3D

114. Montana Medical Center is developing the business associate agreement that will be used by the hospital. When writing the termination agreement, which of the following is appropriate?
A) the business associate should protect information maintained after termination of contract
B) PHI should be returned or destroyed at the time of termination
C) The destruction or return clause should outlast the agreement
D) Both B and C
REFERENCE: OCR 164.502
                Pabrai, p 154, 155, 234, 340-357
                Roach, M., p 47
                Hartley & Jones, p 16
COMPETENCY: Privacy: 2B, 3B, 3C, 3D

115. Los Angeles Medical provides services to a healthcare facility. Many of the services provided require access to PHI. The company has asked their customers to specify in the business associate agreement that they will not be audited any more than 4 times a year. What response should the healthcare facilities take?
A) agree to the request since it is specifically allowed by HIPAA
B) refuse to sign an agreement with the limits
C) agree to the request since it is the only way that Los Angeles Medical will sign the contract
D) agree to the request only if approved by Board of Directors
REFERENCE: Pabrai, p 154-155, 234, 340-357
                Roach, M., p 49
                Hartley & Jones, p 17
COMPETENCY: Privacy: 3B, 3C, 3D, 5A

116.The business associate agreement should contain which of the following clauses
   A) force majeure
   B) "business agreement" clause
   C) indemnification
   D) all of the above
REFERENCE: Pabrai, p 154-155, 234, 340-357
               Roach, M., p 50
               Hartley & Jones, p 16-17
COMPETENCY: Privacy: 2A, 2B, 3A, 3B, 3C, 3D

117.Dr. Brown has just approved the patient's request to amend the medical record. Dr. Brown has routed the request with his approval to the HIM Department. What should the HIM Department do?
   A) file the request where the erroneous information is located
   B) file the request where the erroneous information is located and send a copy of the amendment to anyone who has a copy of the erroneous information
   C) file the request in the front of the chart
   D) file the request where the erroneous information is located and send a copy of the amendment to anyone who has a copy of the erroneous information plus anyone the patient requests
REFERENCE: OCR, 164.526
               Thieleman, p 44
COMPETENCY: Privacy: 2B, 8C

118.As privacy officer, it is my responsibility to assist in policy reviews. This includes ensuring that all of the following policies are developed or revised except
   A) consent for release
   B) ability for patient to request amendment
   C) marketing
   D) awareness training
REFERENCE: OCR 164.308, 164.508, 164.526, 164.530
               Hjort (2001), p 64B
COMPETENCY: Privacy: 4A, 6C, 8C

119.Who is ultimately responsible for security?
   A) vendor
   B) covered entity
   C) chief security officer
   D) none of the above
REFERENCE: Pabrai, p 196-198
               Brandt, p 3
COMPETENCY: Privacy: 2B, 6A
               Security: 5C, 5D

120.The goal of audits should be to provide
  A) data
  B) a list of problems
  C) information
  D) none of the above
REFERENCE: Fuller, p 42
COMPETENCY: Privacy: 6E

121.Kris is a transcriptionist who works at home. She is an employee of the hospital. Which of the following statements apply to her?
  A) she does not need to sign a business associate agreement
  B) she requires patient identifying information
  C) technology can eliminate the need for Kris to have identifying information
  D) both A and C
REFERENCE: OCR, 164.514
               Amatayakul (2002e), p 16A
               Pabrai, p 164, 192-193
COMPETENCY: Privacy: 2B, 4A, 5A, 8C

122.All employees who work at home should have their data or information de-identified. Which of the following statements is a proper response to this comment?
  A) true
  B) This is not true for physicians who access information from home
  C) This is not true for coders who access information from home
  D) none of the above
REFERENCE: OCR, 164.502
               Amatayakul (2002e), p 16b
COMPETENCY: Privacy: 4A, 7D, 8C

123.Risks of privacy violations are _____ at home than at the office.
  A) greater
  B) less
  C) the same
  D) none of the above
REFERENCE: Pabrai, p 196-202
               Amatayakul (2002e), p 16B
COMPETENCY: Privacy: 2B, 4A, 7D, 8C
               Security: 4B, 4P, 7D, 9B

124. Gary was a patient at Tyler Medical Center three months ago. He is requesting to review all of his records. He should have access to everything except
A) any psychotherapy notes
B) any information to be used in court or administrative actions
C) alcohol and drug treatment
D) both A and B
REFERENCE: OCR 164.524
Pabrai, p 144
Hughes (2001a), p 90
Hartley & Jones, p 77
COMPETENCY: Privacy: 2B, 4A, 8B, 8C

125. Adam is an inmate at the Oklahoma State Prison. He is demanding to see his medical records. What action should the HIM staff take?
A) process the request
B) deny the request
C) deny the request if release jeopardizes the patient, other inmates or officer
D) none of the above
REFERENCE: OCR 164.524
Pabrai, p 144
Hughes (2001a), p 90
Hartley & Jones, p 78
COMPETENCY: Privacy: 2B, 4A, 8B, 8C

126. Two months ago Caleb agreed, in writing, to a temporary denial of access to his medical record. This denial will expire at the end of the study in four months. He has decided that he wants to review the medical record now. What action should the HIM staff take?
A) process the request
B) deny the request unless approved by the study project manager
C) deny the request since you have a signed denial of access
D) none of the above
REFERENCE: OCR 164.524
Hughes (2001a), p 90
Davis, p 166
COMPETENCY: Privacy: 2B, 4A, 8A, 8B, 8C

127. Dr. Smith has shadow records which are used during patient care. What action should the Chief Security Officer take?
A) ignore the shadow record since it is not the official record
B) treat them as any other PHI
C) ask the physician to stop using them since they are prohibited by HIPAA
D) computerize the records.
REFERENCE: Pabrai, p 2, 23, 121, 169
Amatayakul (2001b), p 16D
COMPETENCY: Privacy: 2B, 4A, 5A

128. The marketing director at Houston General Hospital has been given four suggestions for marketing. Which one should be eliminated because it requires patient consent?
   A) a face to face discussion with patient on a health-related product
   B) providing the patient with a discount coupon for service
   C) marketing a diaper service provided by a business not owned by the hospital
   D) sending brochures on durable medical equipment available at the hospital

REFERENCE: OCR 164.501, 164.508
               Pabrai, p 173-175
               Johns (2002b), p 229
               Rhodes, p 2, 3
               Davis, p 141
COMPETENCY: Privacy: 2B, 4A, 8B

129. The marketing director is writing the text for the new marketing campaign. Which of the following is not a requirement of HIPAA?
   A) name of the organization marketing the information
   B) any compensation received by the organization
   C) ability of the patient to opt-out of marketing materials.
   D) list of methods used for marketing

REFERENCE: OCR 164.501, 164.508
               Pabrai, p 173-175
               Johns (2002b), p 229
               Rhodes, p 3
COMPETENCY: Privacy   2B, 2C, 2D

130. A notice of privacy practices should contain all of the following except
   A) a header with the specific HIPAA verbiage
   B) a description of each purpose for which PHI could be used
   C) the patient's rights regarding PHI
   D) the specific HIPAA verbiage identifying how records are used for treatment, payment and healthcare operations

REFERENCE: OCR 164.520
               Pabrai, p 133-138
               Johns (2002b), p 213-214
               Hughes (2001b), p 64I
COMPETENCY: Privacy: 2A, 2B, 2C, 2D, 5C, 8B, 8C

131. Physical safeguards include:
1. tools for monitoring access
2. tools to control access to computer systems
3. fire protection
4 tools for preventing unauthorized access to data
A) 1 and 2 only
B) 1 and 3 only
C) 2 and 3 only
D) 2 and 4 only
REFERENCE: OCR 164.310
                        Pabrai, p 235-238
COMPETENCY: Privacy: 6A, 6B
                        Security: 4E, 4F, 4G

132. Research Forum has requested some information on your patients. The information requested does not identify the patients. Under the final rule, what response is appropriate by the healthcare facility?
A) deny the request due to prohibition on outside research
B) release the information if Research Forum signs a data use agreement
C) release the information
D) deny the request due to prohibition to using data for research
REFERENCE: U.S. Department Health and Human Services (2002b), p 3
                        OCR 164.512
                        Pabrai, p 121-126
COMPETENCY: Privacy: 2B, 8A, 8B, 8C

133. As a researcher, I have been asked to sign a data use agreement prior to receiving the data that I requested. Which of the following is one of the purposes of this agreement?
A) to ensure that the data does not identify patient
B) to ensure that the data is used only for purpose identified
C) to ensure that I know the information is protected by HIPAA
D) none of the above
REFERENCE: U.S. Department Health and Human Services (2002b), p 3
                        OCR 164.512
                        Pabrai, p 121-126
COMPETENCY: Privacy: 2B, 8A, 8B, 8C

134. As office manager for a physician practice, I am responsible for getting signed business associate agreements. Which of the following is the appropriate action for the copy machine repair company?
    A) not required because it is specifically omitted by privacy regulations
    B) not required because the copy machine repair technician does not meet the definition of a business associate
    C) required since the technician will be in and out of office
    D) required by HIPAA
REFERENCE: U.S. Office of Civil Rights (2002a), p 5
              OCR (160.102, 164.502
              Pabrai, p 152-153
COMPETENCY: Privacy: 3A, 3B

135. As office manager for a physician practice, I am responsible for getting signed business associate agreements. Which of the following is the appropriate action for the janitorial services company?
    A) not required because work does not require use of PHI
    B) not required because it is specifically omitted by privacy regulations
    C) required because they may come into contact with PHI when emptying trash
    D) required by HIPAA
REFERENCE: U.S. Office of Civil Rights (2002a), p 6
              OCR 160.102, 164.502
              Pabrai, p 152-153
COMPETENCY: Privacy: 3A, 3B

136. Margaret just received a reminder from her physician's office that it is time for her to get a mammogram. According to HIPAA, this is
    A) an example of marketing
    B) not considered marketing
    C) a blatant example of the misuse of PHI
    D) none of the above
REFERENCE: OCR 164.501, 164.508
              Pabrai, p 173-175
              Davis, p 142
COMPETENCY: Privacy: 2B, 2C, 2D, 4A, 8B, 8C

137. The use, access or disclosure of health information limited to the amount necessary for the intended purpose is an example of which concept?
    A) minimum necessary
    B) authorization
    C) privacy
    D) confidentiality
REFERENCE: OCR 165.402
              Johns (2002b), p 198, 212
              Pabrai, p 158, 161-168
              Hartley & Jones, p 5-6
COMPETENCY: Privacy: 8B, 8C

138. In looking at all of the forms being used by my facility, which of the following would I identify as not being HIPAA required?
    A) a complaint form
    B) an individual consent form for disclosure of PHI for treatment
    C) an individual consent to release psychotherapy notes
    D) a work force training certification form to document training
REFERENCE: OCR 165.530
                     Apple & Brandt, p 32
COMPETENCY: Privacy: 2A, 2B, 4A

139. What source of reference would be appropriate in determining the form and content of the health record?
    A) accreditation standards and public health reporting requirements
    B) the needs of individual healthcare organizations
    C) state and federal laws and regulatory requirements
    D) all of the above
REFERENCE: LaTour and Eichenwald, p 202-203
                     Johns (2002b), p 203-205
COMPETENCY: Privacy: 7A

140. Which of the following statements is true of the notice of privacy practice?
    A) The entity must obtain a signed consent to use information for treatment purposes.
    B) It does not give the covered entity permission to use information for TPO purposes.
    C) It must be provided to every individual at the first time of contact or service with the covered entity.
    D) It must be provided to the individual by the covered entity within 10 days after receipt of treatment or service.
REFERENCE: OCR 164.520
                     Johns (2002b), p 213-214
                     Hartley & Jones, p 70
COMPETENCY: Privacy: 2C, 2D, 4A, 8B, 8C

141. Which of the following is true about the directory of patients maintained by a covered entity?
    A) Individuals are not given an opportunity to restrict or deny permission to place information about them in the directory.
    B) Individuals do not need to provide a written authorization before information about them can be placed in the directory.
    C) The directory may contain only identifying information such as the patient's name and birth date.
    D) The directory may contain private information as long at it is kept confidential.
REFERENCE: OCR 164.510
                     Johns (2002b), p 220
COMPETENCY: Privacy: 2B, 7B, 8C

142. In which of the following situations can PHI be disclosed after an individual refuses to provide an authorization?
    A) for disclosures for public health purposes as required by law
    B) for disclosures to health oversight agencies as required by law
    C) for reporting certain types of wounds or other physical injuries as required by law
    D) all of the above
REFERENCE: OCR 154.512
               Johns (2002b), p 223
               Pabrai, p 115-116
COMPETENCY: Privacy: 7D, 8B, 8C

Action Steps to Implement Authorizations
- Document evidence of authority of personal representatives
- Develop a process for implementing revocation of consent/authorizations and restrictions on use
- Develop a process for retaining signed authorizations for a 6 year period
- Develop a mechanism to resolve conflicts between consents and authorizations
    o   more restrictive governs
    o   obtain new consent that clarifies
    o   communicate with individual and document expressed preference
- Maintain psychotherapy notes separate from other medical records of individual (use a separate file for each originator)

---

143. Which of the action steps in the table above relates to the accounting of disclosure mandated in HIPAA Rule?
    A) maintain psychotherapy notes separate from other medical records of individual
    B) develop a process for retaining signed authorizations for a 6 year period
    C) develop a process for implementing revocation of consent/authorizations and restrictions on use
    D) document evidence of authority of personal representatives
REFERENCE: OCR 164.528
               Pabrai, p 146
COMPETENCY: Privacy: 8A, 8B

144. What can you do to mitigate the harmful effects of use or disclosure of information?
    A) notify patients and reassure them
    B) work with police department
    C) revisit policies and procedures about taking records home (may be too much risk of disclosure)
    D) must notify the family/patient of breech of care/disclosure
REFERENCE: OCR 164.530
               Pabrai, p 329
COMPETENCY: Core: 1C, 1M, 1O, 1Q, 1R, 1S, 1U
             Privacy: 2D, 5B, 5C, 8C
             Security: 2E, 4J, 4K, 4M, 9D

---

145. What would constitute wrongful disclosure?
    A) allowing use of e-mail addresses for marketing health care products
    B) attending physician obtaining lab report to monitor patient digoxin levels
    C) allowing a consulting physician to view patient information
    D) sending death information to state office of vital statistics
REFERENCE: Pabrai, p 176
COMPETENCY: Privacy: 8C

146. When may a covered entity terminate its agreement to a restriction?
    A) if the individual agrees to or requests the termination in writing
    B) if the individual requests a termination orally (the oral declaration must still be documented)
    C) if the covered entity informs the individual that it is terminating its agreement to a restriction (effective for protected health information that is created or received after the individual has been informed)
    D) if there is an emergency situation
REFERENCE: OCR 164.522
COMPETENCY: Privacy: 2B, 8B, 8C

147. Which of the following is one of the categories of uses and disclosures of protected health information?
    A) core uses and disclosures, for which no permission is required – although an optional consent can be employed – which includes routine treatment, payment, and other health care operations
    B) those requiring a supplemental authorization, such as research or some kinds of marketing and fundraising.
    C) those requiring an opportunity to agree or object, but no written authorization
    D) not requiring even an opportunity to agree or object
REFERENCE: OCR 164.512
COMPETENCY: Privacy: 8B, 8C

148. Which of the following would need a business agreement?
    A) clergy
    B) coroner
    C) organ procurement organization
    D) record storage company
REFERENCE: OCR 160.102, 164.502
               Pabrai, p 152-156
               Hartley & Jones, p 234
COMPETENCY: Privacy: 3A

149. HIPAA requires a covered entity to include how future revisions of the notice of privacy practices will be communicated. Which of the following is NOT true ?
  A) The law requires a covered entity to provide a paper copy of the revised notice to each individual.
  B) The covered entity can post the revised notice on its web site.
  C) The covered entity can place ads in a local newspaper.
  D) The covered entity can put a notation on the billing statement.
REFERENCE: Johns (2002b), p 213-214
               OCR 164.520
               Hartley & Jones, p 72
COMPETENCY: Privacy: 4A, 5C, 8B, 8C

150. You are the director of a health information management department and often allow your department's volunteer to conduct tours of the health information management department and hospital to the students in the local Health Information Management Program at the university. You just discovered that the volunteer often points out the patients who are HIV-positive or have full-blown AIDS. What principle of liability should you be concerned about?
  A) defamation
  B) negligence
  C) invasion of privacy
  D) vicarious liability
REFERENCE: Abdelhak, p 434-435, 443, 791
               LaTour and Eichenwald, p 201
               Pabrai, p 169-170
               Pozgar, W., p 59-60, 302
               Roach, p 266-268
COMPETENCY: Privacy: 2B, 2C, 2D, 8C

151. Hospitals that destroy their own medical records must have a policy that
  A) insures records are destroyed and confidentiality is protected
  B) notifies patients that their records are destroyed
  C) all records are destroyed annually
  D) the equipment used for destruction of records is properly maintained
REFERENCE: Abdelhak, p 457
               LaTour and Eichenwald, p 171-172
               Roach, W., p 42-43
COMPETENCY: Privacy: 4B, 5B, 7D
               Security: 2A, 5A

152. A written authorization from the patient releasing copies of their medical records is required by all of the following EXCEPT
A) the patient's attorney
B) a physician requesting copies from another physician for the purpose of research
C) an insurance company
D) the hospital attorney for the facility where the patient is treated
REFERENCE: Abdelhak, p 453
               Pabrai, p 129-131, 138
COMPETENCY: Privacy: 8C

153. If the patient record is involved in litigation and the physician requests to make a change to that record, what should the HIM professional do?
A) refer request to legal counsel
B) allow the change to occur
C) notify the patient
D) say the record is unavailable
REFERENCE: Abdelhak, p 439-440
               LaTour and Eichenwald, p 229
COMPETENCY: Privacy: 2B, 2D, 7B, 8C
               Security: 5D, 6A, 6D, 6F, 6G, 10A, 10D, 10E

154. HIM professionals are bound to protect confidentiality by
A) Patient Bill of Rights
B) AHIMA's Code of Ethics
C) Hippocratic Oath
D) JCAHO standards
REFERENCE: Abdelhak, p 442
               Johns (2002b), p 176-179
               LaTour and Eichenwald, p 224-226
COMPETENCY: Privacy: 2C, 2D, 2E

155. In determining which information should be considered confidential, a health information manager should consider and answer yes to all the following questions EXCEPT
A) Is there a patient-provider relationship?
B) Is the information needed to treat or diagnose the patient?
C) Was the information in question exchanged through the professional relationship?
D) Is there a need for all health care providers to access the patient information?
REFERENCE: Abdelhak, p 442
               OCR 160.103
               Pozgar, p 302
COMPETENCY: Privacy: 2B, 2E, 8C

156.A valid authorization for the disclosure of health information should not be
   A) dated prior to discharge of the patient
   B) in writing
   C) addressed to the health care provider
   D) signed by the patient
REFERENCE: OCR 164.508
                LaTour and Eichenwald, p 205-206
                Abdelhak, p 447-450
                Pabrai, p 139-141
COMPETENCY: Privacy: 4A, 8B, 8C

157.Internal disclosures of patient information for patient care purposes should be granted
   A) to legal counsel
   B) on a need to know basis
   C) to any physician on staff
   D) to a family member who is an employee
REFERENCE: OCR 164.514
                LaTour and Eichenwald, p 229
                Abdelhak, p 450-451
COMPETENCY: Core: 1G, 1I
                Privacy: 4A, 8B, 8C

158.According to AHIMA's Position on Transmission of Health Information, the health information manager should engage in all of the following to assure that information is properly sent via facsimile transmission EXCEPT
   A) to always follow-up by sending original record by mail
   B) to pre-program into the machine the number of destination sites
   C) that the sender should contact the recipient prior to transmission
   D) that the sender should contact the recipient after transmission
REFERENCE: Abdelhak, p 448-450
COMPETENCY: Privacy: 2B, 4B, 7C, 7D, 8C

159.All of the following need a proper authorization to access a patient's health information EXCEPT
   A) local and state law enforcement officers
   B) IRS Agents
   C) medical examiners
   D) FBI Agents
REFERENCE: OCR 164.512
                Abdelhak, p 454
                Pabrai, p 146-147
COMPETENCY: Privacy: 2B, 2C, 4A, 4B, 8B, 8C

160. When a person makes a request for his/her records in person, the correspondence clerk should _____ in order to establish safeguards for the security and confidentiality of patient's information.
   A) ask the requester for identification and the request in writing
   B) refuse the request
   C) refer the requester to the facility's attorney
   D) charge an exorbitant fee
REFERENCE: Abdelhak, p 456
COMPETENCY: Privacy: 2B, 2C, 4A, 4B, 8B, 8C

161. Patient authorization to release information is required for
   A) peer review
   B) payment purposes
   C) quality assurance
   D) non identifying research
REFERENCE: OCR 164.502, 164.506
                Abdelhak, p 453
                Pabrai, p 146-147
COMPETENCY: Privacy: 2B, 4A, 8B, 8C

162. With regards to confidentiality, when HIM functions are outsourced (i.e., record copying, microfilming or transcription), the HIM professional should confirm that the outside contractor
   A) costs are not prohibitive, thus compromising confidentiality
   B) hours of operation permit easy access by all health care providers
   C) is contractually bound to handle confidential information appropriately
   D) is located in an easy to find place
REFERENCE: Abdelhak, p 457
                LaTour and Eichenwald, p 156-157
COMPETENCY: Privacy: 3A, 3B, 3C

163. A 21-year-old employee of PRG Publishing was treated in an acute care hospital for an illness unrelated to work. A representative from the personnel department of PRG Publishing calls to request information regarding the employee's diagnosis. What would be the appropriate course of action?
   A) request that the personnel office send an authorization for release of information that is signed and dated by the patient
   B) require parental consent
   C) release the information as the employer is paying the patient's bill
   D) call the patient to obtain verbal permission
REFERENCE: Abdelhak, p 447-450
                Pabrai, p 146-147
COMPETENCY: Privacy: 2B, 2C, 8B, 8C

164. Which of the following is an example of an authorized user of health information?
    A) internet service provider (ISP)
    B) physician for direct patient care
    C) facility employees
    D) private investigator
REFERENCE: Abdelhak, p 460-461
              Pabrai, p 146-147
COMPETENCY: Privacy: 2B, 2C, 8B, 8C

165. A valid authorization for release of information contains
    A) the name, agency or institution to whom the information is to be provided
    B) the name of the hospital or provider who is releasing the medical information
    C) the date and signature of the patient or their authorized representative
    D) all of the above
REFERENCE: OCR 164.508
              Abdelhak, p 445-450
              Johns (2002b), p 171-172, 218-219
              Pabrai, p 138-141
COMPETENCY: Privacy: 2B, 2C, 8B, 8C

166. Release of information without the patient's authorization is permissible in which of the following circumstances?
    A) release to an attorney
    B) release to third party payers
    C) release to state workers' compensation agencies
    D) release to insurance companies
REFERENCE: OCR 164.512
              Johns (2002b), p 223-224
              Abdelhak, p 451
              Davis, p 131, 171
COMPETENCY: Privacy: 2B, 2C, 8B, 8C

167. Because the patient is usually not present when demands for medical information are made, what professional serves primarily as a patient advocate in safeguarding patient confidentiality?
    A) pharmacist
    B) physical therapist
    C) health information professional
    D) radiologist
REFERENCE: Abdelhak, p 428
              Johns (2002b), p 168-170, 218-219
COMPETENCY: Privacy: 2C, 8B

168. A signed authorization for release of information dated October 1, 2003 is received with a request for the chart from the patient's admission of 2/5/2004. Indicate the appropriate response from the options below.
   A) request another authorization that is dated closer, but prior to, the admission date
   B) request another authorization dated after the discharge date
   C) release the requested information
   D) call the patient for a verbal authorization

REFERENCE: OCR 164.508
               Johns (2002b), p 171-172, 218-219
               Abdelhak, p 447-450
               Pabrai, p 138-141
COMPETENCY: Privacy: 2B, 2C, 8B, 8C

169. As a general rule, a person making a report in good faith and under statutory command (i.e., child abuse, communicable diseases, births, deaths, etc.) is
   A) not protected from liability claims
   B) subject to penalties imposed by federal law
   C) subject to penalties imposed by state law
   D) protected

REFERENCE: Pozgar, p 337
               Roach, W., p 140-144
COMPETENCY: Privacy: 2B, 2E

170. According to AHIMA and AHA guidelines, which of the following would be an acceptable authorization for release of information from the medical record of an adult, mentally competent patient hospitalized from 4/16/2003 to 5/10/2003? Authorization dated
   A) 7/10/2003 and presented 8/15/2003
   B) 5/09/2003 and presented 1/15/2004
   C) 3/10/2003 and presented 5/15/2004
   D) 2/15/2003 and presented 1/10/2004

REFERENCE: OCR 164.508
               Johns (2002b), p 171-172, 218-219
               Abdelhak, p 447-450
               Pabrai, p 138-141
COMPETENCY: Privacy: 2E, 8C

171. HIM professionals have a duty to maintain health information by
   A) state statutes
   B) federal statutes
   C) accreditation standards
   D) all of the above

REFERENCE: Abdelhak, p 428, 438-439
               Johns (2002b), p 168-170
               LaTour and Eichenwald, p 224-227
COMPETENCY: Privacy: 2B, 2C, 2E, 8B, 8C

172.The following are four statements regarding release of medical record information. Which statement is the BEST example of a policy?
   A) Medical record information may be released to another local hospital without patient authorization provided it can be ascertained that the patient is currently hospitalized at the requesting hospital and the records are needed for the continuity of care.
   B) The authorization presented by an insurance agent for the purposes of reviewing a chart is to be signed and dated by the viewer and stapled to the inside back of the chart folder.
   C) Receipts for prepayment of medical record information are enclosed when the information is sent.
   D) Correspondence, social service notes and incident reports are removed from the chart folder before it is presented to an insurance representative for review.
REFERENCE: Abdelhak, p 447-450
               LaTour and Eichenwald, p 567-568
COMPETENCY: Privacy: 2B, 2C, 2E, 8B, 8C

173.The minimum record retention period for patients who are minors is
   A) age of majority
   B) age of majority plus period of statute of limitations
   C) five years past treatment
   D) two years past treatment
REFERENCE: Abdelhak, p 438-439
               Johns (2002b), p 206
COMPETENCY: Privacy: 2B, 2D, 2E, 4B, 5A, 5B, 6G

174.The Privacy Act of 1974 permits patients to request amendments to their medical record in which type of facility?
   A) private proprietary health facility
   B) mental health and chemical dependency facility
   C) university based teaching facility
   D) Veterans Administration health facility
REFERENCE: Abdelhak, p 440
               Pabrai, p 188
               Pozgar, p 306-307
COMPETENCY: Privacy: 2B

175.Which of the following is considered confidential information?
   A) patient's name
   B) patient's address
   C) patient's diagnosis
   D) name of insurer
REFERENCE: Abdelhak, p 442
COMPETENCY: Core: 1B
               Privacy: 2A, 7B, 7C

176.It is common practice to forego patient authorization for the release of information when
   A) the patient is an employee
   B) the patient is a physician
   C) the patient has a direct transfer from the hospital to a long-term care facility
   D) the patient is incompetent

REFERENCE: OCR 164.514
               Abdelhak, p 450-451
COMPETENCY: Privacy: 2B, 2C, 8B, 8C

177.Which of the following situations would NOT allow a minor to consent to treatment and refuse disclosure of information?
   A) a minor seeking treatment for suicide attempt
   B) a minor seeking treatment for sexually transmitted disease
   C) a minor seeking treatment for alcohol and substance abuse
   D) a emancipated minor seeking treatment for breast enlargement
REFERENCE: Abdelhak, p 454
COMPETENCY: Privacy: 2B, 2C, 8B, 8C

178.Which of the following should be required to sign a confidentiality statement before having access to patients' medical information?
   A) nursing students
   B) medical students
   C) HIM students
   D) all of the above
REFERENCE: Abdelhak, p 452
               Johns (2002b), p 671
COMPETENCY: Privacy: 4A, 4B, 8B, 8C

179.All of the following are sources for the rules and regulations that define the legal aspects of medical records <u>EXCEPT</u>
   A) institutional policies
   B) laws
   C) paralegals
   D) regulations, governmental and non-governmental
REFERENCE: Abdelhak, p 438-445
               Johns (2002b), p 196-197
COMPETENCY: Privacy: 2B

180. Written authorization from the patient is required for which of the following in order to learn a patient's HIV status?
    A) insurance companies
    B) emergency medical personnel
    C) spouse or needle partner
    D) healthcare workers
REFERENCE: Pozgar, p 377-385
                Roach, W., p 218-230
COMPETENCY: Privacy: 2B, 2C, 4A, 8B, 8C

181. The ideal consent for medical treatment obtained by the physician is
    A) expressed
    B) informed
    C) implied
    D) verbal
REFERENCE: Roach, W., p 67-81
                Pozgar, p 316-320
COMPETENCY: Privacy: 8B, 8C

182. What legislation recognized that the privacy of an individual is directly affected by the collection, maintenance and use of personal information and that confidentiality of that information is a fundamental right guaranteed by the Constitution of the United States?
    A) Privilege Protection Act of 1977
    B) Privacy Act of 1974
    C) TEFRA legislation of 1982
    D) Freedom of Information Act of 1966
REFERENCE: Abdelhak, p 443
                Pozgar, p 97-98
COMPETENCY: Privacy: 2B

183. Mandatory reporting requirements for vital statistics generally
    A) do not require authorization by the patient
    B) require authorization by the physician
    C) require authorization by the payer
    D) do not apply to health care facilities
REFERENCE: OCR 164.512
                Johns (2002b), p 223
                Abdelhak, p 437
                Pabrai, p 188
                Pozgar, p 337
COMPETENCY: Privacy: 2B, 2C, 2E, 4A, 8B, 8C

184.A designated data set includes
   A) the medical record only
   B) any information used to make a decision about the patient
   C) shadow records only
   D) computer records only
REFERENCE: OCR 164.501
               Johns (2002b), p 210
               Amatayakul (2001b), p 16D
               Pabrai, p 172
               Hartley & Jones, p 235
COMPETENCY: Privacy: 7B

185.In determining the designated data set, I can exclude
   A) shadow records
   B) paper records
   C) psychotherapy notes
   D) none of the above
REFERENCE: OCR 164.501
               Amatayakul (2001b), p 16D
               Johns (2002b), p 210
               Pabrai, p 172
               Hartley & Jones, p 235
COMPETENCY: Privacy: 7A, 7B

186.I am evaluating what makes up the designated record set for Birmingham
   Medical Center. Which of the following should not be included?
   A) quality reports
   B) copies of records from other facilities
   C) billing records
   D) authorization for release of information
REFERENCE: OCR, 164.501
               Amatayakul & Waymack, p16A
COMPETENCY: Privacy: 2B, 7A, 7C

187.I have been given the responsibility of mapping the information flow in my
   organization. What would I need to evaluate?
   A) information technology, hardware and communications used to capture store
      and transmit data
   B) how data is captured
   C) transmission of data between business associate and the facility
   D) all of the above
REFERENCE: Apple and Brant, p 30
               Pabrai, p 332-335
COMPETENCY: Privacy: 7D

188. The IRB has approved Dr. Grant's research with the stipulation that only a limited dataset is provided. Which of the following would be a violation of the requirement to remove direct identifiers?
    A) street address
    B) discharge disposition
    C) admission date
    D) diagnosis
REFERENCE: OCR, 164.514
                      Hughes (2002d), p 66
COMPETENCY: Privacy: 2B, 8C

189. Patricia is processing request for medical records. In the record is an operative note and discharge summary from another hospital. The records are going to another physician for patient care. What should Patricia do?
    A) notify the requestor that redisclosure is illegal so they must get records from the source
    B) include the documents from the other hospital
    C) redisclose when necessary for patient care
    D) redisclose when allowed by law
REFERENCE: OCR, 165.408
                      Hughes (2001c), p 72B
COMPETENCY: Privacy: 2B, 4A, 8C

190. Ralph has asked for a list of disclosures of his medical record. He seems surprised not to see his physician, Dr. Emory, on it. What do you tell him?
    A) Dr. Emery has not viewed the medical record
    B) disclosures used for treatment are not recorded
    C) you will run the report again to make sure you ran the report correctly
    D) go talk to Dr. Emory
REFERENCE: OCR, 164.528
                      Hughes (2002C), p 68
COMPETENCY: Privacy: 2B, 4A, 8C

191. Crystal has received a copy of some documents from her medical record. In the request, she had specifically requested the discharge summary, history and physical, operative report, pathology report, laboratory results and x-ray reports. The records that she received only included the discharge summary, history and physical. The enclosed letter said that the other documents were not enclosed because of the minimum necessary rule. What should the director tell Crystal when she calls?
    A) the clerk was appropriate in what was sent
    B) the operative report should have been included too
    C) the operative report and pathology report should have been included
    D) all should have been sent since the patient is an exception to the minimum necessary rule
REFERENCE: OCR, 164.502
                      Hughes (2002b), p 56A
COMPETENCY: Privacy: 2B, 4A, 8C

192. Dr. Brown is treating Amy for her ulcer. She was in Macon General Hospital a year ago. Dr. Brown has asked the hospital for a copy of her discharge summary and endoscopy report. What action should be taken by the hospital?
A) ask Dr. Brown to provide a consent from Amy
B) provide the records to Dr. Brown only if he is on your medical staff
C) provide the records to Dr. Brown since he is treating the patient
D) refuse access to the records
REFERENCE: OCR, 164.506
                    Hughes (2002d), p 65
COMPETENCY: Privacy: 2B, 8C

193. Freda is scheduled to have elective surgery. During the admission process, she is asked to sign a consent allowing the healthcare facility to use the patient information for treatment, payment and healthcare operations. Freda refuses to sign. What action can the healthcare facility take?
A) Refuse to provide treatment until consent is signed.
B) Refuse to provide treatment since she is uncooperative
C) Provide treatment since facilities cannot deny treatment based on refusal to sign
D) None of the above
REFERENCE: Amatayakul (2001c), p 16A
                    Hartley & Jones, p 71-72
COMPETENCY: Privacy: 2B, 2C, 2D, 4A, 4C

194. State law states the hospital must keep a record of disclosures for 10 years. HIPAA says six. What should the hospital do to comply with the conflicting laws?
A) Keep it the 10 years required by the state since it is stricter than HIPAA.
B) Keep it 6 years since HIPAA is a federal law that pre-empts state laws.
C) Keep it 10 years for a state hospital, 6 years if you are not a state hospital.
D) Kept it 6 years if for a federal hospital, 6 years if it is not a federal hospital.
REFERENCE: OCR, 160.203
                    Hughes (2002C), p 68, 70
COMPETENCY: Core: 1A, 1B, 1J
                    Privacy: 2B, 4C, 8C

195. The administrator just received notice that a list of HIV positive patients is being released to the local newspaper. He learned it by reading the paper. Who should he contact to investigate?
A) HIM director
B) hospital attorney
C) his secretary
D) Chief Privacy Officer
REFERENCE: OCR 164.530
                    Johns (2002b), p 195-196, 230
                    AHIMA(2001), p 38
                    Pabrai, p 330-331
COMPETENCY: Privacy: 2B, 5B, 6G

196. Due to the nature of the research that I am scheduled to conduct, the PHI is unable to be de-identified and it would be difficult to perform the research if consent was requested. The correct action should be:
   A) amend research until the data can be identified since HIPAA does not allow you to have access to PHI under any circumstances without patient consent
   B) ask for a list of patients and their contact information so that you can call them and gain permission
   C) ask for an IRB waiver of authorization
   D) conduct the research study since you are an employee of a covered entity
   REFERENCE: HIPAAdvisory, p 1
   COMPETENCY: Privacy: 2B, 2D, 8A, 8C

197. As a member of the IRB, I have the responsibility of reviewing requests for waivers to the authorization requirement. In reviewing the request, which of the following would I not look for as justification?
   A) risk of disclosure is minimal
   B) research would not be practical if the researchers had to gain authorization
   C) researchers are employees of covered entity
   D) the PHI was instrumental to the research
   REFERENCE: HIPAAdvisory, p 2
   COMPETENCY: Privacy: 2B, 2D, 8A, 8C

198. I have been given the responsibility to write the data use agreement that we will require researchers to sign prior to providing access to limited data sets. Which of the following is NOT required?
   A) that the researcher will only use the data for the purpose of the research
   B) that there be limitations on who has access to the data
   C) that the data must be protected from disclosure
   D) a list of identifiers to be included
   REFERENCES: HIPAAdvisory, p 3
   COMPETENCY: Privacy: 2B, 2D, 8A, 8C

199. Ed insists that the IRB can provide exemptions to the authorization requirement for research. Crystal insists that it is the Privacy Board that must authorize exemptions. Who is right?
   A) Crystal
   B) Ed
   C) both Crystal and Ed
   D) Neither Crystal nor Ed
   REFERENCE: HIPAAdvisory, p 1
   COMPETENCY: Privacy: 2B, 2D, 8A, 8C

200.Dr. Jones has just told Dr. Warren that he would send some PHI via email so that Dr. Warren can consult on a patient's care. Dr. Warren is concerned that it would be a breech of the HIPAA privacy regulation and expresses his concern. Dr. Jones' appropriate response should be:

A) You are right. I wasn't thinking.

B) You are wrong. As long as the necessary security measures are in place, it is perfectly appropriate to email PHI.

C) You are wrong. HIPAA specifically supports the use of email.

D) You are right. I need a signed patient authorization before I can send it to you.

REFERENCE: Health Privacy Project, p 1
COMPETENCY: Privacy: 2B, 2D, 6A, 8A, 8C

1. D

2. C The release of childbirth information is acceptable since it is related to the reason for admission. The mass mailing of samples violates giving out confidential information to outside agencies.

3. B The chest x-ray has no bearing on the finger fracture.

4. C

5. B

6. B

7. B

8. B

9. B

10. B

11. B

12. B

13. D

14. D

15. B

16. C

17. D

18. A

19. B

20. D

21. B

22.   D   If the healthcare provider agrees, then it cannot violate the request
           except in emergency care so the providers should notify patient even
           through they have the patient authorization.

23.   C

24.   B

25.   A   Even through he works in the lab, the information is more than the
           minimum necessary to perform the task at hand.

26.   D

27.   A

28.   A

29.   D

30.   B

31.   A

32.   B

33.   B

34.   C

35.   D

36.   B

37.   C

38.   A

39.   D

40.   D

41.   B

42.   D

43.   B

44. B

45. C

46. C

47. C

48. C

49. C The device identifier could be used to backtrack and identify the patient.

50. D

51. C

52. C

53. C

54. A

55. D

56. D

57. D A covered facility may post the information on the website, but it is not required unless the facility has a website.

58. D

59. B

60. B

61. A

62. D

63. A

64. A

65. B

66. A

67.	D
68.	D
69.	C
70.	C
71.	A
72.	D
73.	D
74.	A
75.	D
76.	B
77.	A
78.	B
79.	A
80.	B
81.	B
82.	B
83.	C
84.	A
85.	A
86.	C
87.	B
88.	C
89.	C

90. C

91. C

92. B

93. C

94. C

95. D The first accounting should be free. The covered entity may charge for subsequent requests within a 12 month period. First, the patient should be notified of the fee, so that he/she may withdraw or modify the request. This would enable the patient to avoid or reduce the fee.

96. B

97. B

98. C

99. C

100. C

101. C

102. A

103. C

104. D

105. C The person who recorded the documentation in question should be the one who authorizes the change. While this reference does not come out and explicitly state this, it does state that the form should have a place for the provider's signature and comments.

106. D

107. B

108. C

109. C

110. D

Answer Key for Privacy Questions for the CHP

111. D

112. C

113. C

114. D

115. B

116. C

117. D

118. C

119. B

120. C

121. D

122. B

123. A

124. D

125. C

126. C

127. B

128. D

129. D

130. D

131. C

132. B

133. B

134. B

135. A

136. B

137. A

138. A

139. D

140. C

141. B

142. D

143. B

144. A

145. A

146. D

147. C

148. D

149. A Although it is an option, the covered entity is not required to provide a paper copy of the revised notice to all individuals whose protected health information it maintains. The covered entity can post the revised notice on its web site, place ads in newspapers, send e-mail, put a notation on the billing statement or use a combination of approaches.

150. C

151. A

152. D

153. A

154. B

155.   D

156.   A

157.   B

158.   A

159.   C

160.   A

161.   B

162.   C

163.   A

164.   B

165.   D

166.   C

167.   C

168.   B

169.   D

170.   A

171.   D

172.   A

173.   B

174.   D

175.   C

176.   C

177.   A

178. D

179. C

180. A

181. B

182. B

183. A

184. B

185. C

186. C

187. D

188. A

189. B

190. B

191. D

192. C

193 C The signature is just to document receipt. The hospital should note the refusal but cannot refuse to treat patient.

194. A

195. D

196. C

197. C

198. D

199. C

200. B

REFERENCES FOR PRIVACY QUESTIONS

Abdelhak, M., Grostick, S., Hanken, M., & Jacobs E. (Eds.) (2001). *Health information: Management of a strategic resource*. Philadelphia: W.B. Saunders Company.

Abraham, P. R. (2002). HIPAA changes home health, hospice documentation practices. *Journal of AHIMA, 73*(2), 39-40.

AHIMA (2001). Help wanted: Privacy officer. *Journal of AHIMA, 72*(6), 37-39.

Amatayakul, M. (2000). Getting ready for HIPAA privacy rules. *Journal of AHIMA*, 71(4), 34-36.

Amatayakul, M. (2001a). HIPAA on the job series: Five steps to reading the HIPAA Rules. *Journal of AHIMA,* 72(8), 16A-C.

Amatayakul, M. (2001b). HIPAA on the job series: Managing individual rights requirements under HIPAA privacy. *Journal of AHIMA,* 72(6), 16A-D.

Amatayakul, M. (2001c). HIPAA on the Job: Forms and documentation for HIPAA privacy – a closer look. *Journal of AHIMA, 72*(5), 16A-D.

Amatayakul, M. (2002a). HIPAA on the job: A reasonable approach to physical security. *Journal of AHIMA, 73*(4), 16A-C.

Amatayakul, M. (2002b). AHIMA Practice brief: Implementing the minimum necessary standard. *Journal of AHIMA, 73*(9), 96A-F.

Amatayakul, M. (2002c). The first line of defense against privacy complaints. *Journal of AHIMA, 73*(9), 24A-C.

Amatayakul, M. (2002d). HIPAA on the Job: United under HIPAA: A comparison of arrangements and agreements. *Journal of AHIMA, 73*(8), 24A-D.

Amatayakul, M. (2002e). Make your telecommuting program HIPAA compliant. *Journal of AHIMA, 73*(2), 16A-C.

Amatayakul, M., & Walsh, T. (2001). HIPAA on the job series: Selecting strong passwords. *Journal of AHIMA,* 72(9), 16A-D.

Amatayakul, M., & Waymack, P. (2002). What's your designated record set. *Journal of AHIMA, 73*(6), 16A-C.

REFERENCES FOR PRIVACY QUESTIONS

Apple, G. J., & Brandt, M. D. (2001). Ready, set, assess: An action plan for conducting a HIPAA privacy risk assessment. *Journal of AHIMA, 72*(6), 26-32.

Brandt, M. (2001). HIPAA security standards: Working with your information technology vendors. *AHIMA Convention Proceedings.* Retrieved January 16, 2003 from http://www.ahima.org.

Callahan-Dennis, J. (2000). Privacy and Confidentiality of Health Information. San Francisco: Jossey-Bass.

Cassidy, B. S. (2000). HIPAA on the job: Understanding chain of trust and business partner agreements. *Journal of AHIMA, 71*(9), 16A-C.

Cassidy, B. S. (2001). HIPAA on the job: The next challenge: Employee training on privacy, security. *Journal of AHIMA, 72*(1), 16A-C.

Choy, A., Pritts, J., & Goldman, J. (2002). E-health: What's outside the privacy rule's jurisdiction? *Journal of AHIMA, 73*(5), 34-39.

Davis, J. B. (2003). HIPAA Compliance manual: *A comprehensive guide to the administrative simplification provisions for health care professionals.* Practice Management Information Corporation: Los Angeles, CA

Dougherty, M. (2001). AHIMA Practice Brief: Accounting and tracking disclosure of protected health information. *Journal of AHIMA, 72*(10), 72E-H.

Dougherty, M. (2002). It's time to finalize your privacy policies. *Journal of AHIMA 73*(10), 61-64.

Fuller, S. (1999). Implementing HIPAA security standards – are you ready? *Journal of AHIMA, 70*(9), 38-44.

Health Privacy Project. Myths and Facts about the HIPAA privacy rule. Printed on November 3, 2004, from http://www.healthprivacy.org/info-url_nocat2303/info-url_nocat_show.htm?doc_id=173435

HIPAAdvisory. Research. Printed on November 3, 2004 at http://www.hipaadvisory.com/regs/finalprivacymod/gresearch.htm

Hjort, B. (2001). AHIMA Practice Brief: A HIPAA privacy checklist. *Journal of AHIMA 72*(6), 64A-C.

Huffman, E. (1995). Health Information Management (10th edition). Berwyn, IL: Physician Record Company.

REFERENCES FOR PRIVACY QUESTIONS

Hughes, G. (2001a). Managing exceptions to HIPAA's patient access rule. *Journal of AHIMA,* 72(9), 90-92.

Hughes, G. (2001b). AHIMA Practice Brief: Consent for the use or disclosure of individually identifiable health information. Journal of AHIMA, 72(5), 64E – F.

Hughes, G. (2001c). AHIMA Practice Brief: Redisclosure of PHI. *Journal of AHIMA, 72(8), p 72A-72B*

Hughes, G. (2002a). AHIMA Practice Brief: Understanding the minimum necessary standard. *Journal of AHIMA* 73(1), 56A-B.

Hughes, G. (2002b). AHIMA Practice Brief: Notice of Information Practices (updated). *Journal of AHIMA 72(5), p 64I-64M*

Hughes, G. (2002c). AHIMA Practice Brief: Laws and regulations governing the disclosure of health information (Updated November, 2002). Retrieved February 1, 2003, from http://www.ahima.org

Hughes, G. (2002d). AHIMA Practice Brief: Understanding the privacy rule amendments *Journal of AHIMA* 73(10), p 64-66.

Hughes, G. (2002e). Creating Privacy Rule Implementation Efficiency. *Journal of AHIMA,* 73(9), p 97-99.

Hughes, G. (2002f). AHIMA Practice Brief: Preemption of the HIPAA privacy rule. *Journal of AHIMA,* 73(2), 56A-C.

Hughes, G. (2002g). Simple steps to tracking disclosures. *Journal of AHIMA*, 73(7), p 68-70

Johns, M. L. (2002b). *Health information technology: An applied approach.* Chicago, IL: American Health Information Management Association.

Nicholson, R. (2002). The dilemma of psychotherapy notes and HIPAA. *Journal of AHIMA* 73(2), 38-39.

Pabrai, Uday. (2003). *Getting Started with HIPAA.* Boston, MA: Premier Press

Pozgar, G. D. (1999). *Legal aspects of healthcare administration (7th ed.).* Gaithersburg, MD: Aspen Publications.

Roach, M. (2001). HIPAA compliance questions for business partner agreements. *Journal of AHIMA,* 72(2), 45-51.

REFERENCES FOR PRIVACY QUESTIONS

Roach, Jr., W. (1998). *Medical records and the law* (3rd edition). Boston, MA: Jones and Bartlett Publishers.

Rhodes, H. (2001). Marketing privacy: HIPAA's new sales pitch. *AHIMA convention proceedings.* Retrieved January 16, 2003 from http://www.ahima.org.

Rode, D. (2001). Final privacy rule puts health information in national spotlight. *Journal of AHIMA, 72*(2), p 32A-C.

Rode, D. (2002). Quest for patient's trust only just begun. *Journal of AHIMA 73*(10), p 16, 18.

Sullivan, T. (2002). Mind your business associate access: Six steps. *Journal of AHIMA, 73*(9), 92, 94, 96.

Thieleman, W. (2002). A patient friendly approach to the record amendment process. *Journal of AHIMA*, 73(5), 46-47.

U.S. Office of Civil Rights (2002a). *Frequently asked questions about the HIPAA privacy rule.* Retrieved December 19, 2002 from http://www.benefitslink.com/articles/hipaa-faq-10-02-2002.pdf.

U. S. Department of Health and Human Services (2002b). *HHS Fact Sheet: Modifications to the standards for privacy of individually identifiable health information – final rule.* Retrieved on August 25, 2002 from http://www.hhs.gov/news/press/2002pres/20020809.html

U. S. Department of Health and Human Services (2003) HHS Fact Sheet*: Protecting The Privacy Of Patients' Health Information* (April 14, 2003) Retrieved January 15, 2004, from http://www.hhs.gov/news/facts/privacy.html

OCR
U.S. Department of Health and Human Services Office for Civil Rights (2003) *Standards for Privacy of Individually Identifiable Health Information Security Standards for the Protection of Electronic Protected Health Information General Administrative Requirements Including, Civil Money Penalties: Procedures for Investigations, Imposition of Penalties, and Hearings Regulation Text* (Unofficial Version) (45 CFR Parts 160 and 164) December 28, 2000 as amended: May 31, 2002, August 14, 2002, February 20, 2003, and April 17, 2003 Retrieved January 15, 2004, from http://www.hhs.gov/ocr/combinedregtext.pdf

REVIEW SECTION
FOR THE
CHS EXAMINATION

Core Questions for the CHS Examination

Core Questions
For the CHS Examination

1. You are looking at your policies, procedures, training program, etc. and comparing it to the HIPAA regulations. You are conducting a
   A) policy assessment
   B) risk assessment
   C) compliance audit
   D) gap analysis
   REFERENCE: OCR 164.308, 164.530
                   Amatayakul, et al., p 29-31
                   Pabrai, p 223-224, 336-337, 477-483
                   Johns (2002a), p 107
                   Hjort (2001), p 64A
   COMPETENCY: Core: 1K, 1M, 1U
                   Security: 4B

2. I am planning our new training program on privacy issues. I need to ensure that which of the following attends the training sessions?
   A) both current and new employees
   B) physicians
   C) volunteers
   D) all of the above
   REFERENCE: OCR 164.530
                   Amatayakul, et al., p 55-57
                   Pabrai, p 229, 327-328
                   Callahan-Dennis (2000), p 69-72, 74
   COMPETENCY: Core: 1D, 1E

3. As Chief Privacy Officer, you have been asked why you are conducting a risk assessment. Which reason would you give?
   A) get rid of problem staff
   B) change organizational culture
   C) prevent breach of confidentiality
   D) none of the above
   REFERENCE: OCR 164.308, 164.530
                   Pabrai, p 223-224, 336-337, 477-483
                   Callahan-Dennis (2000), p 31-32, 36
   COMPETENCY: Core: 1M, 1T

4. Florida Beach Hospital is reviewing the following new policy for approval and implementation. What problem with the policy do you have?

> Policy: Because of recent legislation, Florida Beach Hospital will track release of confidential patient identifiable information in the following circumstances as required by law:
>
> employers
> attorneys
> patient
> external researcher

A) tracking release to employers is exempted from legislation
B) tracking release to attorneys is exempted from legislation
C) tracking release to patient is exempted from legislation
D) tracking release to external researcher is exempted from legislation

REFERENCE: OCR 164.316, 164.528
               Amatayakul, et al., p 24-27
               Pabrai, p 146, 243-244
               Hartley & Jones, p 81
               Dougherty (2001), p 72E
COMPETENCY: Core: 1B, IT
               Privacy: 2B, 8C

5. Mark is in charge of the training department. While he does not conduct all of the training classes, he is responsible for maintaining documentation on the training provided. Which of the following documentation should he maintain?
A) attendance roster, content of course, handouts, announcements and quiz results
B) sign-in sheet and agenda only
C) content of course, handouts and transcript of questions asked by staff
D) handouts, attendance roster, content of course and list of people scheduled to attend but who did not show up.

REFERENCE: OCR 164.308, 164.530
               Amatayakul, et al., p 55-57
               Pabrai, p 229, 327-328
               Callahan-Dennis (2000), p 71-72
               Hjort (2002), p 60A
               Hartley & Jones, p 118
COMPETENCY: Core: 1D, 1E
               Privacy: 4A
               Security: 8C

6. You are on a task force that has the assignment of evaluating your privacy program. Which of the following should the task force do?
   A) evaluate policies and procedures
   B) ask the Chief Executive Officer to support your activities
   C) appoint a privacy officer
   D) all of the above
REFERENCE: OCR 164.308, 164.530
              Pabrai, p 330-332, 336-338, 477-483
              Johns (2002b), p 229-231
              Hjort (2001), p 64A
COMPETENCY: Core: 1I, 1J, 1K, 1L
              Privacy: 2A, 5A

7. Michaela tells Bob, the pharmacy tech, that only the HIM department is subject to privacy and security restrictions because they are responsible for the record. What should be Bob's response?
   A) I know. I am glad that I do not work in HIM.
   B) I disagree. Everyone who works in a covered entity is responsible for complying with privacy and security regulations.
   C) I disagree. Healthcare providers like physicians and nurses also have a responsibility to keep patient's confidential information private.
   D) none of the above
REFERENCE: Amatayakul, et al., p 55-57
              Pabrai, p 229
              Callahan-Dennis (2000), p17
              Hjort (2002), p 60A
              Hartley & Jones, p 24
COMPETENCY: Core: 1B, 1D, 1E
              Privacy: 2B, 4C

8. Employees should receive training on privacy at least
   A) upon hiring
   B) annually
   C) when something changes
   D) both A and C
REFERENCE: OCR 164.308, 164.530
              Amatayakul, et al., p 55-57
              Pabrai, p 229, 327-328
              Hjort (2002), p 60D
              Hartley & Jones, p 118
COMPETENCY: Core: 1D, 1E

9. You have been asked to define privacy. Which of the following definitions would you use?
   A) the patient has the right to control who reviews his or her medical record
   B) patients have rights regarding their individually identifiable health information
   C) access to medical record information has to be controlled by technical controls
   D) access to patient identifiable health information is available only to healthcare professionals
   REFERENCE: LaTour and Eichenwald, p 233
                Amatayakul, et al., p 3-4
                Pabrai, p 15
                Cassidy, (2000), p 16A
   COMPETENCY: Core: 1B, 1E, 1F

10. The agreement that you are looking at designates that all of the separate facilities that your organization owns are designated as a single covered entity. This must be a(n)
    A) affiliated covered entity
    B) organized healthcare arrangement
    C) traditional partner agreement
    D) data use agreement
    REFERENCE: OCR 164.105
                 Amatayakul, et al., p 20-22
                 Amatayakul (2002d), p 24C
    COMPETENCY: Core: 1I, 1J

11. HIPAA requires a healthcare facility to conduct privacy training at various points. These points include
    A) prior to the compliance date of HIPAA
    B) for new employees
    C) when new privacy policies impact employees
    D) all of the above
    REFERENCE: OCR 164.308, 164.530
                 Amatayakul, et al., p 55-57
                 Pabrai, p 229, 327-328
    COMPETENCY: Core: 1E, 1F

12. Sabrina is sorting through a large stack of old policies and procedures trying to determine which ones can be discarded. Which of the following policies could she retire?
    A) policy revised 2 years ago
    B) policy replaced 7 years ago
    C) policy implemented 5 years ago
    D) none of the above
REFERENCE: OCR 164.316
                Amatayakul, et al., p 24-26
                Pabrai, p 237-328, 243-244
                Dougherty (2002), p 64
COMPETENCY: Core: 1H, 1J
                Privacy: 2B, 4B

13. Thomas has identified a need to update a policy and procedure that is referred to on the notice of information practices. Which of the following is an appropriate step for him to take?
    A) change the policy whether or not the notice of information practices notifies the patient that the policy and procedure may be changed
    B) change policy if notice of information practice has a statement allowing change
    C) change policy whether or not the notice of information practice notifies the patient that the policy and procedure may be changed and then update the notice of information practice
    D) none of the above
REFERENCE: OCR 164.530
                Amatayakul, et al., p 24-27
                Pabrai, p146, 243-244
                Dougherty (2002), p 61
                Hartley & Jones, p 72
COMPETENCY: Core: 1H, 1J
                Privacy: 2A, 2B, 4A, 4B

14. Training is a key component of HIPAA. Which of the following types of training should be conducted?
    A) general privacy and security training
    B) job specific privacy and security training
    C) management specific privacy and security training
    D) all of the above
REFERENCE: OCR 164.308, 164.530
                Amatayakul, et al., p 55-57
                Pabrai, p 229, 327-328
                Amatayakul & Johns, p 16C
                Hartley & Jones, p 118
COMPETENCY: Core: 1D, 1E
                Security: 8A, 8B

15.Randy is developing the training plan for the privacy and security training. He should
   A) include policies and procedures
   B) consider using various training methods based on the audience
   C) provide core training for all staff
   D) do all of the above
REFERENCE: OCR 164.308, 164.530
               Amatayakul, et al., p 55-57
               Pabrai, p 146, 229, 243-244, 327-328
               LaTour and Eichenwald, p 581-592
               Abdelhak, p 615-616
               Johns (2002b), p 230
               Amatayakul & Johns, p 16D, 16 E
COMPETENCY: Core: 1D, 1E
               Security: 2C

16.The agenda for the core privacy and security training has been established. Which of the following should be excluded from the agenda?
   A) definition of confidentiality
   B) definition of privacy
   C) patient right to his/her medical information
   D) copy of final privacy and security regulations
REFERENCES: Amatayakul, et al., p 55-57
               LaTour and Eichenwald, p 582-588
               Pabrai, p 146, 229, 243-244, 327-328
               Johns (2002b), p 171
               Amatayakul & Johns, p 16D
COMPETENCY: Core: 1D, 1E

17.Training is an important part of HIPAA privacy and security rules. Which of the following statements is a true statement regarding this training?
   A) the privacy and security rule mandates lecture training
   B) HIPAA mandates training and documentation requirements but not the method to be used
   C) requires training to be conducted upon hire and then on a semi-annual basis thereafter
   D) self directly learning is mandated
REFERENCE: OCR, 164.308, 164.530
               Amatayakul, et al., p 55-57
COMPETENCY: Core: 1D, 1E

18. Janie is asked the difference between privacy and security. She explains it as
  A) privacy is the management of disclosures and security is controlling access from inappropriate disclosure
  B) security is the management of disclosures and privacy is controlling access from inappropriate disclosure
  C) privacy is protecting data from destruction and security determines who can have access to PHI
  D) security is protecting data from destruction and privacy determines who can have access to PHI

REFERENCE: LaTour and Eichenwald, p 223-224
              Amatayakul, et al., p 3, 9
              Pabrai, p 15
              Sullivan, p 92
COMPETENCY: Core: 1B, 1I

19. Violation of a patient's privacy may occur when using information in which of the following formats?
  A) paper
  B) verbal
  C) computer
  D) all of the above

REFERENCE: OCR 160.103
              Pabrai, p 2, 110-111, 119-121
              Amatayakul, et al., p 3-8
              Dougherty (2001), p 72E
              Hartley & Jones, p 241
              Davis, p 50
COMPETENCY: Core: 1I, 1K, 1Q

20. Dr. Thomas has a solo practice specializing in orthopedics. He does not file electronic claims. What is his status with regard to the privacy regulations?
  A) he must abide by the tenets of the privacy regulations since he is a healthcare provider
  B) he is not a covered entity since he does not transmit health claims electronically
  C) he is covered since he is a business associate
  D) none of the above

REFERENCE: OCR 160.102
              Amatayakul, et al., p 19
              Pabrai, p 190
              Choy, Pritts, & Goldman, p 35
              Hartley & Jones, p 5, 235
COMPETENCY: Core: 1B, 1I

21. The student clinic at the University of Macon treats students for a variety of services. The clinic provides free or low cost services and only accepts self-pay form of reimbursement. According to HIPAA, the student clinic is
    A) a covered entity because it is a health plan
    B) a covered entity because it is a clearinghouse
    C) not a covered entity
    D) a covered entity because it is a provider
REFERENCE: OCR 160.102, 164.104
               Amatayakul, et al., p 19
               Pabrai, p 190
               Choy, Pritts, & Goldman, p 34-35
               Hartley & Jones, p 5, 235
COMPETENCY: Core: 1B, 1I

22. Respond to the following comment. The VA Medical Center is not subject to HIPAA privacy requirements.
    A) This is wrong since governmental facilities are subject to HIPAA
    B) This is wrong since they submit electronic claims
    C) This is right since governmental facilities are not subject to HIPAA
    D) This is right since they do not submit electronic claims
REFERENCE: OCR 164.512
               Amatayakul, et al., p 18-19
               Pabrai, p 117, 185-186
COMPETENCY: Core: 1B, 1I

23. HIPAA's privacy rule was established by
    A) Department of Health and Human Services
    B) Congress
    C) CMS
    D) Centers for Disease Control
REFERENCE: Johns (2002b), p 673
               Pabrai, p 4-6
               Amatayakul (2000), p 34
               Doscher (2002), p 11
COMPETENCY: Core: 1B

24. Fred is responsible for privacy training and Bob is responsible for security training. Which of the following is true?
    A) they can work together since the training requirements are similar
    B) they must keep their efforts separate due to differences
    C) they must ensure that training is conducted by May
    D) none of the above
REFERENCE: OCR 164.308, 164.530
               Amatayakul, et al., p 9, 55-57
               Callahan-Dennis (2000), p 17, 67-76
               Pabrai, p 225-226, 474-475
               Hjort (2002), p 60B
COMPETENCY: Core: 1I
               Security: 10E

25. Mickey's job as a release of information coordinator just underwent substantial changes. He received privacy training 6 months ago. Which of the following is true?
    A) Mickey will not need to be trained again for 6 months
    B) Mickey should be given additional training on the changes
    C) Mickey should only receive training if he is a paid employee of the hospital
    D) Mickey should receive training only if he requests it
REFERENCE: OCR 164.308, 164.530
               Amatayakul, et al., p 55-57
               Pabrai, p 146, 229, 243-244, 327-328
               Hjort (2002), p 60D
COMPETENCY: Core: 1D, 1E

26. Greg is conducting a privacy training session. At the beginning of the course, he asks what role in the organization each participant has. He learns that there are people from environmental services, nursing, health information management and the business office. What problem does he have?
    A) he cannot proceed because of diverse group
    B) he should proceed with an extensive training program
    C) maybe none if he is conducting general awareness training
    D) none of the above
REFERENCE: OCR 164.308, 164.530
               Amatayakul, et al., p 55-57
               Pabrai, p 146, 229, 243-244, 327-328
               Johns (2002b), p 230,676
               LaTour and Eichenwald, p 586-588
               Hjort (2002), p 60B, 60D
               Hartley & Jones, p 118
COMPETENCY: Core: 1D, 1E

27. Michaela works at home for a covered entity. Because she does not work on the hospital campus, she is exempt from the training requirements. React to this comment.
    A) all employees must undergo training
    B) the training must be appropriate for her role
    C) she is exempt
    D) both A and B
REFERENCE: OCR 164.308, 164.530
              Amatayakul, et al., p 55-57
              Pabrai, p 146, 229, 243-244, 327-328
              LaTour and Eichenwald, p 586-588
              Johns (2002b), 230, 676
              Hjort (2002), p 60B
COMPETENCY: Core: 1D, 1E
              Privacy: 2B, 4A

28. If privacy training is divided into three levels of training (I, II and III) with level III being the most intense, at which level would you expect to find specifics on the disclosure of patient information?
    A) I – General
    B) II – Job specific
    C) III – Management specific
    D) Not included in any training
REFERENCE: OCR 164.308
              Amatayakul, et al., p 55-57
              Hjort (2002), p 60C
              LaTour and Eichenwald, p 581
COMPETENCY: Core: 1D, 1E

29. Which of the following formats could be used for HIPAA training?
    A) lecture
    B) computer based training
    C) handouts
    D) any of the above
REFERENCE: OCR 164.308, 164.530
              Amatayakul, et al., p 55-57
              LaTour and Eichenwald, p 590-592
              Pabrai, p 146, 243-244, 327-328
              Hjort (2002), p 60D
COMPETENCY: Core: 1D, 1E

30.At which level should the privacy officer operate?
   A) Vice president
   B) Department director
   C) Leadership
   D) None of the above
   REFERENCE: OCR 164.530
                   Pabrai, p 326, 330-331
                   Johns (2002b), p 165-196, 229-230
                   Hjort (2001), p 64A
   COMPETENCY: Core: 1C, 1O, 1S

31.Madison Medical Center, which is owned by Hospital Corporation of California, is
   _____ bound by the Privacy Act of 1974.
   A) not
   B) absolutely
   C) partially
   REFERENCE: Abdelhak, p 440
                   Pabrai, p 188
                   Callahan-Dennis (2000), p 12
                   Hughes (2002c), p 64A
   COMPETENCY: Core: 1B, 1I

32.Which law allows for patients to amend information?
   A) HIPAA
   B) Privacy Act of 1974
   C) Confidentiality of Alcohol and Drug Abuse Patient records
   D) Both A and B
   REFERENCE: OCR 164.526
                   Pabrai, p 145-146
                   Abdelhak, p, 439-440, 443
                   Johns (2002b), p 226-227
                   Hughes (2002c), p 64A, 64B
   COMPETENCY: Core: 1B, 1I

33.Ben and Jason have a difference of opinion. Ben says that the Confidentiality of
   Alcohol and Drug Abuse Patient Records rule supercedes HIPAA. Jason says it is
   the reversed. Who is right?
   A) Ben
   B) Jason
   C) both since neither law covers all of the clauses of the other
   D) neither since it depends on which part of the law is stricter
   REFERENCE: OCR 160.201, 160.203
                   Johns (2002b), p 209
                   Hughes (2002c), p 64B
   COMPETENCY: Core: 1B, 1I

34. The Confidentiality of Alcohol and Drug Abuse Patient Records rule includes all of the following except
   A) identity of patient
   B) diagnosis of patient
   C) treatment of patient
   D) payment of bill
REFERENCE: Callahan-Dennis (2000), p 70
               Johns (2002b), p 70
               Hughes (2002c), p 64B
COMPETENCY: Core: 1B, 1I

35. The Whitaker Clinic is an exclusive alcohol and drug treatment facility. They do not receive federal funds. Which of the following statements are true?
   A) They are not subject to the Confidentiality of Alcohol and Drug Abuse Patient Records rule since it is not a federally assisted program.
   B) They are subject to the Confidentiality of Alcohol and Drug Abuse Patient Records rule since they provide alcohol and drug abuse treatment.
   C) They are not subject to the Confidentiality of Alcohol and Drug Abuse Patient Records rule since they are privately owned.
   D) They are subject to the Confidentiality of Alcohol and Drug Abuse Patient Records rule since they are privately owned.
REFERENCE: Callahan-Dennis (2000), p12-14
               Johns (2002b), p 70-71
               Hughes (2002c), p 64B
COMPETENCY: Core: 1B, 1I

36. Laws and regulations that apply to confidentiality include
   A) HIPAA
   B) Privacy Act of 1974
   C) Medicare Conditions of Participation
   D) all of the above
REFERENCE: Callahan-Dennis (2000), p 12-14
               Hughes (2002c), p 64B
COMPETENCY: Core: 1B, 1I

37. The Conditions of Participation for _____ requires patient access to his/her medical records information within 24 hours.
   A) hospitals
   B) long term care
   C) home health
   D) hospice
REFERENCE: Hughes (2002c), p 64B
COMPETENCY: Core: 1B, 1I

38. The Joint Commission of Healthcare Organizations requires
    A) the maintenance of secure paper records
    B) the maintenance of secure computerized records
    C) the maintenance confidentiality, security and integrity of data and information
    D) protection of the patient's privacy
REFERENCE: LaTour and Eichenwald, p 187
               Johns (2002b), p 829-835
               Hughes (2002c), p 64B
COMPETENCY: Core: 1A

39. Reason(s) for conducting a privacy risk assessment is (are)
    A) HIPAA compliance
    B) reducing liability
    C) both A and B
    D) none of the above
REFERENCE: OCR 164.308, 164.530
               Amatayakul, et al., p 10, 29-31
               Pabrai, p 223-224, 336-337, 477-483
               LaTour and Eichenwald, p 188-189
               Johns (2002b), p 339-347
               Callahan-Dennis (2000), p 31-33
               Callahan-Dennis (2001a), p 2
COMPETENCY: Core: 1T, 1U

40. Bob has been asked to specify the difference between risk assessment and gap analysis. He should reply
    A) "Risk assessment is an evaluation of potential risks, gap analysis is comparing HIPAA requirements to actual practices."
    B) "Gap analysis is an evaluation of potential risks, risk assessment is comparing HIPAA requirements to actual practices."
    C) "Risk assessment requires computer software and security assessment does not."
    D) "Risk assessment is required for privacy regulations and gap analysis is required for privacy regulations."
REFERENCE: Johns (2002b), p 107, 339, 345-348
               Pabrai, p 338-339
               Callahan-Dennis (2000), p 31-33
               Callahan-Dennis (2001a), p 1
COMPETENCY: Core: 1L, 1M, 1T, 1U

41. The purpose of privacy risk assessment is to investigate
    A) the facility for HIPAA deficits
    B) the facility to identify privacy problems related to HIPAA only
    C) the facility to identify privacy deficits whether it is related to HIPAA or not
    D) the facility's policies and procedures
REFERENCE: OCR 164.308, 164.530
                Amatayakul, et al., p 10, 29-31
                Pabrai, p 223-224, 336-337, 447-483
                Johns (2002b), p 107, 339, 345-348
                Callahan-Dennis (2000), p 31-33
                Callahan-Dennis (2001a), p 1
COMPETENCY: Core: 1L, 1M, 1T, 1U

42. The Chief Privacy Officer's required role in training is
    A) conducting the training
    B) ensuring that the appropriate training policies and procedures are followed
    C) developing a training plan
    D) all of the above
REFERENCE: OCR 164.308, 164.530
                Amatayakul, et al., p 13, 46, 127-128
                Pabrai, p 229, 327-328
                Callahan-Dennis (2000), p 67-72
                Callahan-Dennis (2001b), p 35
COMPETENCY: Core: 1D, 1E

43. You have been asked by the administrator how successful the privacy program
    is. You can answer by giving him
    A) the number of breeches
    B) the number of complaints
    C) the rate of privacy training being conducted on time
    D) all of the above
REFERENCE: Callahan-Dennis (2000), p 67-76
                Amatayakul, et al., p 45-46, 58-60, 66
                Callahan-Dennis (2001b), p 37
COMPETENCY: Core: 1B, 1F, 1K, 1S

44. A healthcare facility is developing a policy on how to document privacy training. Which of the following should be included in the policy?
    A) biometrics to record attendance
    B) showing driver's license
    C) signing a statement that training has been received
    D) signing a statement that training has been received and that employee will honor policies and procedures
REFERENCE: OCR 164.308, 164.530
               Amatayakul, et al., p 55-57
               Pabrai, p 229, 327-328
               Callahan-Dennis (2000), p 67-76
               LaTour and Eichenwald, p 584-588
               Cassidy (2001), p 16A
COMPETENCY: Core: 1D, 1E

45. I have been given the assignment of evaluating the HIPAA training provided. Which of the examples below demonstrates an outcome that can indicates effectiveness?
    A) The admission clerk is able to answer patient's questions regarding the notice of practices
    B) The health information technician is able to document the disclosure of PHI as mandated.
    C) The nurse knows where to look up a policy and procedure on privacy as needed.
    D) all of the above
REFERENCE: OCR 164.308
               Amatayakul, et al., p A 55-57, 66
               LaTour and Eichenwald, p 599
COMPETENCY: Core: 1D, 1E

46. The new training policy identifies the frequency of retraining on privacy and security training. This retraining should occur
    A) when the recertification occurs
    B) when there is a substantial change in policies and procedures
    C) every six months
    D) none of the above
REFERENCE: OCR 164.308, 164.530
               Amatayakul, et al., p 55-57
               Pabrai, 229, 327-328
               Johns (2002b), p 230-231
               Cassidy (2001), p 16A
COMPETENCY: Core: 1D, 1E

47. Which of the following security training is not required by HIPAA?
   A) password management
   B) virus protection
   C) awareness training
   D) audit trails
REFERENCE: OCR 164.308
               Amatayakul, et al., p 55-57
               Pabrai, p 229
               Johns (2002b), p 676
               Cassidy (2001), p 16B
COMPETENCY: Core: 1C, 1D
               Security: 8A, 8B, 9B

48. The facility transmits health information. Which of the following is required by the security standard?
   A) assessment of risk
   B) using HL-7
   C) using ASTM standards
   D) encryption
REFERENCE: OCR 164.308
               Amatayakul, et al., p 10, 29-31
               Pabrai, p 223-224, 336-337, 477-483
               Johns (2002b), p 669
               Hartley & Jones, p 129
COMPETENCY: Core: 1A
               Security: 7A, 7D, 7E

49. Security awareness must be based on
   A) the employee's role in the organization
   B) policies and procedures
   C) HIPAA regulation
   D) past experiences with security violations
REFERENCE: OCR 164.308
               Amatayakul, et al., p 55-57
               Pabrai, p 229
               Johns (2002b), 366-337
               Hartley & Jones, p 144
COMPETENCY: Core: 1D, 1E
               Security: 2C, 8A

50. Law enacted by a legislative body is referred to as
    A) public law
    B) private law
    C) administrative law
    D) statute
REFERENCE: Johns (2002b), p 199
COMPETENCY: Core: 1B
              Privacy: 2B, 2E

51. There are laws that include a body of criminal law that bar conduct considered being harmful to society and set forth a system for punishment for bad acts. This type of law involves the government and its relationships with individuals or organizations and is referred to as
    A) administrative law
    B) public law
    C) tort law
    D) private law
REFERENCE: Johns (2002b), p 199
COMPETENCY: Core: 1B
              Privacy: 2B, 2E

52. The concept of preemption as used in the HIPAA privacy rule refers to
    A) stricter state statutes related to the confidentiality of healthcare information will take precedence over the provisions of the HIPAA privacy rule
    B) the mandate of a notice of privacy practice should include a statement that explains that individuals may complain to the secretary of the Department of Health and Human Services when they believe that their privacy rights have been violated
    C) the fact that Joint Commission on Accreditation of Healthcare Organizations sets the official record retention standards for hospitals and other healthcare facilities
    D) research projects in which new treatments and tests are investigated to determine whether they are safe and effective
REFERENCE: OCR 160.202, 160.203
              Amatayakul, et al., p 4
              Pabrai, p 9, 117
              Johns (2002b), p 209
              Hartley & Jones, p 112
COMPETENCY: Core: 1A, 1B

53. The leader of the HIPAA compliance team wants all of her team members to clearly understand the compliance process. Which of the following would be the best tool for accomplishing this objective?
    A) flowchart
    B) force-field analysis
    C) pareto chart
    D) scatter diagram
REFERENCE: Johns (2002b), p 736-737
COMPETENCY: Core: 1I, 1K, 1L, 1N

54. The primary functions of the Chief Privacy Officer are
    A) overseeing the development, implementation and enforcement of the healthcare organization's policies and processes for protecting patient-identifiable information from unauthorized access or disclosure
    B) overseeing the development, implementation and enforcement of the healthcare organization's policies and processes for complying with all federal, state and accreditation rules and regulations related to the confidentiality and privacy of health-related information
    C) assessing the healthcare organization's information needs, establishing information systems priorities and overseeing information systems implementation projects
    D) overseeing the healthcare organization's information resource management functions and leading the strategic information systems planning process
REFERENCE: OCR 164.530
              Pabrai, p 326, 330-331
              Johns (2002b), p 582, 826-827
COMPETENCY: Core: 1B, 1C, 1E, 1F, 1I, 1S

55. The training objectives for the privacy and security training
    A) should be what you expect to cover during the training session
    B) should be based on deficiencies that have been identified
    C) should be used during evaluation
    D) all of the above
REFERENCE: 164.308
              Amatayakul, et al., p 55-57
              LaTour and Eichenwald, p 599
COMPETENCY: Core: 1D, 1E

56. Which of the following is not true about a privacy gap analysis?
    A) A privacy gap analysis should be one of the first steps the privacy officer takes to prepare for HIPAA compliance.
    B) The privacy gap analysis compares where you are now with where you need to be.
    C) As part of beginning the privacy gap analysis, gather the existing policies and procedures and a copy of the HIPAA regulations.
    D) When your privacy gap analysis is completed, communicate your results to the Security Officer.
REFERENCE: Pabrai, p 336-339, 478-483
               Callahan-Dennis (2000), p 81-83
COMPETENCY: Core: 1L, 1M

57. Annualized Loss Expectancy (ALE) refers to
    A) the financial impact or loss to the organization should the system fail
    B) the calculated financial cost for an occurrence of a harmful event
    C) the calculated relative attractiveness of a target to the perpetrators (i.e. the attractiveness of hacking into a system)
    D) the probability of a harmful event happening
REFERENCE: OCR 164.308
               Miller & Gregory, p 119
               Johns (2002a), p 342
COMPETENCY: Core: 1P

58. The first step in conducting a risk analysis is to
    A) evaluate assets in terms of value to the organization
    B) identify the information assets
    C) calculate the risk based on types of intentional/unintentional occurrences
    D) calculate a risk measurement index
REFERENCE: OCR 164.308
               Amatayakul, et al., p 29-33
               Johns (2002a), p 345
               Pabrai, p 336-337, 477-483
               Hartley & Jones, p 130
COMPETENCY: Core: 1F, 1I, 1L, 1M, 1T, 1U
               Security: 4B

59. Which of the following statements is NOT true of methodologies of determining risk?
A) a methodology may consider level of risk of unintentional occurrences happening based on probability of occurrence and cost impact
B) methodology may consider level of risk of potential intentional occurrence based on attractiveness of system to a specific perpetrator and impact of success of the attack on the targeted system
C) methodology may be based on specific, objective verifiable information in determining level of risk
D) methodology may use historical statistical data or arbitrary measurements to determine level of risk
REFERENCE: Johns (2002a), p 344
COMPETENCY: Core: 1F, 1I, 1L, 1M, 1T, 1U
                         Security: 4B

60. Coastal Hospital is a covered entity under HIPAA. In order to comply with the requirements they must train their workforce on Policies and Procedures with respect to Protected Health Information (PHI). Which of the following levels of the work force would be exempt from training?
A) HIM staff because they have already received training in release of information
B) Staff Physicians because they have taken the Hippocratic Oath
C) Administrative Staff because they do not perform hands on care
D) None of the above would be exempt from training.
REFERENCE: OCR 164.308, 164.530
                         Pabrai, p 229, 327-328
                         Callahan-Dennis (2000), p 1
                         Hjort (2002), p 60C
COMPETENCY: Core: 1D
                         Security: 8D

61. In determining how a person in a position in a department uses health information, the HIPAA Privacy and Security trainer would most certainly review the
A) past performance evaluations of persons in the position
B) job description
C) facility policy on protecting health information
D) facility policy and procedure on documenting training
REFERENCE: LaTour and Eichenwald, p 598-600
                         Hjort (2002), p 60C
COMPETENCY: Core: 1D, 1E

62. The general New Employee Orientation training would most likely cover which of the following HIPAA components?
   A) marketing issues
   B) business associate agreements
   C) physical/workstation security
   D) Job specific training (example: patient right to amend record)
REFERENCE: OCR 164.308
                      LaTour and Eichenwald, p 582-584
                      Hjort (2002), p 60C
COMPETENCY: Core: 1D, 1E

63. The teaching method selected by an instructor influences the student's ability to understand the material. Instructor-led classrooms may work best when
   A) in-depth training and interaction is desired
   B) there are 3 shifts of employees to train
   C) you want to minimize cost for training
   D) employees from all departments must be trained
REFERENCE: OCR 164.308
                      LaTour and Eichenwald, p 590-592
                      Hjort (2002), p 60D
COMPETENCY: Core: 1N

64. To ensure consistency of coverage among trainers, you may want to develop
   A) training manuals
   B) meeting handouts and minutes
   C) signed confidentiality statements acknowledging receipt and understanding of any training attended
   D) ongoing training to keep the issues in front of the work force
REFERENCE: OCR 164.308
                      LaTour and Eichenwald, p 598-600
                      Hjort (2002), p 60D
COMPETENCY: Core: 1N

65. In developing a training "to do list", you would consider the staff and what general training and specialized training topics would be necessary. What tool would be most helpful in organizing this information?
   A) a GANTT chart to show who gets trained when
   B) a spreadsheet with grids identifying who needs what type of training
   C) a "Train-the-Trainers" training manual to help in consistency in training
   D) documentation of previous orientation training to see what has already been covered.
REFERENCE: OCR 164.308
                      LaTour and Eichenwald, p 580-584
                      Hjort (2002), p 60D
COMPETENCY: Core: 1N

Use the following information to answer questions 66-68.

The training staff in the Human Resources Department is proposing a computer based training program for 200 employees and needs to prepare a budget for the time and cost of the training.
- The training program will be 30 minutes in length.
- The employees may take the training on line at any time.
- There are 200 employees to be trained.
- The rate of pay for 50 of the employees is $15.50 per hour.
- The rate of pay for 50 of the employees is $12.00 per hour.
- The rate of pay for the other 100 employees is $18.00 per hour.

66. How many employee clock hours will be needed to complete the training?
    A) 200 hours
    B) 150 hours
    C) 100 hours
    D) 50 hours
REFERENCE: Basic math calculation
              Amatayakul, et al., p 133-135
COMPETENCY: Core: 1E, 1P

67. In submitting the cost of training, how much should the training staff request in the budget for doing the computer based training?
    A) $3,175.00
    B) $1,975.00
    C) $1,887.50
    D) $1,587.50
REFERENCE: Basic math calculation
COMPETENCY: Core: 1E, 1P

68. What would be the average cost for training an employee?
    A) $15.87
    B) $15.50
    C) $ 9.00
    D) $ 7.94
REFERENCE: Amatayakul, et al., p 133-135
COMPETENCY: Core: 1E, 1P

69. One of the greatest threats to the confidentiality of health data is
    A) when medical information is reviewed as a part of Quality Assurance activities
    B) re-disclosure of information for purposes not authorized in writing by the patient
    C) lack of written authorization by the patient
    D) when medical information is used for research or education
REFERENCE: Abdelhak, p 456-457
COMPETENCY: Core: 1C, 1I
                       Privacy: 2B, 2E

Case Study:
William is a 16-year-old male who lives at home with his parents and works part-time as a dishwasher at one of the local restaurants. While performing his duties William is severely scalded and rendered unconscious while emptying the dishwasher. He is taken to the emergency room of the local acute care hospital for emergency treatment.

70. Referring to the Case Study, in order to provide treatment to William, who should the health care provider receive consent from?
    A) the employer
    B) the parents
    C) the patient
    D) no consent is needed for emergency care
REFERENCE: Pozgar, p 331
                       Roach, W., p 76-77
COMPETENCY: Core: 1B

71. Referring again, to the Case Study, in order to release information to his employer, the hospital must receive
    A) a consent signed by the patient
    B) a court order
    C) no consent is needed
    D) a consent signed by the patient's parent
REFERENCE: Abdelhak, p 454-455
                       Pozgar, p 76-77
COMPETENCY: Core: 1G, 1H
                       Privacy: 4B, 8B

72. Which of the following is an example of the breach of confidentiality?
    A) a nurse speaking with the physician in the patient room
    B) staff members discussing patients in the elevator
    C) the admission clerk verifying over the phone that the patient is in house
    D) the hospital operator paging code blue in room 3 north
REFERENCE: Abdelhak, p 434
                Amatayakul, et al., p 5-8
                Pabrai, p 169
                Pozgar, p 302
COMPETENCY: Core: 1K, 1L, 1M, 1Q
                Privacy: 4A, 8B, 8C

73. HIPAA mandated the collection of information on healthcare fraud and abuse.
    As a result, what data bank was developed?
    A) the National Practitioner Data Bank
    B) the Healthcare Integrity and Protection Data Bank
    C) the National Health Provider Inventory
    D) the Nationwide False Claims Data Bank
REFERENCE: Johns, (2002b), p 152
COMPETENCY: Core: 1K, 1L
                Privacy: 2B, 2C, 5B

74. The administrator needs to be notified of a privacy breech. Who would be the
    most likely person or group who would tell him?
    A) Chief Privacy Officer
    B) privacy oversight committee
    C) HIM director
    D) Chief Information Officer
REFERENCE: OCR 164.308, 164.530
                Amatayakul, et al., p 46, 58-60
                Pabrai, p 236, 330-331
                Johns (2002b), p 230, 826-827
                AHIMA, p 37
COMPETENCY: Core: 1K, 1L, 1Q, 1R, 1S

75. The Chief Privacy Officer feels overwhelmed. He has been trying to do
    everything by himself. What actions should he take?
    A) develop privacy oversight committee
    B) work with attorney
    C) work more hours
    D) both A and B
REFERENCE: Johns (2002b), p 195-196, 826-827
                Pabrai, p 326, 330-331
                AHIMA, p 37
COMPETENCY: Core: 1K, 1L, 1Q, 1R, 1S

76. An evaluation of the privacy and security training has determined that there is a deficit in the training program. What should be done?
   A) determine where problem occurred and make necessary change
   B) change instructor
   C) change teaching method
   D) change content
REFERENCE: OCR 164.308
                Amatayakul, et al., p 55-56, 66
                LaTour and Eichenwald, p 599
                Pabrai, p 229, 327-328
COMPETENCY: Core: 1D, 1E

77. I am describing what I expect from my Chief Privacy Officer. My expectations include all of the following except
   A) the CPO must be able to function at a high level within the organization
   B) the CPO must have a reputation as being credible
   C) the CPO must understand patient data
   D) the CPO must have a master's degree
REFERENCE: Johns (2002b), 195, 826-827
                Pabrai, p 326, 330-331
                Apple and Brandt, p 28
COMPETENCY: Core: 1I
                Privacy: 2D

78. I am looking for people to help with the risk assessment. What would I want these people to have a strong understanding of?
   A) HIPAA laws
   B) health information management
   C) flow of information
   D) data quality
REFERENCE: OCR 164.308
                Amatayakul, et al., p 31, 127-128
                Dennis-Callahan (2000), p 81-90
                Pabrai, p 223-224, 336-337, 477-483
                Apple and Brandt, p 28
COMPETENCY: Core: 1T
                Privacy: 7D

79. HIPAA requires which of the following to be a part of the risk assessment?
    A) follow the steps specified in the regulations
    B) develop policies and procedures that best suit the organization and meet the requirements of the rule
    C) use project management skills
    D) use technology

REFERENCE: OCR 164.308, 164.530
               Amatayakul, et al., p 24-27, 36-38, 108
               Pabrai, p 223-224, 336-337, 477-483
               Dennis-Callahan (2000), p 31-34, 81-90
               Apple and Brandt, p 28
COMPETENCY: Core: 1M, 1T, 1U

80. Risk assessment should look at
    A) organizational level risks
    B) departmental level risks
    C) both A and B
    D) none of the above

REFERENCE: OCR 164.308, 164.530
               Amatayakul, et al., p 34-38
               Pabrai, p 223-224, 336-337, 477-483
               Dennis-Callahan (2000), p 31-34, 81-90
               Apple and Brandt, p 30
COMPETENCY: Core: 1M, 1T, 1U

81. The covered entity should _____ risk assessment tools.
    A) ask each department director to develop
    B) develop uniform
    C) use tables as
    D) conduct training on

REFERENCE: Dennis-Callahan (2000), p 31-34, 81-90
               Pabrai, p 223-224, 336-337, 477-483
               Apple and Brandt, p 30
COMPETENCY: Core: 1M, 1N, 1T, 1U

82. Tools that could be used in mapping information flow include all of the following except
    A) data flow diagrams
    B) checklist
    C) project management software
    D) flow chart

REFERENCE: Johns (2002a), p 153-154
               Pabrai, p 332-335
COMPETENCY: Core: 1N
               Privacy: 7D

83. Twenty-five areas of concern were identified in the risk assessment. Which of the following is a good tool to identify which area needs to be addressed first?
   A) assign weight to each of the issues based on seriousness of risk
   B) handle in the order identified
   C) patient care areas first
   D) GANTT chart
REFERENCE: OCR 164.308
                Amatayakul, et al., p 38-41, 108
                Johns (2002b), 339, 344-347, 504-505
                Pabrai, p 223-224, 336-337, 477-483
                LaTour and Eichenwald, p 188-189
                Apple and Brandt, p 31
COMPETENCY: Core: 1F, 1M, 1T, 1U

84. I am concerned about the risks involved with using a business associate. I am specifically concerned with releasing large amounts of PHI. Which of the following would I most likely be concerned about?
   A) collection agency
   B) contract coder
   C) hospital to which you refer patients
   D) environmental services
REFERENCE: OCR 164.308, 164.530
                Amatayakul, et al., p 22, 66-68
                Pabrai, p 234, 152-155, 340-342
                Johns (2002b), p 222-223
                Apple and Brandt, p 32
COMPETENCY: Core: 1F
                Privacy: 3C

85. Risk assessment should include all of the following except
   A) business associate agreements
   B) policies and procedures
   C) forms
   D) hardware
REFERENCE: OCR 160.103, 164.308
                Amatayakul, et al., p 36-38, 108
                Pabrai, p 223-224, 336-337, 477-483
                LaTour and Eichenwald, p 188-189
                Apple and Brandt, p 32
COMPETENCY: Core: 1F, 1M, 1T, 1U
                Security: 8E

86.The outcome of the risk assessment currently being conducted should include all of the following except
A) identifying business associates
B) forms
C) policies and procedures
D) hardware inventory
REFERENCE: OCR 164.308
Amatayakul, et al., p 36-38, 108
Pabrai, p 223-224, 336-337, 477-483
LaTour and Eichenwald, p 188-189
Apple and Brandt, p 32
COMPETENCY: Core: 1M, 1T, 1U
Privacy: 3A, 3B, 4A, 4C
Security: 8E

87.Which of the following is not the purpose of risk assessment?
A) educate administration on HIPAA regulations
B) train staff on the HIPAA regulations
C) it is the basis for planning for HIPAA compliance
D) evaluate privacy policies and procedures
REFERENCE: OCR 164.304, 164.308
Amatayakul, et al., p 29-31, 108
Pabrai, p 223-224, 336-337, 477-483
LaTour and Eichenwald, p 188-189
Apple and Brandt, p 32
COMPETENCY: Core: 1M, 1S, 1T, 1U
Security: 8E

88.I have developed an inventory of privacy and security policies and procedures. This was primarily done
A) to meet requirement of HIPAA
B) as good management practice
C) because I was asked to complete it by my supervisor
D) because I did not have anything better to do
REFERENCE: OCR 164.304, 164.308, 164.316, 164.530
Amatayakul, et al., p 24-27, 131-132
Pabrai, p 243-244, 336-337, 477-483
Apple and Brandt, p 32
COMPETENCY: Core: 1H

89. The chief financial officer needs to develop a budget for implementation of HIPAA. Which of the following types of budgets would be the most appropriate for this type of project?
A) flexible budget
B) fixed budget
C) activity-based budget
D) zero-based budget
REFERENCE: LaTour and Eichenwald, p 622
                        Amatayakul, et al., p 133-135
COMPETENCY: Core: 1P

90. Based on the risk assessment, Macon General Hospital identified a need to renovate nursing units in order to protect privacy. What type of budget should these expenses come under?
A) capital
B) operating
C) personnel
D) fixed
REFERENCE: LaTour and Eichenwald, p 618
                        Amatayakul, et al., p 133-135
COMPETENCY: Core: 1P

91. The new policies and procedures required as part of the new HIPAA regulations have been written. What is the key to change implementation?
A) communication
B) type of training provided
C) policy format
D) all of the above
REFERENCE: OCR 164.308, 164.560
                        Amatayakul, et al., p 127-128
                        LaTour and Eichenwald, p 230, 656
                        Pabrai, p 229, 327-328
COMPETENCY: Core: 1G

92. The project plan is being developed for changes resulting from the HIPAA requirements. The initial budget for the proposed changes should be
A) detailed
B) the same as the final budget
C) estimates
D) none of the above
REFERENCE: LaTour and Eichenwald, p 638
                        Amatayakul, et al., p 133-135
COMPETENCY: Core: 1P

93. Marjorie has the responsibility of implementing the new policies and procedures. Upon which management skill will she be drawing?
A) controlling
B) planning
C) leadership
D) organizing
REFERENCE: LaTour and Eichenwald, p 499
               Amatayakul, et al., p 46, 128
COMPETENCY: Core: 1G

94. Thomas has just completed teaching a privacy and security awareness training program. Which of the following would not be an appropriate assessment of the results?
A) evaluation
B) feedback from participant's supervisor
C) follow-up in a week or two with the employee
D) input from supervisor
REFERENCE: OCR 164.308
               LaTour and Eichenwald, p 588
               Amatayakul, et al., p 55-57
COMPETENCY: Core: 1D, 1E

95. The administrator wants to be kept apprised of the privacy and security issues. Which of the following communication tools could be used?
A) bulletin boards
B) daily contact with employees
C) weekly status report
D) quarterly reports
REFERENCE: LaTour and Eichenwald ,p 570
COMPETENCY: Core: 1O, 1S

96. JCAHO security requirements are
A) mandatory for everyone
B) voluntary for everyone
C) mandatory for those choosing to be JCAHO accredited
D) more stringent than HIPAA
REFERENCE: LaTour and Eichenwald, p 203
COMPETENCY: Core: 1A

97. The security rule specifically identifies two instructions to be included in the incidence response system. Which of the following is not an example of ways these instructions could be implemented?
    A) contact Chief Privacy Officer immediately
    B) interview appropriate staff
    C) document findings
    D) revise forms
REFERENCE: OCR 164.308
               Amatayakul, et al., p 58-60
               Pabrai, 203-231
COMPETENCY: Core: 1Q, 1R

98. An employee just was found to have violated a patient's privacy. The proper disciplinary step has been taken. Which of the following statements is the most likely to made by the Chief Privacy Officer to the administrator?
    A) there may still be financial ramifications to the healthcare facility
    B) the problem has been resolved
    C) the employee is the only one that has any risk from legal action
    D) none of the above
REFERENCE: OCR 164.308
               Amatayakul, et al., p 58-60
               Pabrai, p 224-225, 230-231
COMPETENCY: Core: 1P

99. Randall is reading a privacy manual and watching a video. These are examples of
    A) self-directed learning
    B) formal training
    C) seminar
    D) traditional methods
REFERENCE: LaTour and Eichenwald, p 590
COMPETENCY: Core: 1D

100. Which of the following steps are REQUIRED by the HIPAA requirements?
    A) documentation of an incident response process
    B) documentation of a damage mitigation system
    C) notification of OCR of incident
    D) both A and B
REFERENCE: OCR 160.308, 164.530
               Amatayakul, et al., p 58-60
               Pabrai, p 230-231, 328-329
               Ruano, p 68
COMPETENCY: Core: 1K, 1Q, 1U

1. B

2. D Although physicians are not technically under the control of the facility, they still need to be included in the HIPAA training program.

3. C

4. C

5. A

6. D

7. B

8. D

9. A

10. A

11. D

12. B

13. B

14. D

15. D

16. D

17. B

18. A

19. D There is not a restriction in the format used, only that the information is released.

20. B The physician does not meet the definition of a covered entity since he/she does not file claims electronically.

21. C

22. A

23. A

24. A

25. B

26. C

27. D

28. B

29. D

30. C

31. A

32. D

33. D

34. D

35. A Confidentiality of alcohol and drug abuse patient record regulation only applies to federally assisted programs.

36. D

37. B

38. C

39. C

40. A

41. C

42. B

43. D

44. D

45. D

46. B

47. D

48. A

49. A

50. D

51. B

52. A

53. A

54. B

55. D

56. D The privacy officer should be communicating with the security officer as well as others on a team formed to work through the gap analysis to avoid duplication of efforts. With a variety in staff team members, each member will have special perspectives and insights to help in detecting potential risks.

57. A ALE is usually defined as the financial impact or loss to the organizations should the system fail. It is typically calculated by multiplying the financial cost per each occurrence of a harmful event times the number of times the event is expected to happen in one year.

58. B The first step in conducting a risk analysis is to know what constitutes the organizational information assets.

59. C Ultimately, the determination of risk is based on management judgment. The probability estimates can be based on historical statistical data or could be arbitrary measurements based on judgment and experience of the organizational security team.

60. D

61. B

62. C

63. A

64.   A

65.   B

66.   C   Calculation: 200 employees X .5 hour for training=100 clock hours

67.   D   Calculation:
      50 employees X .5 hour X $15.50 per hour = $387.50
      50 employees X .5 hour X $12.00 per hour = $300.00
      100 employees X .5 hour X $18.00 per hour = $900.00
      387.50 + 300.00 + 900.00= $1587.50

68.   D   Calculation: $1587.50 divided by 200 employees = $7.94 per employee

69.   B

70.   D

71.   D

72.   B

73.   B

74.   A

75.   D

76.   A

77.   D

78.   C

79.   B

80.   C

81.   B

82.   B

83.   A

84.   B

85.   D

86.   D

87.   B

88.   A

89.   C   This type of budget is used for projects that affect many groups or departments.

90.   A

91.   A

92.   C

93.   C

94.   D

95.   C

96.   C

97.   D

98.   D

99.   A

100. D

CORE REFERENCES

Abdelhak, M., Grostick, S., Hanken, M., & Jacobs E. (Eds.) (2001). *Health information: Management of a strategic resource*. Philadelphia: W.B. Saunders Company.

AHIMA (2001). Help wanted: Privacy officer. *Journal of AHIMA, 72*(6), 37-39.

Amatayakul, M. (2000). Getting ready for HIPAA privacy rules. *Journal of AHIMA, 71*(4), 34-36.

Amatayakul, M. (2002d). HIPAA on the Job: United under HIPAA: A comparison of arrangements and agreements. *Journal of AHIMA, 73*(8), 24A-D.

Amatayakul, M., et al. (2004) *Handbook for HIPAA Security Implementation.* AMA Press.

Amatayakul, M., & Johns, M. L. (2002). HIPAA on the job series: Compliance in the crosshairs: Targeting your training. *Journal of AHIMA. 73*(10), 16A-F.

Apple, G. J., & Brandt, M. D. (2001). Ready, set, assess: An action plan for conducting a HIPAA privacy risk assessment. *Journal of AHIMA, 72*(6), 26-32.

Callahan-Dennis, J. (2000). Privacy and confidentiality of health information. San Francisco: Jossey-Bass.

Callahan-Dennis, J. (2001a) Leading the HIPAA privacy risk assessment. *AHIMA Convention Proceedings.* Retrieved January 16, 2003, from http://www.ahima.org.

Callahan-Dennis, J. (2001b). The new privacy officer's game plan. *Journal of AHIMA, 72*(2), 33-37.

Cassidy, B. S. (2000). HIPAA on the job: Understanding chain of trust and business partner agreements. *Journal of AHIMA, 71*(9), 16A-C.

Choy, A., Pritts, J., & Goldman, J. (2002). E-health: What's outside the privacy rule's jurisdiction? *Journal of AHIMA, 73*(5), 34-39.

Dougherty, M. (2001). Practice brief: Accounting and tracking disclosure of protected health information. *Journal of AHIMA, 72*(10), 72E-H.

Dougherty, M. (2002). It's time to finalize your privacy policies. *Journal of AHIMA 73*(10), 61-64.

Hjort, B. (2001). AHIMA practice brief: A HIPAA privacy checklist. *Journal of AHIMA 72*(6), 64A-C.

Hjort, B. (2002). Privacy and security training. *Journal of AHIMA, 73*(4), 60A-G.

CORE REFERENCES

Hughes, G. (2002c). AHIMA practice brief: Laws and regulations governing the disclosure of health information (Updated November, 2002). Retrieved February 1, 2003, from http://www.ahima.org

Johns, M. L. (2002a). *Information Management for Health Professions.* Albany, NY: Delmar Publishing.

Johns, M. L. (2002b). *Health information technology: An applied approach.* Chicago, IL: American Health Information Management Association.

LaTour, K. M., & Eichenwald, S. (2002). *Health information management: Concepts principles, and practice.* Chicago, IL: American Health Information Management Association.

Pozgar, G. D. (1999). *Legal aspects of healthcare administration (7th ed.).* Gaithersburg, MD: Aspen Publications.

Roach, Jr., W. (1998). *Medical records and the law* (3rd edition). Boston, MA: Jones and Bartlett Publishers.

Ruono, M. (2003). Moving toward a unified information security program. *Journal of AHIMA, 74*(1), 66, 68.

Sullivan, T. (2002). Mind your business associate access: Six steps. *Journal of AHIMA, 73*(9), 92, 94, 96.

U. S. Department of Health and Human Services (2003) HHS Fact Sheet: *Protecting The Privacy Of Patients' Health Information (*April 14, 2003) Retrieved January 15, 2004, from http://www.hhs.gov/news/facts/privacy.html

OCR
    U.S. Department of Health and Human Services Office for Civil Rights (2003) *Standards for Privacy of Individually Identifiable Health Information Security Standards for the Protection of Electronic Protected Health Information General Administrative Requirements Including, Civil Money Penalties: Procedures for Investigations, Imposition of Penalties, and Hearings Regulation Text* (Unofficial Version) (45 CFR Parts 160 and 164) December 28, 2000 as amended: May 31, 2002, August 14, 2002, February 20, 2003, and April 17, 2003 Retrieved November 5, 2004, from http://www.hhs.gov/ocr/combinedregtext.pdf

Security Questions
for the
CHS Examination

Security Questions
for the CHS Examination

1. Mary processed a request for information and mailed it out last week. Today, the requestor, an attorney, called and said that all of the requested information was not provided. Mary pulls the documentation including the authorization and what was sent. She believes that she sent everything that was required. She confirms this with her supervisor. The requestor still believes that some extra documentation is required. Given the above information, which of the following statements is true?
   A) Mary is not required to release the extra documentation because the facility has the right to limit access to PHI.
   B) Mary is required to release the extra documentation because the requestor knows what is needed.
   C) Mary is required to release the extra documentation because in the customer service program for the facility, the customer is always right.
   D) Mary is not required to release the additional information because her supervisor agrees with her.
   REFERENCE: OCR 164.502
                          Pabrai, p 160
                          Hughes (2002a), p 56A
   COMPETENCY: Security: 10A, 10B, 10D, 10F

2. Your multi-facility system has decided to use a WAN. You suggest to the Data Security Committee that data encryption would offer such advantages as
   A) converting outgoing data into unintelligible transmissions
   B) increasing the speed at which the data is transmitted
   C) eliminating the need for patient identification security
   D) automatic data dictionary development
   REFERENCE: OCR 164.312, 164.304
                          Amatayakul, et al., p 92
                          Pabrai, p 238-241
                          Johns (2002a), p 225, 357
                          LaTour and Eichenwald, p 58-59
                          Johns (2002b), p 679
                          Abdelhak, p 681
                          Rada, p 50
   COMPETENCY: Privacy: 6C
                          Security: 7A, 7D, 7E

3. The computer system containing the computerized patient record was located in a room that was flooded. As a result, the system is inoperable. Which of the following would be implemented?
   A) SWOT analysis
   B) information systems strategic planning
   C) request for proposal
   D) business continuity processing
REFERENCE: OCR 364.308, 164.310
                Amatayakul, et al., p 71
                Pabrai, p 235-236
                Johns (2002a), p 359-362
                Johns (2002b), p 670
                Hartley & Jones, p 152
COMPETENCY: Privacy: 6C
                Security: 3A, 3D

4. You are walking around the facility to identify any privacy and security issues. You walk onto the 6W nursing unit and are able to watch the nurse entering confidential patient information. You make a note of this. What are you doing?
   A) gap analysis
   B) risk assessment
   C) monitoring audit trail
   D) none of the above
REFERENCE: OCR, 164.306
                Amatayakul, et al., p 77-78, 84, 112-113
                Hjort (2001), p 64A
                Hartley & Jones, p 130
                Pabrai, p 206-208, 447
COMPETENCY: Core: 1M
                Privacy: 2B, 6A, 8B
                Security: 4B, 4C, 4E, 10A, 10B, 10C

5. You are walking around the facility to identify any privacy and security issues. You walk onto the 6W nursing unit and are able to watch the nurse entering confidential patient information. How can you best improve the privacy of the patients?
   A) ask the nurse to type the data at another computer
   B) turn the computer screen so that the public cannot see it.
   C) give the nurse additional training
   D) none of the above
REFERENCE: Amatayakul, et al., p 77-78, 112-113
                Pabrai, p 206-208, 447
                Amatayakul (2002a), p 16C
COMPETENCY: Privacy: 2B, 6A
                Security: 4B, 4C, 4E, 5C, 10A, 10B, 10C

6. I am conducting an environmental risk assessment. Which of the following would be excluded from my assessment?
   A) placement of water pipes in the facility
   B) verifying that virus checking software is in place
   C) status of fire protection
   D) presence of back-up power
REFERENCE: OCR 164.310
               Amatayakul, et al., p 35, 173
               Pabrai, p 235-238
               Callahan-Dennis (2000), p 18
COMPETENCY: Privacy: 6A, 8C
               Security: 3A, 3D, 4B, 5C

7. In reviewing your new employee presentation on privacy, you realize that you have never added technology to the content. In updating the presentation to include privacy issues surrounding technology, which of the following would not be added?
   A) need to back up data
   B) talking about patient while reviewing computer screen in public area. (monitor faces away from public)
   C) need to face monitors away from public area
   D) locking doors to computer rooms
REFERENCE: OCR 164.312
               Amatayakul, et al., p 74-75
               Pabrai, p 238-241
               Amatayakul (2002a), p 16A-16C
COMPETENCY: Privacy: 2B, 8B, 8C

8. You are writing policies and procedures on what is and what is not confidential information. Which of the following would you include under the not confidential information in most cases?
   A) diagnosis
   B) date of service
   C) allergy
   D) none of the above
REFERENCE: Callahan-Dennis (2000), p 10
COMPETENCY: Privacy: 2B, 7A, 7C, 8C
               Security: 10A, 10F

9. Your transcription system is set up to back up your hard drive every five minutes. The back-up is on the hard drive of another computer. This computer is located in the room next door to the primary computer. What should be done to improve the back-up process?
A) place the back-up on optical disk
B) back-up daily
C) back-up on a diskette
D) move back-up computer to an office across town
REFERENCE: OCR 164.308
Amatayakul, et al., p 60-61, 83
Abdelhak, p 167
COMPETENCY: Privacy: 6C
Security: 3A, 3D

10. Today is June 30, 2003. Barbara has received a written authorization from an attorney for records on John Marshall. The dates of service requested by the authorization are for the admission of June 2, 2003 through June 8, 2003. The authorization is dated June 3, 2003. Which if the following is the appropriate response?
A) release the records as requested
B) return authorization and request one dated after June 8, 2003
C) ask supervisor to process request
D) none of the above
REFERENCE: LaTour, p 205-206
Callahan-Dennis (2000), p 37
Pabrai, p 139-140
COMPETENCY: Privacy: 8C
Security: 10A

11. Pam is determining whether or not the information she is reviewing is confidential. Which one of the following issues is not a part of her decision making process?
A) information is part of the patient care process
B) determining whether or not there was a relationship between the patient and the healthcare provider
C) determining if information was collected as part of any patient and healthcare provider relationship
D) stored in medical record
REFERENCE: OCR, p 160.103
Callahan-Dennis (2000), p 36
COMPETENCY: Security: 10A

12. The local newspaper has notified the hospital that they have received a computer listing of the names of patients receiving HIV treatment in your facility. What method(s) could be used to identify the source of this breach of confidentiality?
    A) a review of computer audit trails to determine who may have accessed such information
    B) identify where, when, and by whom such data is originated and distributed
    C) identify all employees whose passwords would permit access to such information
    D) all of the above
REFERENCE: OCR 164.312
                Amatayakul, et al., p 93-96, 116-118
                Pabrai, p 110-114, 238-241
                Abdelhak, p 678-680
COMPETENCY: Privacy: 6A, 6B, 6E
                Security: 4B, 4D, 4E, 4F, 4I

13. Plans for a manual back-up system for locating patient records in the event the computer system is not operating would include
    A) converting from terminal digit filing to alphabetic filing
    B) issuing all patients WORM smart cards indicating their medical record number
    C) using the same number for the patient account number and medical record number
    D) using an MPI card system or maintaining a paper/microfilm copy of an alphabetic MPI listing
REFERENCE: OCR 164.308
                Amatayakul, et al., p 60-61, 83
                Pabrai, p 1231-232
                Abdelhak, p 188
COMPETENCY: Privacy: 6C
                Security: 3A, 3D

14. You have been asked to provide examples of technical security measures. Which of the following would not be included in your examples?
    A) audit trail
    B) automatic log-out
    C) passwords
    D) training
REFERENCE: OCR 164.310, 164.312
                Amatayakul, et al., p 86, 91-96
                Pabrai, p 238-247
                Johns (2002b), p 677-679
                Davis, p 212
                Hartley & Jones, p 157
COMPETENCY: Privacy: 6A
                Security: 6A, 6C, 6F

15. You have been given the responsibility of deciding which access control to use. Which of the following is not one of your options?
    A) audit trail
    B) biometrics
    C) password
    D) key cards
REFERENCE: OCR 164.312
               Amatayakul, et al., p 99-102
               Pabrai, p 238-241
               Fuller, p 40
               Davis, p 214
               Rada, p 35
               Hartley & Jones, p 158
COMPETENCY: Privacy: 6A
             Security: 6A, 6C, 6F

16. Your organization is sending confidential patient information across the Internet using technology that will transform the original data into unintelligible code that can be re-created by authorized users. This technique is called
    A) a firewall
    B) validity processing
    C) a call back process
    D) data encryption
REFERENCE: OCR 164.312
               Pabrai, p 210, 213
               Amatayakul, et al., p 92, 103-105, 123
               Abdelhak, p 222
               Rada, p 50
               Hartley & Jones, p 236
               Davis, p 26
COMPETENCY: Privacy: 6A
             Security: 6C, 7A

17. Which of the following policies should be implemented regarding passwords?
    A) they should be changed periodically
    B) they should not be something that can be easily guessed like spouse's name
    C) passwords should not be repeated
    D) all of the above
REFERENCE: OCR 164.310
               Amatayakul, et al., p 100-101
               Johns (2002a), p 356-357
               Amatayakul & Walsh, p 16C
COMPETENCY: Privacy: 6A, 6B, 8C
             Security: 4D, 6A, 6C

18. One method of disaster recovery in the event of corrupted, lost, or damaged electronic data is to
   A) create regular back-ups that are stored in a safe location off premises
   B) establish passwords and audit trails
   C) make duplicate copies of all paper records and store them in an off-site location
   D) submit all electronic records to a community health information network (CHIN)

REFERENCE: OCR 164.308
               Amatayakul, et al., p 60-62, 109
               Pabrai, p 231-232
               Abdelhak, p 167
COMPETENCY: Privacy: 6C
               Security: 3A, 3C, 3D, 4A, 4G

19. Tracking when employees were logged on the system and what they did is called
   A) error detection
   B) audit trail
   C) data misuse
   D) data recovery

REFERENCE: OCR 164.310
               Amatayakul, et al., p 93-96, 116-118, 205
               Pabrai, p 239-241
               Johns (2002a), p 367
               Abdelhak, p 157
               Davis, p 10
COMPETENCY: Privacy: 6A
               Security: 4D, 4E, 4F, 6F

20. ABC hospital has conducted extensive privacy training for their employees. They trust their employees because it is a small community. They have not had any breeches in the past. They feel that monitoring compliance through an audit trail is not necessary. Is this good practice?
   A) yes
   B) no
   C) under certain circumstances
   D) none of the above

REFERENCE: OCR 134.310, 164.312
               Amatayakul, et al., p 93-96, 116-118
               Pabrai, p 239-240
               LaTour and Eichenwald, p 58-60
               Fuller (1999), p 40
               Hartley & Jones, p 116
COMPETENCY: Core: 1D, 1E
               Privacy: 8B
               Security: 4D, 4E, 4F, 6F, 9C

21. Your facility had a hacker break in and data was altered in your facility's electronic information. What is the best way to ensure someone from the outside cannot do this again?
A) password
B) training
C) audit trail
D) firewall
REFERENCE: OCR 164.312
                Amatayakul, et al., p 121
                LaTour and Eichenwald, p 58-59
                Pabrai, p 264
                Abdelhak, p 680-681
COMPETENCY: Privacy: 6A
                Security: 4D, 4F, 4G, 4I,6A, 6C, 6G, 7C, 7D, 7E

22. General Hospital accidentally uploaded confidential patient information onto the Internet. Based on a civil penalty of $100.00, how much would the hospital have to pay in civil penalties if there were 100 patients involved?
A) $1,000
B) $10,000
C) $100,000
D) $25,000
REFERENCE: U.S. Department of Health and Human Services (2003), p 3
                Amatayakul, et al., p 136-137
COMPETENCY: Security: 4A, 4B, 4G, 6B, 7E

23. You are reviewing a report that shows when an employee logged on, off, and what they did. This is a(n):
A) audit trail
B) product report
C) password database
D) encryption
REFERENCE: OCR 164.312
                Amatayakul, et al., p 93-96, 116-118, 205
                LaTour and Eichenwald, p 58-60
                Johns (2002a), p 367
                Abdelhak, p 157
                Davis, p 10
COMPETENCY: Privacy: 6A
                Security: 4D, 4E, 4F, 6C

24. Which of the following should be the most appropriate means of protecting data being passed over the Internet?
    A) password
    B) firewall
    C) encryption
    D) audit trail
REFERENCE: OCR 164.310
                Amatayakul, et al., p 92, 103-105, 123
                LaTour and Eichenwald, p 58-60
                Pabrai, p 210, 213, 240
                Johns (2002b), p 679
                Rada, p 50
                Hartley & Jones, p 236
                Davis, p 26
COMPETENCY: Privacy: 6A, 6B
                Security: 6F, 7A, 7E, 9E

25. Marvin has trouble remembering his password. He is trying to come up with a solution that will help him remember. He reads the policies on passwords. Based on the policy, he eliminates all of his ideas except to
    A) use the same password all of the time
    B) use his children's names
    C) write the password down and place the paper under his calendar
    D) select a password that is based on something related to the time of the year.
REFERENCE: OCR 164.308
                Amatayakul, et al., p 57-58, 100-101
                Amatayakul & Walsh, p 16C
                Johns (2002b), p 664
COMPETENCY: Privacy: 6A, 6B
                Security: 4D, 6A, 6C

26. You have been asked to identify the goals of your security program. What would be your response?
    A) protect privacy of patient
    B) ensure integrity of data
    C) ensure availability
    D) all of the above
REFERENCE: OCR, 164.306
                Amatayakul, et al., p 4-5
                Johns, (2002a), p 327
                Pabrai, p 219, 476
COMPETENCY: Security: 2C, 4A

27. Jonathan noticed on the audit log that someone from outside of the organization logged into the system last night. This person is not an employee and does not have the authority to log into the system. This person is a (an)
A) hacker
B) Trojan horse
C) unauthorized employee use
D) None of the above
REFERENCE: Amatayakul, et al., p 87, 208
                      Johns (2002a), p 329
COMPETENCY: Privacy: 6E
                      Security: 4B, 4D, 4F, 4G, 4I, 5D, 6G, 7B, 7C, 7E

28. Which of the following displays evidence of unauthorized user activity?
A) employee logged into a system they did not have authorization to log into
B) hacker logged into system
C) multiple levels of security
D) none of the above
REFERENCE: Amatayakul, et al., p 87-88
                      Pabrai, p 204
                      Johns (2002a), p 328
COMPETENCY: Privacy: 2B, 8C
                      Security: 4B, 4D, 4F, 4G, 4I, 5D, 6G, 7B, 7C, 7E

29. Fred is proud of the security measures that his team has developed for the data on the file server. Fred is concerned about the security of personally identifiable data if it is removed from the secured server. Which of the following policies could he implement to protect this data?
A) prevent users from downloading files
B) implement virus checking software
C) conduct risk analysis
D) develop a business continuity plan
REFERENCE: OCR 164.308
                      Amatayakul, et al., p 47, 78-80, 124
                      Johns (2002a), p 32
COMPETENCY: Security: 6B, 6E, 6F, 7A, 9C

30. Steve is horrified. Confidential information has been compromised. A software program has copied files from the secure server to an unsecured area. This is an example of what a _____ can do.
A) virus
B) Trojan horse
C) worm
D) none of the above
REFERENCE: Amatayakul, et al., p 211
                      Pabrai, p 203
                      Johns (2002a), p 329-330
COMPETENCY: Security: 6B, 6F, 6G, 7A, 7B, 7C, 7E

31. As security officer, I am responsible for ensuring that data is available when needed. Threats to this responsibility include all of the following except a
    A) worm
    B) natural disaster
    C) system accidentally unplugged
    D) forgotten password
REFERENCE: OCR 164.312
                Amatayakul, et al., p 72-80
                Pabrai, p 202-204
                Johns (2002a), p 332
COMPETENCY: Security: 4A, 4B, 4C

32. You are the Chief Security Officer. You have been asked why you created a security policy team to assist in the security. Your response would be
    A) to take some of the pressure off you
    B) to determine if you have the necessary skills to develop a successful plan
    C) to help obtain buy-in for the enterprise wide security plan
    D) all of the above
REFERENCE: Amatayakul, et al., p 13, 46, 127-128
                Pabrai, p 205
                Johns, (2002a), p 337
COMPETENCY: Security: 2A, 2B, 2D, 2E, 4A, 4B, 4M, 4N

33. The security policy team should
    A) be established by the CEO
    B) be clear on the responsibilities of the team
    C) be marketed to the entire organization
    D) both A and B
REFERENCE: Amatayakul, et al., p 13, 46, 127-128
                Johns (2002b), p 669
                Johns (2002a), p 336-338
COMPETENCY: Security: 2A, 2B, 2D, 2E, 4A, 4B, 4M, 4N

34. Mary has been given the responsibility of selecting the access control model to be used in assuming compliance with the minimum necessary rule. Which of these is not one of her choices?
    A) user based access control
    B) role-based access control
    C) passwords
    D) context based access control
REFERENCE   OCR 164.308, 164.312
                Amatayakul, et al., p 88-89, 114
                Pabrai, p 215-216, 236
                Johns (2002b), p 678
                Johns (2002a), p 367
                Hartley & Jones, p 213
                Amatayakul (2002b), p 96B
COMPETENCY: Security: 4A, 4D, 6A

35. Marvin is creating a list of unintentional threats to data. Which of the following would not be included on the list?
A) fire
B) power failure
C) malicious alteration of software
D) spilled soft drink in equipment
REFERENCE: OCR 164.308, 164.310, 164.312
                        Amatayakul, et al., p 72-80
                        Pabrai, p 198-204
                        Johns (2002b), p 666-668
                        Johns (2002a), p 341
COMPETENCY: Security: 4A, 4B, 4C, 4E

36. Steve is calculating the annualized loss expectancy of system failure. He has determined that an extended power failure would cost the facility $100,000. How did he calculate this figure?
A) determine per hour cost of system being down
B) estimate the number of times that the system will be down and multiply it by the criticality of the system
C) multiply the cost of the system being down by the number of times that he expects it to be down
D) none of the above
REFERENCE: OCR 164.308
                        Miller and Gregory, p 118-119, 368
                        Johns (2002a), p 341
COMPETENCY: Security: 3A, 6B

37. Limiting access to data based on the need to know is an example of
A) personnel security
B) physical security
C) hardware security
D) communications security
REFERENCE: OCR 164.308, 164.312, 164.514
                        Amatayakul, et al., p 52-53
                        Pabrai, p 158-159, 226-227, 235-238
                        Johns (2002a), p 341, 367
                        Hartley & Jones, p 47
COMPETENCY: Privacy: 2B, 4A, 5A, 8C
                        Security: 2D, 4B, 4F, 4G, 6A, 6G

38. Sam suspects Brett of intentionally altering the amount that he owes the healthcare organization for a surgery that he had last year. Brett works in the Business Office so he had the capability to make the necessary alteration. How can Sam prove this?
A) ask Brett
B) check audit trail
C) access control
D) status message

REFERENCE: OCR 164.312
                Amatayakul, et al., p 93-96, 117
                Pabrai, p 211
                LaTour and Eichenwald, p 58-60
                Johns (2002a), p 358
COMPETENCY: Privacy: 6B
                Security: 4G, 5C

39. Martin has been given the responsibility to determine the physical security of the planned new computer center. Which of the following should be excluded from his deliberations?
A) ensure that the computer center is not near any electromagnetic radiation
B) fire detection and suppression systems
C) encryption
D) inventory of computer components

REFERENCE: OCR 164.310
                Amatayakul, et al., p 73, 79, 83-84
                Pabrai, p 235-238
                Johns (2002a), p 352-353
                Rada, p 65-67
COMPETENCY: Privacy: 6B
                Security: 4G, 5C

40. The healthcare facility has determined that in the event of a total system failure, they need to have the billing system up and running in just a few days. One way of doing this would be
A) to have a hot site
B) to have the ability to reconstruct the database
C) to have a cold site
D) both A and B

REFERENCE: OCR 164.308
                Amatayakul, et al., p 62-65, 109-110
                Johns (2002a), p 360
COMPETENCY: Privacy: 6C
                Security: 3A, 3D, 4A, 4B

41. Stan is stunned at the request for a redundant hard drive. His data management background has taught him to eliminate redundancy. What can you tell him that would change his mind?
    A) redundancy eliminates the possibility of losing data
    B) redundancy reduces the risk of losing data
    C) redundancy saves money
    D) redundancy is never necessary and Stan should refuse the request
REFERENCE: Amatayakul (2002a), p 16B
COMPETENCY: Security: 3A, 3C, 3D, 4G

42. Craig is creating a database that will be used to establish the minimum necessary decisions. What data does he need?
    A) condition surrounding access
    B) role
    C) type of protected health information needed
    D) all of the above
REFERENCE: OCR 164.308, 164.312
              U. S. Office of Civil Rights (2002c), p 2-3
              Amatayakul, et al., p 5-8, 52
              Pabrai, p 228, 238-241
COMPETENCY: Privacy: 2A, 2B, 7A, 7C, 7D, 8B
              Security: 10A, 10F

43. How can the privacy and security officers work together?
    A) they cannot because the roles are too different
    B) they can jointly develop the policies and procedures
    C) they can establish safeguards to protect patient identifiable health information
    D) none of the above
REFERENCE: OCR 164.308
              Amatayakul, et al., p 13, 46, 127-128
              Pabrai, p 225, 244, 324-326
              Amatayakul (2000), p 36
COMPETENCY: Privacy: 4A, 5A
              Security: 4A, 4M, 4N, 10E

44. Which of the following is not a requirement of the HIPAA security rule?
    A) awareness training
    B) training on password management
    C) virus training
    D) accessing patient information
REFERENCE: OCR 164.308
              Amatayakul, et al., p 55-56
              Pabrai, p 229
              Hjort (2002), p 60B
COMPETENCY: Security: 8A, 8B

45. Which of the following is not a part of important security training issues?
    A) identifying viruses
    B) faxing
    C) reporting breech of security
    D) awareness training
REFERENCE: OCR, 164.308
              Amatayakul, et al., p 55-56
              Rada, p 19
              Hjort (2002), p 60C, 60D
COMPETENCY: Security: 5B, 6C, 6F

46. Password management includes all of the following except
    A) the confidentiality of password
    B) procedures for creating passwords
    C) procedures for changing passwords
    D) a database of passwords
REFERENCE: OCR, p 164.308
              Amatayakul, et al., p 57-58, 100-101
              Johns (2002a) p 356-357
              Hartley & Jones, p 143
              Hjort (2002), p 60C
COMPETENCY: Security: 4D, 6A, 6C

47. The HIPAA security rule says that implementation of the rule
    A) should be technology neutral
    B) requires the CE to use specific hardware
    C) requires the CE to use specific software
    D) none of the above
REFERENCE: Amatayakul, et al., p 10-11
              Pabrai, p 218-220
              Hartley & Jones, p 127
COMPETENCY: Security: 4A, 9E

48. When listing examples of administrative safeguards, which of the following
    would be left off?
    A) evaluation of network security
    B) policies regarding levels of access
    C) incident procedures
    D) access controls
REFERENCE: OCR 164.304, 164.308
              Amatayakul, et al., p 52-55, 58-60, 66
              Pabrai, p 222-233
              Brandt, p 2
              Hartley & Jones, p 105, 233
              Rada, p 23
COMPETENCY: Security: 4A, 4K, 4L, 6F

49. The vendor's role in security includes all of the following except
    A) a system back-up
    B) activity reports
    C) the termination of passwords
    D) awareness training
REFERENCE: Brandt, p 2
COMPETENCY: Privacy: 2B, 6A
                 Security: 2D, 6B, 9B, 9D

50. The new physical security program includes all of the following except
    A) continuity of operations
    B) keeping maintenance records
    C) work station security
    D) encryption
REFERENCE: OCR 164.310
                 Amatayakul, et al., p 69-70
                 Brandt, p 3
                 Pabrai, p 216
                 Hartley & Jones, p 152-153
COMPETENCY: Privacy: 2B, 6A
                 Security: 5C, 5D

51. Who is ultimately responsible for security?
    A) vendor
    B) covered entity
    C) chief security officer
    D) chief privacy officer
REFERENCE: OCR, 164.306
                 Amatayakul, et al., p 19
                 Pabrai, p 196-198
                 Brandt, p 3
                 Hartley & Jones, p 6
COMPETENCY: Privacy: 2B, 6A
                 Security: 5C, 5D

52. Event reporting is an example of a/an
    A) physical security safeguard
    B) access control safeguard
    C) administrative security safeguard
    D) network security safeguard
REFERENCE: OCR 164.308
                 Amatayakul, et al., p 58-60
                 Pabrai, p 230-231
                 Johns (2002a), p 365
                 Brandt, p 3
                 Davis, p 10
COMPETENCY: Security: 4E, 4F, 4G

53. Risks of privacy violations are _____ at home than at the office.
   A) greater
   B) less
   C) the same
   D) easier eliminated
   REFERENCE: Pabrai, p 196-202
                  Amatayakul (2002e), p 16B
   COMPETENCY: Privacy: 2B, 4A, 7D, 8C
                Security: 4B, 4P, 7D, 9B

54. Which of the following training topics is not mandated by HIPAA?
   A) password management
   B) disaster recovery
   C) awareness training
   D) audit trails
   REFERENCE: OCR 164.308
                  Amatayakul, et al., p 55-56
                  Pabrai, p 229
                  Cassidy (2001), p 16B
   COMPETENCY: Core: 1C, 1D
                Security:8A, 8B, 9B, 9E

55. Which of the following steps should be used to identify employees who need to be trained?
   A) employee records in HR
   B) accounting to determine who has received payroll check
   C) education department to identify interns
   D) all of the above
   REFERENCE: OCR 164.308
                  Amatayakul, et al., p 55-57
                  Pabrai, p 229
                  Cassidy (2001), p 16B
   COMPETENCY: Core: 1C, 1D
                Security: 2B, 8C

56. The facility wishes to begin using electronic signatures. Which of the following characteristics should the electronic signatures assume?
   A) identity the individual signing the document
   B) ensure integrity of a document's content
   C) allow repudiation
   D) all of the above
   REFERENCE: OCR 164.312
                  Amatayakul, et al., p 115-116, 208
                  Pabrai, p 245-248
   COMPETENCY: Security: 4D, 6E, 9B

57. The facility transmits health information. Which of the following is required by the security standard?
   A) assessment of risk
   B) using HL-7
   C) using ASTM standards
   D) encryption
   REFERENCE: OCR 164.308
                  Amatayakul, et al., p 10-11, 29-30
                  Pabrai, p 223
                  Rada, p 14
                  Hartley & Jones, p 128
   COMPETENCY: Security: 7A, 7D, 7E

58. Physical safeguards include:
                  1. tools monitoring access
                  2. tools to control access to computer systems
                  3. fire protection
                  4. tools preventing unauthorized access to data
   A) 1 and 2 only
   B) 1 and 3 only
   C) 2 and 3 only
   D) 2 and 4 only
   REFERENCE: OCR 164.310
                  Amatayakul, et al., p 69-70
                  Pabrai, p 235-238
                  Hartley & Jones, p 106-107
                  Rada, p 66-67
   COMPETENCY: Privacy: 6A, 6B
                  Security: 4E, 4F, 4G

59. Which of the following would be included in the facilities security incident procedures?
                  1. reporting process
                  2. response procedures
                  3. notifying administration
                  4. notifying OCR
   A) 1 and 2 only
   B) 1 and 3 only
   C) 2 and 3 only
   D) 2 and 4 only
   REFERENCE: OCR 164.308
                  Amatayakul, et al., p 58-60
                  Pabrai, p 230-231
                  Johns (2002a), p 365
                  Hartley & Jones, p 140
                  Rada, p 24
   COMPETENCY: Core: 1Q, 1R
                  Security: 4A, 4E, 4J, 4N

60. An employee has resigned from the facility. Which of the following security processes must be followed according to the security rule?
    1. follow incident reporting process
    2. removal from access lists
    3. turn in keys and access cards
    4. send notice of termination to all employees
  A) 1 and 2 only
  B) 1 and 3 only
  C) 2 and 3 only
  D) 2 and 4 only
REFERENCE: OCR 164.308
                Amatayakul, et al., p 50-51
                Pabrai, p 227
                Johns (2002a), p 366
COMPETENCY: Security: 4D, 4E, 4F, 4I, 4G

61. Contingency planning does not require which of the following processes?
  A) data backup
  B) disaster planning
  C) hot site
  D) testing
REFERENCE: OCR 164.308
                Amatayakul, et al., p 60-65
                Pabrai, p 231-233
                Johns (2002a), 359-362, 364-365
                Hartley & Jones, p 146-147, 152
                Rada, p 27
COMPETENCY: Privacy: 6C
                Security: 3A, 3D, 9B

62. The security rule requires _____ of the implementation of security measures.
  A) validation
  B) evaluation
  C) configuration
  D) certification
REFERENCE: OCR 164.308
                Amatayakul, et al., p 66
                Pabrai, p 233
                Johns (2002a), p 364
COMPETENCY: Security: 4K, 4L

63. My administrator just told me that we have to begin thorough background checks on all employees and new hires because of the final security rule. My response to him is that he is right,
    A) since it is a requirement for all organization
    B) if we are a small organization
    C) if we are a large organization
    D) if we have evaluated this scalable requirement and found that the background checks are the most appropriate for our organization.
REFERENCE: OCR 164.308
               Amatayakul, et al., p 49
               Davis (2003), p 216
COMPETENCY: Security: 2A, 2B, 4K, 9B

64. The facility must conduct an information system activity review. Examples of this includes all of the following except
    A) logins
    B) file accesses
    C) security incidents
    D) policy evaluation
REFERENCE: OCR 164.308, 164.312
               Amatayakul, et al., p 45-46
               Pabrai, p 225, 233
               Hartley & Jones, p 137
               Rada, p 23
COMPETENCY: Privacy: 6D, 6E
               Security: 4A, 4F, 4G, 4I, 4J

65. Facility personnel can be a security risk. How can this risk be reduced?
    A) security training
    B) personnel clearance processes
    C) monitoring access activities
    D) all of the above
REFERENCE: OCR 164.308
               Amatayakul, et al., p 47-49
               Pabrai, p 222-331
COMPETENCY: Security: 2C, 4E, 9B

66. You have been asked to define a security incident procedure. How would you respond?
   A) It is a formal process to be followed to ensure that security processes are handled appropriately.
   B) It is a formal written process to be followed to ensure that security violations are reported and handled appropriately.
   C) It is specifically a policy and procedure for physical safeguards.
   D) It is specifically a policy and procedure for technical safeguards.
   REFERENCE: OCR 164.308
                  Amatayakul, et al., p 58-60
                  Pabrai, p 230
                  Hartley & Jones, p 145, 242
   COMPETENCY: Security: 2C, 4A, 4J, 9B

67. The security incident procedures must include:
                  1. Process to report violations
                  2. Procedure to respond to violations
                  3. Notification of OCR
                  4. Notification of administrator

   A) 1 and 2 only
   B) 2 and 3 only
   C) 1 and 4 only
   D) 2 and 4 only
   REFERENCE: OCR 164.308
                  Amatayakul, et al., p 58-60
                  Pabrai, p 230-231
                  Hartley & Jones, p 145
   COMPETENCY: Core: 1Q, 1R
                  Security: 4A, 4G, 4J, 4M

68. Required security management processes include all of the following except
   A) risk analysis
   B) termination process
   C) risk management
   D) a sanction policy
   REFERENCE: OCR 164.308
                  Amatayakul, et al., p 43-45
                  Pabrai, p 223
                  Hartley & Jones, p 136-137
   COMPETENCY: Security: 4A, 4B, 4I, 9B

69. Monitoring access controls, accountability, data backup and disposal are examples of
   A) device and media controls
   B) physical safeguards
   C) security methods
   D) ASTM standards
   REFERENCE: OCR 164.310
                   Amatayakul, et al., p 69-70, 79-81
                   Pabrai, p 235-237
                   Davis, p 209
                   Hartley & Jones, p 152
   COMPETENCY: Security: 4D, 4E, 6C, 6F

70. All facilities must have sign-in sheets and escorts for visitors who have access to hardware.
   A) true
   B) false
   C) the requirement is actually only required "if appropriate"
   D) none of the above
   REFERENCE: OCR 164.310
                   Amatayakul, et al., p 74-76
                   Rada, p 65-66
   COMPETENCY: Security: 4A, 4E, 4G

71. Do the security standards specifically require a Chief Security Officer to be responsible for the security process?
   A)   no, it just requires an individual to be in charge
   B)   yes
   C)   no, there is no requirement
   D)   no, it requires a committee to be in charge
   REFERENCE: OCR 164.308
                   Amatayakul, et al., p 46
                   Pabrai, p 225-226
                   Rada, p 18
                   Hartley & Jones, p 6
                   Johns, p 336-338
   COMPETENCY: Security: 4A, 4M

72. Physical safeguards requirements include all of the following except
   A) maintenance requirements
   B) need-to-know procedures
   C) workstation use
   D) access control
   REFERENCE: OCR, 164.310
                   Amatayakul, et al., p 76-79
                   Rada, p 91
   COMPETENCY: Security: 4E, 4F, 4G, 6A, 6C

73. Security training is required for
   a) business associates
   b) contractors
   c) agents
   d) all workforce members
REFERENCE: OCR 164.308
                Amatayakul, et al., p 55-56
                Pabrai, p 229
                Hjort (2002), p 60C
COMPETENCY: Core: 1D
                Security: 8A, 8B, 8D

74. Julia must write the policies and procedures for the security management
    process. These policies must address which of the following:
                1. correction of security breeches
                2. prevention of security breeches
                3. detection of security breeches
                4. reporting of security breeches
   A) 1 and 2 only
   B) 1 and 3 only
   C) 1, 2, and 3 only
   D) 1, 2, 3, and 4
REFERENCE: Amatayakul, et al., p 44
                Davis (2003), p 207
COMPETENCY: Security: 2A 2B, 3A, 4B, 9B

75. Is encryption is required for access control?
   A) yes
   B) no, it is addressable
   C) not if ASTM standards are met
   D) not if role-based access is used
REFERENCE: OCR 164.312, 164.314
                Amatayakul, et al., p 86
                Pabrai, p 238
                Hartley & Jones, p 160
COMPETENCY: Security: 5A, 6C. 6E

76. Which of the following techniques would a facility employ for access control?
1. automatic logoff
2. passwords
3. token
4. unique user identification
A) 1 and 4
B) 1 and 2 only
C) 2 and 4 only
D) all of the above techniques
REFERENCE: OCR 164.312
Amatayakul, et al., p 87-92, 99-102
Hartley & Jones, p 157
COMPETENCY: Security: 4D, 4F, 6A, 6C

77. You have been asked how you can corroborate that data has not been altered. How would you respond?
A) check sum
B) security incident
C) information system activity review
D) evaluation
REFERENCE: OCR 164.312
Amatayakul, et al., p 97
Rada, p 38
COMPETENCY: Security: 4D, 4E, 4F, 4G, 4P, 6A, 6B, 6G

78. Access controls, audit controls, encryption and integrity controls are examples of
A) data security
B) physical security
C) technology safeguards
D) all of the above
REFERENCE: OCR 164.312
Amatayakul, et al., p 86-99
Pabrai, p 238-241
Rada, p 35
Hartley & Jones, p 105
COMPETENCY: Security: 4D, 4E, 4F, 4G, 4P, 6A, 6B, 6G

79. Which of the following are required technical safeguards?
A) unique user identifier
B) encryption
C) automatic logoff
D) integrity controls
REFERENCE: OCR 164.312
Amatayakul, et al., p 86, 90-91
Pabrai, p 238-241
Hartley & Jones, p 157-158
COMPETENCY: Security: 6F, 7A

80. Which of the following are required technical safeguards?
    A) audit controls
    B) automatic shutoff
    C) integrity
    D) both A and B
REFERENCE: OCR 164.312
                Amatayakul, et al., p 86, 93-96
                Pabrai, p 238-241
                Hartley & Jones, p 157-158
COMPETENCY: Security: 6F, 7A

81. The purpose of transmission security is to
    A) protect PHI from unauthorized access over electronic communication networks
    B) protect security
    C) ensure that health information transmitted electronically over open networks is not easily intercepted
    D) ensure that health information transmitted electronically over closed networks is not easily intercepted.
REFERENCE: OCR 164.312
                Amatayakul, et al., p 103-105
                Pabrai, p 238-241
COMPETENCY: Security: 6C, 7A

82. Encryption is required by the security rule.
    A) true
    B) false, it is addressable
    C) only if ASTM standards are not used
    D) if the facility is over 200 beds in size
REFERENCE: OCR 164.312
                Amatayakul, et al., p 103-104
                Hartley & Jones, p 158
COMPETENCY: Security: 7A, 7E

83. Heath has been given the responsibility of writing the security incident procedure for his facility. He looks up the required components according to the final security rule. He finds that the procedure must include:
                    1. notification process
                    2. response procedure
                    3. risk analysis
                    4. documentation of incident
   A) 1 and 2 only
   B) 1 and 4 only
   C) 2 and 3 only
   D) 2 and 4 only
REFERENCE: OCR 164.308
                Amatayakul, et al., p 58-60
                Davis (2003), p 207
                Pabrai, p 230-231, 329
COMPETENCY: Core: 1G, 1Q, 1R
                Security: 2A, 2B, 3A, 4B, 9B

84. Mark, Dan and John are arguing over network security. Mark says that encryption is required for a VPN. Dan says that it is not required because it is a secure network. John says that it is required for facilities with more than 10 employees. Who is right?
   A) Mark
   B) Dan
   C) John
   D) None of them
REFERENCE: OCR 164.312
                Amatayakul, et al., p 92
                Davis (2003), p 215
COMPETENCY: Security: 4I, 6F, 7A

85. I have been asked to discuss the types of attacks that can be used to breech network security. I would not discuss
   A) the man-in-the middle attack
   B) a virus
   C) sniffing
   D) tampering
REFERENCE: Cisco (n.d.a), p 2
COMPETENCY: Security: 4I, 7E

86. I want to select the simplest way to share keys. I would choose
   A) passwords
   B) RSA
   C) public keys
   D) certificates
REFERENCE: Amatayakul, et al., p 115-116
                Cisco (n.d.a), p 2
COMPETENCY: Security: 6E, 6F, 7A, 7D

87. My organization uses a public key infrastructure. I just received a certificate from another user. Before my system accepts it, the computer will check to ensure that the certificate has
A) valid dates
B) been created by a computer system that we trust
C) been through the firewall
D) both A and B
REFERENCE: Amatayakul, et al., p 116
               Cisco (n.d.a), p 2
               Pabrai, p 17, 265
COMPETENCY: Security: 6E, 6F, 7A, 7D

88. Health plans, health care providers and health care clearinghouses are required to follow the security standards if they
A) maintain health information
B) receive federal funding
C) maintain or transmit health information electronically
D) share information with external organizations
REFERENCE: OCR 164.302, 134.306
               Amatayakul, et al., p 1-2, 9-10
               Pabrai, p 197
               Hartley & Jones, p 125
               Rada, p 7-8
COMPETENCY: Core: 1B, 1I
               Security: 9E

89. The private key is created by
A) the user's computer
B) the operating system
C) functional software
D) any of the above
REFERENCE: Cisco (n.d.a), p 1
COMPETENCY: Security: 6E, 6F, 7A, 7D

90. I have decided to place my electronic protected health information on a computer on the outermost perimeter network. This is
A) appropriate because you need to get access quickly in a medical emergency
B) appropriate because it makes the data more secure
C) inappropriate because this is the most vulnerable place on the network
D) inappropriate because this is where financial data should be stored
REFERENCE: Cisco (n.d.b), p 10
COMPETENCY: Security: 6F, 7A, 7E

91. I have positioned my firewall between routers that control both internal and external data. The advantage of this is that I can
   A) reduce the amount of data passing through the firewall
   B) improve the quality of both internal and external security of our network
   C) improve the quality of the external security
   D) reduce the cost of network security
REFERENCE: OCR 164.312
               Amatayakul, et al., p 121
               Cisco (n.d.b), p 10
COMPETENCY: Security: 6F, 7A, 7E

92. The primary reason that healthcare organizations develop business continuity plans is to minimize the effects of
   A) employees who deliberately introduce computer viruses into the system
   B) malfunctions of hardware and software
   C) computer shutdowns during natural disasters
   D) damage to information systems cause by computer hackers
REFERENCE: OCR 164.308
               Amatayakul, et al., p 60-63
               Pabrai, p 164.308
               Johns (2002b), p 670-671, 674
               Hartley & Jones, p 146
COMPETENCY: Security: 3A
               Privacy: 6C

93. The administrative provisions of the HIPAA security rule require healthcare organizations to develop
   A) access establishment and modification
   B) an emergency mode operation plan
   C) application and data criticality
   D) testing and revision process
REFERENCE: OCR 164.310, 164.312
               Amatayakul, et al., p 60, 62-63
               Johns (2002b), p 674
COMPETENCY: Security: 4D, 4G

94. Which of the following options should I select in order to protect my network?
   A) only computers with electronic protected health information is behind the firewall
   B) computers with confidential information of any type on is behind the firewall
   C) all communications from networks inside and outside of our network is controlled by the firewall
   D) communications from untrusted networks must be routed through the firewall
REFERENCE: OCR 164.312
               Amatayakul, et al., p 121
               Cisco (n.d.a), p 9
COMPETENCY: Security: 6F, 7A, 7E

95. Safeguarding system reliability is a function of ensuring the _____ of data.
    A) privacy
    B) integrity
    C) availability
    D) media control
REFERENCE: OCR 164.312
                Amatayakul, et al., p 64
                Johns (2002b), p 665
                Johns (2002a), p 331-332
COMPETENCY: Security: 10E
                Privacy: 8C

96. Policies for tracking hardware and electronic media coming into the organization, leaving the organization and its movement within the organization would fall under
    A) application controls
    B) audit controls
    C) device and media controls
    D) network controls
REFERENCE: OCR 164.310
                Amatayakul, et al., p 79-83
                Pabrai, p 235-238
                Johns (2002b), p 670
                Hartley & Jones, p 155-156
COMPETENCY: Security: 4D, 4E, 4F, 5A, 5D, 6G

97. The most common threat to the security of healthcare data is
    A) natural disasters
    B) fires
    C) employees
    D) equipment malfunctions
REFERENCE: Amatayakul, et al., p 35
                Johns (2002b), p 666-667
                Pabrai, p 198-204
COMPETENCY: Security: 5D
                Privacy: 6C

98. An example of a technical safeguard is
    A) access control
    B) integrity control
    C) audit control
    D) all of the above
REFERENCE: OCR 164.312
               Amatayakul, et al., p 86
               Pabrai, 238-241
               Johns (2002b), p 670
               Hartley & Jones, p 104-105
COMPETENCY: Security: 6A, 6C
             Privacy: 6A

99. How often should the organization's security policies and procedures be
    reviewed to ensure that they are appropriate for current regulations and
    practice?
    A) once every six months
    B) periodically
    C) every two years
    D) every five years
REFERENCE: OCR 164.316
               Amatayakul, et al., p 24-27
               Johns (2002b), p 671
COMPETENCY: Core: 1B, 1T
             Security: 2A, 2B, 2E

100. Which of the following is not true in reference to data security? Data integrity
     means to
     A) protect programs from unauthorized change
     B) ensure that data entered into the system are protected from unauthorized
        modifications or deletion
     C) protect authorized users from corrupting data through mistakes
     D) protect data from unauthorized modification or deletion of data
REFERENCE: OCR 164.312
               Amatayakul, et al., p 34, 99
               Johns (2002a), p 266, 359
               Pabrai, p 240-241
COMPETENCY: Security: 4B, 4G

101. The contingency plan provides an alternative means of processing data when natural or human disasters strike as well as for
    A) providing for alternative site processing
    B) providing for recovery of data
    C) reducing the duration of outage of the system
    D) all of the above.
REFERENCE: OCR 164.308
                Amatayakul, et al., p 60-64
                Pabrai, p 231-233
                Johns (2002a), p 360
COMPETENCY: Security: 3A, 3C, 3D

102. The contingency plan is based on
    A) information gathered in a risk analysis and assessment
    B) having a "hot site" for system backup
    C) having a "cold site" that is ready for use in case of a disaster
    D) cost of the plan
REFERENCE: OCR 164.308
                Amatayakul, et al., p 60-64
                Pabrai, p 206-208, 217-219, 223-224, 231-233
                Johns (2002a), p 339, 360
COMPETENCY: Security: 3A, 3C, 3D

103. Intentional threats to security could include
    A) a natural disaster (flood)
    B) equipment failure (software failure)
    C) human error (data entry error)
    D) data theft (unauthorized downloading of files)
REFERENCE: Amatayakul, et al., p 35-36
                Johns (2002a), p 341
                Pabrai, p 202-204
COMPETENCY: Security: 3A, 3C, 3D

104. The object of countermeasures is to either prevent a harmful event or control the damage. Countermeasures may be grouped into personnel, physical hardware, and software, and communications security. One of the greatest threats to security is
    A) natural disasters
    B) employees
    C) hardware failures
    D) software viruses
REFERENCE: Amatayakul, et al., p 34-36
                Johns (2002a), p 347-348
                Pabrai, p 198, 203
COMPETENCY: Core: 1Q, 1R
                Security: 3A, 3C, 3D

105.All of the following are physical security measures EXCEPT
   A) automatic power-down capabilities
   B) keeping an updated inventory of hardware
   C) systematic testing of software prior to implementation
   D) keeping a contact log of vendors, support personnel and service personnel
      for emergencies
REFERENCE: OCR 164.310
                       Amatayakul, et al., p 69-70
                       Johns (2002a), p 353-354
                       Pabrai, p 237-238
COMPETENCY: Security: 5C, 5D, 6F, 6G

106.I just received a message from a VPN. This message is considered to have
   come from a _____ network.
   A) untrusted
   B) unknown
   C) trusted
   D) secured
REFERENCE: Cisco (n.d.b), p 8
                       Amatayakul, et al., p 126
COMPETENCY: Security: 6A, 6C, 6F, 7A, 7E

107.The security policy should include the ability to log all transactions, including
   additions, deletions, or changes in the data. This log is part of the
   A) software control inventory
   B) access control
   C) hardware inventory log
   D) physical protection
REFERENCE: OCR 164.312
                       Amatayakul, et al., p 87-96
                       Johns (2002a), p 358
                       Pabrai, p 219-210, 246
COMPETENCY: Security: 6G, 9C

108. A print out of data on the activity of the record as it crosses through various processes is shown in the table provided below. What inconsistency in the data would be investigated?

	Registration	Nursing Assessment	Lab Order Entry	Pharmacy Order Entry	Patient File	Encounter File
Record Activity Across Processes						
Patient Number	049184	049584	049584	049584	049584	049584
Patient Last Name	Hunter	Hunter	Hunter	Hunter	Hunter	Hunter
Patient First Name	Robin	Robin	Robin	Robin	Robin	Robin
Patient M. Initial	B	B	B	B	V	B
Birth Date	07-23-38	072338	07/23/38	07-23-38	07-23-38	07-23-38
Patient Sex						

A) birth date in nursing assessment and lab order entry have different format
B) patient middle initial in patient file is different
C) patient number is different in the registration file
D) B and C

REFERENCE: Amatayakul, et al., p 96-98
Johns (2002a), p 257
COMPETENCY: Security: 6B, 6G

109. The privacy and security rule requires that training be documented. What methods of documenting training efforts need to be used?
A) retention of training aids, and handouts
B) meeting handouts and minutes
C) training content, training dates, and attendee names
D) signed confidentiality statements

REFERENCE: OCR 164.308
Amatayakul, et al., p 55-56
Pabrai, p 229, 327-328
Johns (2002b), p 230
Hjort (2002), p 60E
Hartley & Jones, p 118
COMPETENCY: Security: 8C

110. When a health care facility fails to monitor the activities of its employees, it can be held liable under
    A) respondeat superior
    B) corporate negligence
    C) contributory negligence
    D) general negligence
REFERENCE: Abdelhak, p 433, 781
COMPETENCY: Core: 1B, 1I, 1K, 1L
              Security: 2D, 2E, 4P

111. Hospitals that destroy their own medical records must have a policy that
    A) insures records are destroyed and confidentiality is protected
    B) notifies patients that their records are destroyed
    C) all records are destroyed annually
    D) the equipment used for destruction of records is properly maintained
REFERENCE: OCR 164.310
              LaTour and Eichenwald, p 171-172
              Abdelhak, p 199
              Roach, W., p 42-43
COMPETENCY: Privacy: 4B, 5B, 7D
              Security: 2A, 5A

112. To develop a record retention policy, the HIM professionals should first
    A) analyze current storage space
    B) calculate the past 5 years of discharges
    C) consult microfilm vendors
    D) consult all applicable statutes and regulations
REFERENCE: LaTour and Eichenwald, p 171-172
              Johns (2002b), p 205-208
              Abdelhak, p 198-199
              Pozgar, p 305
COMPETENCY: Security: 5A, 5B

113. If the patient record is involved in litigation and the physician requests to make a change to that record, what should the HIM professional do?
    A) refer request to legal counsel
    B) allow the change to occur
    C) notify the patient
    D) say the record is unavailable
REFERENCE: Abdelhak, p 439-440
COMPETENCY: Privacy: 2B, 2D, 7B, 8C
              Security: 5D, 6A, 6D, 6F, 6G, 10A, 10D, 10E

114. Which of the following security measures should a health care facility incorporate into its institution wide confidentiality plan?
   A) verification of employee identification
   B) locked access to data processing areas
   C) locked access to record areas
   D) all of the above
REFERENCE: OCR 164.310
               Amatayakul, et al., p 69-71
               Pabrai, p 235-238
               Abdelhak, p 460-461
COMPETENCY: Security: 4D, 4E, 4F, 4G, 6A, 6C

115. What advice should be given to a physician who has just informed you that she has just discovered that a significant portion of a discharge summary she dictated last month was left out?
   A) Squeeze in the information omitted by writing in available spaces such as the top, bottom, and side margins.
   B) Dictate the portion omitted with the heading "Discharge Summary-Addendum" and make a reference to the addendum with a note that is dated and signed on the initial Discharge Summary (e.g., "9/1/03— See Addendum to Discharge Summary" — Signature).
   C) Re-dictate the discharge summary and replace the old one with the new one.
   D) Inform the physician that nothing can be done about the situation.
REFERENCE: Abdelhak, p 439
               Johns (2002b), p 140-141
COMPETENCY: Security: 2A, 2C, 4E, 4G, 5D, 6G

116. Access control of electronic health data is achieved by which method?
   A) original signature
   B) personal signature stamp
   C) unique identification code
   D) institutional code
REFERENCE: OCR 164.312
               Amatayakul, et al., p 90-91
               Pabrai, p 208, 211-212, 239, 241
               Abdelhak, p 440
COMPETENCY: Security: 6A, 6G

117. Insecure information systems can result in
   A) lost productivity
   B) lost revenue
   C) corrupted data
   D) all of the above
REFERENCE: Amatayakul, et al., p 29-31
               Beaver, p 47
               Pabrai, p 205-207
COMPETENCY: Security: 5D, 6B, 6G

118.My CIO believes that as long we use a firewall, data encryption, antivirus software and other technical tools, our data is safe.
  A) this belief is true
  B) this belief is false
  C) this is advocated by HIPAA
  D) this is advocated by HIMSS
REFERENCE: Amatayakul, et al., p 35-36
              Beaver, p 47
              Pabrai, p 206-207
COMPETENCY: Security: 6E, 6F, 7A

119.I just received a message from a computer that is located on another network from within my organization. It is behind the firewall. This message came from which type of network
  A) untrusted
  B) unknown
  C) trusted
  D) secured
REFERENCE: Cisco (n.d.b), p 8
COMPETENCY: Security: 6A, 6C, 6F, 7A, 7E

120.The weakest part of any security program is
  A) people
  B) technical tools
  C) physical security
  D) data access
REFERENCE: Amatayakul, et al., p 35
              Pabrai, p 198-204
              Beaver, p 48
COMPETENCY: Security: 4B, 8A, 8D

121.Security policies should address
  A) access to information systems
  B) maintenance of information system
  C) job description of Chief Security Officer
  D) both A and B
REFERENCE: OCR 164.216, 164.308
              Amatayakul, et al., p 24-27
              Pabrai, p 223-224
              Beaver, p 48
COMPETENCY: Security: 2D, 2E, 4A

122.Administration's role in security includes all of the following except
    A) empowering employees
    B) developing buy-in by employees,
    C) implementation of security plan
    D) enforce policies
REFERENCE: OCR 164.308
                Amatayakul, et al., p 128
                Pabrai, p 224-225
                Beaver, p 48
COMPETENCY: Security: 2B, 2C, 2D, 4A

123.According to the final security rule, the maintenance log should record which of
    the following:
    A) locks on the computer housing EPHI
    B) installation of new electrical plug in the computer room
    C) painting of hall of hospital
    D) all of the above
REFERENCE: OCR 164.310
                Amatayakul, et al., p 76-77
                Hartley & Jones (2004), p 153
                Pabrai, p 237
COMPETENCY: Security: 7C, 9A, 9B

124.Incidence response in the event of a security breach
    A) is required by HIPAA
    B) should be a formal process
    C) should be implemented within 12 hours of incident
    D) both A and B
REFERENCE: OCR 164.308
                Amatayakul, et al., p 58-60
                Pabrai, p 230-231
                Ruano, p 68
COMPETENCY: Security: 4J

125. A computer was sold as surplus. Electronic protected health information that was not destroyed before it was sold was printed out and given to the San Francisco Telegraph. The CEO heard about the incident on the nightly news. What step(s) should he and his staff take according to the final security rule?
      1. call patients affected
      2. take necessary steps to mitigate effects of this type of public incident
      3. notify the OIG
      4. notify the OCR
A) 1 and 2 only
B) 2 only
C) 1, 2, and 3
D) 1, 2, and 4
REFERENCE: OCR 164.308, 164.310
                        Amatayakul, et al., p 58-61, 81-82
                        Hartley & Jones (2004), p 145
                        Pabrai, p 230-231, 329
COMPETENCY: Security: 4G, 4O, 5A, 9B

126. Controls and countermeasures
A) reduce vulnerabilities
B) help meet established security policy
C) will eliminate risks
D) Both A and B
REFERENCE: Wagner, p 39-42
                        Pabrai, p 206-207
COMPETENCY: Security: 5D, 6F, 7A, 7E

127. Marty is responsible for backing up data. He conducts routine testing of the back-ups. This includes error checking and restoration. The back-ups are stored in a cabinet beside the hardware. How can this process be improved?
A) conduct testing daily
B) use a team to back up the data
C) move back-ups to safer location
D) none of the above
REFERENCE: OCR 164.308, 164.312
                        Amatayakul, et al., p 60-61
                        Amatayakul (2002a), p 16B
COMPETENCY: Security: 3C, 3D, 6G

128. Brody was the supervisor of the 4-West Neurology unit until last month, when he stepped down to be a RN on the night shift so he could go to school during the day. A routine audit of access found that he still had access to the same electronic protected health information. The system was updated to reflect his new role. What should the security representative who caught it do?
1. document change of access capabilities
2. send a monthly report of this type of change to the CIO
3. maintain documentation for six years
4. send letter to Brody describing the steps taken

A) 1 and 2 only
B) 1 and 3 only
C) 1 and 4 only
D) 2 and 3 only
REFERENCE: OCR 164.308, 164.312
               Amatayakul, et al., p 26, 52-55, 87-90
               Hartley & Jones (2004), p 142
               Pabrai, p 228
COMPETENCY: Security: 2A, 2B, 2D, 2E, 4B, 4D, 4E, 4F, 4G

129. A record destruction program should include all of the following except
A) the method of destruction
B) securing materials awaiting destruction
C) stating what can be shredded
D) for daily destruction
REFERENCE: OCR 164.310
               Amatayakul, et al., p 81-82
               LaTour and Eichenwald, p 171-172
               Pabrai, p 235-237
               Abdelhak, p 199
               Amatayakul (2002a), p 16B
COMPETENCY: Security: 5A

130. Claims Processing of America is a healthcare clearinghouse that is a subsidiary of Abbott Media. Birmingham Hospital is concerned that Abbott Media could request electronic protected health information. Claims Processing of America and Birmingham Hospital, who is a business associate of Claims Processing of America, discuss the issue. Which one of the following statements is the MOST appropriate directions for Birmingham Hospital to give them?
A) you are responsible to Abbott Media so must you comply with their request
B) Claims Processing of America must notify Abbott Media of the penalties for inappropriate access to electronic protected health information.
C) deny any request for any reason
D) do not address the situation
REFERENCE: Amatayakul, et al., p 66-68, 136
               Hartley & Jones (2004), p 141
               Pabrai, p 34, 152-156, 192-193
COMPETENCY: Security: 2A, 2C, 2E, 9B

131.An agreement where two business partners share information electronically is a
   A) business associate agreement
   B) policy and procedure
   C) contingency plan
   D) none of the above
REFERENCE: OCR 164.314
                Amatayakul, et al., p 206
                Pabrai, p 242
COMPETENCY: Security: 4A, 4G

132.The security incident response that I am developing should have which of the
   following:
   A) documentation of actions to be taken
   B) immediate termination of guilty employee
   C) notification of OCR
   D) turning off affected system while investigation is underway
REFERENCE: OCR 164.308
                Amatayakul, et al., p 58-60
                Pabrai, p 230
                Rada, p 27
                Hartley & Jones, p 145
COMPETENCY: Security: 4G, 4J, 4L, 6F

133.Brandon is suspected of a serious security breech. According to the security
   rule, potential sanctions would include which of the following:
   A) termination
   B) civil penalties
   C) criminal penalties
   D) all of the above
REFERENCE: OCR 164.308
                Amatayakul, et al., p 136
                Pabrai, p 114-115, 224-225
COMPETENCY: Security: 4G, 4J, 9A, 9B

134.The covered entity plans to de-identify patient information and provide that
   information to researchers. The covered entity plans to include a code that will
   allow them to re-identity the information. Under the HIPAA requirements, this is
   A) allowed
   B) not allowed
   C) allowed if the code is not connected to the subject of the information (i.e.
      derivative of social security number)
   D) allowed if the code follows ASTM standards
REFERENCE: OCR 164.514
                Pabrai, p 120-124
                Johns (2002b), p 220-223
COMPETENCY: Security: 4O

135. The covered entity has provided de-identified patient information to researchers. This information included a code that can re-identify the information. Six months later, the researchers ask for the mechanism to be able to de-code the information. How should the covered entity respond?
    A) provide the mechanism
    B) ask them why they want the mechanism and supply if a good reason is provided
    C) do not provide the mechanism
    D) provide the mechanism if they have IRB approval for the research
REFERENCE: OCR 164.514
              Pabrai, p 120-124
              Johns (2002b), p 220-223
COMPETENCY: Security: 4O

136. Which of the following methods are appropriate for use in de-identification of data?
    A) statistical method
    B) safe harbor
    C) scientific methods
    D) all of the above
REFERENCE: OCR 164.514
              Pabrai, p 120-124
              Johns (2002b), p 220-223
COMPETENCY: Security: 4O

137. The administrator states that he should not have to participate in privacy and security training. How should you respond?
    A) "All employees are required to participate in the training including top administration."
    B) "I will record that in my files."
    C) "Did you read the privacy rules?"
    D) "You are correct. There is no reason for you to participate in the training."
REFERENCE: OCR 164.308, 164.530
              Amatayakul, et al., p 55-56
              Pabrai, p 229
              Johns (2002b), p 230
              Amatayakul & Johns, p 16D
              Rada, p 19
              Hartley & Jones, p 118
COMPETENCY: Security: 8D

138. The training director, Juan, made the comment, "everyone from housekeeping to the administrator should be trained using the same manner". How should you respond?
A) "I totally agree since it will make training efficient."
B) "Training methods may vary to the different groups."
C) "Self-directed learning can be used by physicians and administration only, everyone else should attend classes."
D) "HIPAA mandates that all members of the workforce be trained in the same manner"

REFERENCE: OCR 164.308, 164.530
                Amatayakul, et al., p 55-56
                Pabrai, p 229
                Johns (2002b), p 230
                Amatayakul & Johns, p 16D
                Rada, p 19
COMPETENCY: Security: 8D

139. Chan is responsible for the retention of training records. He is running out of space and wants to destroy old records. How many years does he need to maintain?
A) 2
B) 5
C) 6
D) 8

REFERENCE: OCR 164.316, 164.530
                Amatayakul, et al., p 26-27
                Pabrai, p 244, 327-328
                Hjort (2002), p 60A
COMPETENCY: Security: 8C

140. Rosa is developing a training record retention policy. In the policy, she writes that the records should be maintained
A) in writing
B) electronically
C) either A or B
D) in both paper and electronic formats

REFERENCE: OCR 164.316, 164.530
                Amatayakul, et al., p 26-27, 55-56
                Pabrai, p 244, 327-328
                Hjort (2002), p 60A
COMPETENCY: Security: 8C

141. Juanita is comparing a list of employees who attended HIPAA training with a list of all employees. She notes that 10 people have not been trained. These 10 employees are either part time or work in maintenance. How should she react?
A) take the necessary steps to ensure these 10 people receive training
B) take no actions since training for these staff members is optional
C) take no actions since training for these staff members is not required
D) notify the employees that they must receive the training within the next year
REFERENCE: OCR 164.316, 164.530
                       Amatayakul, et al., p 55-56
                       Pabrai, p 244, 327-328
                       Hjort (2002), p 60C
                       Rada, p 19
COMPETENCY: Security: 8C

142. Data criticality analysis is part of the _____ process.
A) data access
B) contingency planning
C) contract negotiation
D) authorization
REFERENCE: OCR 164.308
                       Amatayakul, et al., p 38-41
                       Pabrai, p 231-233
                       Hartley & Jones, p 148
COMPETENCY: Security: 3B

143. Data criticality can be defined as:
A) assessment of vulnerability, sensitivity and security of the data under its control
B) assessment of software used to maintain data
C) a view of how administration views data collected
D) none of the above
REFERENCE: OCR 164.308
                       Amatayakul, et al., p 60-63, 65
                       Pabrai, p 231-233
COMPETENCY: Security: 3B

144. Physicial security requirements mandate which of the following hardware and software actions?
A) security testing
B) inventory
C) review of maintenance performed
D) none of the above
REFERENCE: OCR, 164.310
                       Amatayakul, et al., p 76-77
COMPETENCY: Security: 4H, 6F

145. Bonnie says that the Board of Directors are exempt from privacy and security training requirements since they have no access to PHI. Adam says they are not. Who is right?
    A) Bonnie
    B) Adam
    C) both are wrong since the board is exempt from privacy but not security
    D) both are wrong since the board is exempt from security but not privacy
REFERENCE: OCR 164.310
                Amatayakul, et al., p 47-49
                Pabrai, p 235-238
                Hjort (2002), p 60C
                Rada, p 19
COMPETENCY: Security: 8A, 8D

146. Conducting internal audits to ensure compliance with plan is part of the security requirements. Which of the following is true?
    A) sanctions should be consistent throughout organization
    B) information system activity reviews should follow your policies
    C) outcomes of audits should be usable information
    D) all of the above
REFERENCE: OCR 164.308
                Amatayakul, et al., p 66
                Pabrai, p 224-225, 230-231
                Fuller, p 42
COMPETENCY: Security: 9A

147. Los Angeles Memorial Hospital has contracted with a business associate to code medical records. Many of the coders will work out of his or her home. What should the hospital do to protect privacy and security?
    A) cancel contract as this is inappropriate
    B) conduct the required training themselves
    C) mandate security measures taken
    D) put a clause in the business associate agreement that ensures that staff is trained, information is protected and that they will comply with HIPAA requirements
REFERENCE: OCR 164.308, 164.314
                Amatayakul, et al., p 66-68
                Pabrai, p 324, 241-242, 152-156
                Amatayakul (2002e), p 16C
COMPETENCY: Security: 8A, 8D

148. The Chief Privacy Officer and the Chief Security Officer are responsible for protecting PHI. Because of this, the following is recommended:
   A) because of differences a facility should evaluate an individual's skills when determining whether one or two people have these roles
   B) they should be the same person
   C) they have the same skills
   D) their responsibilities should be divided so there is no overlap in responsibilities
REFERENCE: Callahan-Dennis (2001b), p 36
               Amatayakul, et al., p 13, 46-47, 128
               Pabrai, p 225, 326, 330-331
COMPETENCY: Core: 1D
               Security: 10E

149. The security rule is essentially a set of
   A) business rules
   B) technology rules
   C) policy rules
   D) all of the above
REFERENCE: Beaver, p 46
COMPETENCY: Security: 9B, 9D

150. Rachel is a cafeteria employee at Valdosta Medical Center. The security team has just checked to see what she has access to. She has access to patient room number and dietary orders only. This follows the procedure that was developed in the security plan that was developed jointly with her director and the security team. This is an example of _____ at work.
   A) workforce clearance procedure
   B) security rule implementation
   C) accessibility
   D) access authorization
REFERENCE: OCR 164.308
               Amatayakul, et al., p 52-55
               Hartley & Jones (2004), p 140
               Pabrai, p 226
COMPETENCY: Security: 2A, 2D, 2E, 4D, 4E, 4F, 4G, 6A

151. We have conducted an analysis of our organization and decided that one of the addressable security measures, password management is not appropriate. What actions should we take?
　　　　　　　　1. document reasons for decision
　　　　　　　　2. implement a comparable security measure
　　　　　　　　3. apply for dispensation from the Office of Civil Rights
　　　　　　　　4. apply for dispensation from the Office of the Inspector General
A) 1 and 2 only
B) 1 and 3 only
C) 2 and 3 only
D) 2 and 4 only
REFERENCE:　　OCR 164.308, 164.312
　　　　　　　　Amatayakul, et al., p 10-13, 75-76
　　　　　　　　Hartley & Jones (2004), p 124-125, 133
　　　　　　　　Pabrai, p 217-218
COMPETENCY:　Security: 2A, 2D, 4A, 4B, 4C

152. In developing my security plan, I am using which of the following factors to determine what techniques to put in place?
　　　　　　　　1. the size of my organization
　　　　　　　　2. the type and level of technology that exist in my organization
　　　　　　　　3. expense of security measures
　　　　　　　　4. level of risk
A) 1 and 2 only
B) 1, 2, and 4 only
C) 1 and 3 only
D) 1, 2, 3, and 4
REFERENCE:　　Amatayakul, et al., p 10-13
　　　　　　　　Hartley & Jones (2004), p 132
　　　　　　　　Pabrai, p 197-198, 217-218
COMPETENCY:　Security: 2A, 2D, 4A, 4B, 4C

153. HIPAA requires the facility to be able to gain access to data in event of an emergency. Which of the following could be used to accommodate this?
A) integrity
B) at least two people having full access
C) use role access
D) entity authentication
REFERENCE:　　OCR 164.310
　　　　　　　　Amatayakul, et al., p 71
　　　　　　　　Pabrai, p 240
　　　　　　　　Hartley and Jones, p 157
COMPETENCY:　Security: 6A, 6C, 6D

154. In the event of an emergency, the facility should implement
    A) the disaster recovery plan
    B) the emergency operation plan
    C) the back-up plan
    D) all of the above as appropriate
REFERENCE: OCR 164.308
                Amatayakul, et al., p 60-63
                Pabrai, p 231-233
COMPETENCY: Security: 3A, 3B, 3C, 3D, 6D

155. We have a problem with one of the computers that contain PHI. Which of the following steps should I take?
    A) destroy computer and reinstall data from back-up
    B) document maintenance performed to solve problem
    C) verify access control
    D) conduct background check
REFERENCE: OCR 164.308
                Amatayakul, et al., p 76-77
                Davis, p 211
                Hartley & Jones, p 153
COMPETENCY: Security: 5B, 5D

156. Ongoing security awareness training
    A) must be formal training
    B) must be extensive, self-directed learning
    C) can take the form of screen saver reminders and posters
    D) is not be necessary
REFERENCE: OCR 164.308
                Amatayakul, et al., p 55-56
                Pabrai, p 229
                Beaver, p 48
COMPETENCY: Security: 8A, 8B

157. I am conducting the risk assessment for the ambulatory care center where I work. I am evaluating the medical record file room for security rule violations. The statement that best describes this situation is that this is
    A) a requirement of the security rule
    B) a recommendation of the security rule
    C) not necessary since the security rule only addressed electronic protected health information
    D) not necessary since the ambulatory care center is JCAHO accredited
REFERENCE: Hartley & Jones (2004), p 128
                Pabrai, p 197
COMPETENCY: Core: 1B
                Security: 2A, 2B

158. A plan to comply with the security regulations cannot be established until
   A) the risk assessment is completed
   B) a Chief Privacy Officer has been hired
   C) the policies have been reviewed
   D) none of the above
REFERENCE: OCR 164.308
                Amatayakul, et al., p 29-31
                Pabrai, p 205-207, 223, 477-478, 480-483
                Klein, p 3
COMPETENCY: Security: 5B, 5D

159. I have a plan to conduct a risk analysis at least annually, monitor compliance
   with policies and procedures monthly, and monitor the audit log daily. This is an
   example of
   A) due care
   B) due diligence
   C) policies and procedures
   D) administrative safeguards
REFERENCE: Amatayakul, et al., p 14, 30, 43-44, 66
                Proctor, Davis, & Rosenblum (2003), p 36
COMPETENCY: Security: 2A, 2B, 2C, 2D, 2E, 4A, 4B, 4C, 6G

160. Identify an example of due care.
   A) we develop our security plan in such a way as to cover security threats that
      are reasonable
   B) we develop our security plan to cover everything possible
   C) we monitor compliance monthly
   D) gaining approval of consultants to confirm plan
REFERENCE: OCR 164.308
                Amatayakul, et al., p 43
                Proctor, Davis, & Rosenblum (2003), p 36
                Pabrai, p 197-198, 217-218
COMPETENCY: Security: 2A, 2B, 4A, 4B, 4C

161. I have to choose the type of encryption to be used for the new CPR.
   What are my choices?
   A) symmetric and conventional
   B) asymmetric and public-key
   C) symmetric and asymmetric
   D) public-key and integrity
REFERENCE: OCR 164.312
                Miler & Gregory, p 172-180
                Stallings (2000), p 651
COMPETENCY: Core: 1I
                Privacy: 6A, 6B
                Security: 6E, 6F, 7A, 7D

162. As the network administrator, I am responsible for which of the following network security requirements?
1. confidentiality
2. integrity
3. availability
4. public-key

A) 1 and 2 only
B) 2 and 3 only
C) 1 and 4 only
D) 1, 2 and 3 only
REFERENCE: OCR 164.304, 164.312
Amatayakul, et al., p 85-86
Stallings (2000), p 651
Johns (2002a), p 328-332
Pabrai, p 209-213, 219
COMPETENCY: Core: 1I
Privacy: 6A, 6B
Security: 6E, 6F, 7A, 7D

163. Macon General Hospital has just discovered that someone is monitoring transmissions of confidential data. This is an example of a (an)
A) integrity issue
B) passive attack
C) active attack
D) traffic analysis
REFERENCE: Miller & Gregory, p 235-237
Stallings (2000), p 651
Pabrai, p 202, 212, 216
COMPETENCY: Core: 1G, 1M, 1R,
Security: 2D, 2E, 4C, 5D, 6A, 6E, 7A

164. The purpose of the encryption algorithm is to
A) transform message back into original format
B) control the transformations made
C) send the scrambled message
D) alter the message to be sent
REFERENCE: OCR 164.312
Amatayakul, et al., p 92
Miller & Gregory, 169, 172-173
Stallings (2000), p 653
Johns (2002a), 225, 357
Pabrai, p 210, 213, 240
COMPETENCY: Security: 7A, 7E

165. Active attacks are a (an)
    A) alteration of data being sent
    B) monitoring of data sent
    C) terrorist action
    D) elimination of infrastructure
REFERENCE: Stallings (2000), p 652
                      Pabrai, p 202, 212
COMPETENCY: Security: 7A

166. I have a choice between DES and triple DES. I must choose a method of
    A) conventional security
    B) message authentication
    C) conventional encryption
    D) message repudiation
REFERENCE: Miller & Gregory, p 166, 174-175
                      Stallings (2000), p 652-653
COMPETENCY: Security: 4D, 6C, 6E, 6F, 7A

167. The secret key and the original message controls the
    A) ciphertext
    B) plaintext
    C) decryption algorithm
    D) public key
REFERENCE: Miller & Gregory, p 166, 170-171
                      Stallings (2000), p 653
COMPETENCY: Security: 4D, 6C, 6E, 6F, 7A

168. Encryption is an important part of network security. One method of encryption
    requires the user to have:
                1. private key
                2. public key
                3. cryptographic hashing
                4. password
    A) 1 and 2 only
    B) 1 and 3 only
    C) 1 only
    D) 1 and 4 only
REFERENCE: Miller & Green, p 176-179
                      Comer (1999), p 493
COMPETENCY: Security: 4D, 6C, 6E, 6F, 7A

169. Your administrator has asked you how you authenticate who sent a message. Your response is a
    A) private key
    B) public key
    C) digital signature
    D) password
REFERENCE: Miller & Gregory, p 180-181
              Comer (1999), p 493
              Pabrai, p 209, 211-212
COMPETENCY: Security: 4D, 6C, 6E, 6F, 7A

170. The key to your authentication process is the digital signature. Which of the following tools creates the digital signature?
    A) public key
    B) private key
    C) encryption
    D) decryption
REFERENCE: Miller & Gregory, p 180-181
              Comer (1999), p 493
              Pabrai, p 210, 213, 247-248
COMPETENCY: Security: 4D, 6C, 6E, 7A

171. The hospital, as part of the network security process, is developing a packet filter that will protect their information systems from access by Internet traffic. This is called
    A) a public key
    B) a private key
    C) repudiation
    D) a firewall
REFERENCE: Miller & Gregory, p 88-89
              Comer (1999), p 496
              Pabrai, p 264, 490-491
COMPETENCY: Security: 4D, 6C, 6E, 7A

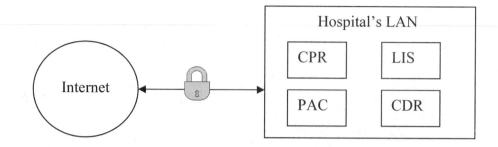

Hospital's LAN

CPR   LIS

PAC   CDR

Internet

172.In the diagram above, the padlock represents
   A) a public key
   B) a firewall
   C) a private key
   D) a digital signature
REFERENCE: Miller & Gregory, p 88-93
               Comer (1999), p 496
               Pabrai, p 264, 490-491
COMPETENCY: Security: 4D, 6C, 7A

173.Eavesdropping is a risk of the LAN. I want to reduce my risk. How should I
   proceed?
   A) wireless LAN
   B) wired LAN
   C) eliminate the LAN
   D) use the Internet
REFERENCE: Nichols & Lekkas (2002), p 335
COMPETENCY: Security: 6C, 6F, 7A, 7D, 7E

174.The administrator wants to know why we have implemented spread spectrum
   technology. Your response is to
   A) create interference
   B) reduce risk of eavesdropping and interference of wired network
   C) reduce risk of eavesdropping and interference of wireless network
   D) route messages
REFERENCE: Nichols & Lekkas (2002), p 337
COMPETENCY: Security: 6F, 7A, 7E

175.Which of the following is not a technology used to reduce the risk of
   interference?
   A) spread spectrum
   B) infrared
   C) broadband
   D) narrowband
REFERENCE: Nichol & Lekkas (2002), p 339
COMPETENCY: Security: 4K, 6F, 7A, 7E

176.To protect the patient's privacy, we need to confirm that messages are authentic. This can be done with
A) message authentication
B) a firewall
C) data flow
D) eavesdropping monitoring
REFERENCE: Miller & Gregory, p 170, 180-181
                        Stallings (2000), p 662
                        Pabrai, p 209, 211-212
COMPETENCY: Security: 4K, 6F, 7A, 7E

177.When verifying the message authentication, I need to confirm which of the following?
1. message has not been altered
2. timeliness of receipt of message
3. source of message is valid
4. absence of virus
A) 1, 2, and 3 only
B) 1 and 3 only
C) 1 and 2 only
D) 1 and 4 only
REFERENCE: Miller & Gregory, p 180-182
                        Stallings (2000), p 662
                        Pabrai, p 209, 211-212
COMPETENCY: Security: 4K, 6F, 7A, 7E

178.Cryptography is demonstrated by
A) encryption and decryption
B) protecting data from Trojan horses
C) nonrepudiation
D) message authentication
REFERENCE: Miller & Gregory, p 371
                        Amatayakul, et al., p 164-167
                        Nichols & Lekkas (2002), p. 85
                        Pabrai, p 213
                        Rada, p 50
COMPETENCY: Security: 4K, 6E, 6F, 7A, 7E

179. Matthew has the responsibility of choosing the type of encryption to be used. His options include:

           1. substitution
           2. permutation
           3. number theoretical methods
           4. coding

A) 1 and 2 only
B) 2 and 3 only
C) 1 and 3 only
D) 1, 2, and 3 only

REFERENCE: Miller & Gregory, p 165-169
                    Nichols & Lekkas (2002), p 85
COMPETENCY: Security: 6F, 7A, 7E

180. Marty has been accused by the CSO of tampering with confidential patient information. He denies the charges. The CSO is able to prove that Marty initiated the changes. He was able to prove it because of the use of

A) authorization
B) non-repudiation
C) SSL
D) passwords

REFERENCE: Miller & Gregory, p 170, 180-181
                    Nichols & Lekkas (2002), p 356
                    Pabrai, p 209-210
COMPETENCY: Security: 4D, 4I, 6F, 6G

181. I am writing the policy on internal security audits. Which of the following monitors would I not include?

A) monitoring logons
B) monitoring file access
C) security incidents
D) repudiation

REFERENCE: Amatayakul, et al., p 66, 116-117
                    Davis, p 206
COMPETENCY: Security: 2B, 2D, 2E, 4A, 4B, 4D, 4F, 4I

182. SSL is a(n) _____ protocol.

A) audit trail
B) encryption
C) private key
D) wireless transmission

REFERENCE: Miller & Gregory, p 187
                    Nichols & Lekkas (2002), p 367
COMPETENCY: Security: 6F, 7A, 7E

183.In developing a security plan, I am most concerned about
   A) external threats
   B) internal threats
   C) viruses
   D) access controls
REFERENCE: Amatayakul, et al., p 34-36
              Pelletier, Bresee, & Hill (2003), p 50
              Pabrai, p 203
COMPETENCY: Core: 1T, 1U
              Security: 2D, 2F, 4B

184.My security plan should include precautions for which of the following?
   A) electronically stored and transmitted PHI
   B) paper-based PHI
   C) verbal PHI
   D) all of the above
REFERENCE: OCR 164.501
              Amatayakul, et al., p 1
              Pelletier, Bresee & Hill (2003), p 50
              Pabrai, p 196
COMPETENCY: Security: 2A, 2D, 4A

185.Nurses need access to physician orders, progress notes, nursing notes, and medication records of patients under their care. The use of _____ will provide them with access to what they need and prevent them from gaining access to other PHI.
   A) passwords
   B) user based access
   C) context based access
   D) role-based access
REFERENCE: OCR 164.312
              Amatayakul, et al., p 88-89, 114
              Pelletier, Bresee, & Hill (2003), p 50
              Pabrai, p 236
COMPETENCY: Security: 4D, 4E, 4F, 6A, 10A

186.The term "addressable" is used in the security standards. What does this mean?
A) required for large hospitals
B) required for small physician practice
C) required if reasonable and appropriate for organization
D) required if data is shared over the Internet
REFERENCE: Amatayakul, et al., p 12-13
                 Proctor, Davis, & Rosenblum (2003), p 35
                 Pabrai, p 217-218
                 Hartley & Jones, p 124-125
                 Rada, p 9
COMPETENCY: Security: 2A, 2B, 4A, 4B, 4C

187.Evaluate this statement. Our facility has decided that encryption is too costly to implement so we are able to omit this portion since it is an addressable option and not required by the security statement.
A) this is a true statement
B) this is a false statement since there is no flexibility in the standard
C) this is a false statement since encryption is actually required
D) encryption does not have to be implemented but an alternative security method does
REFERENCE: Amatayakul, et al., p 12-13, 103-104
                 Proctor, Davis, & Rosenblum (2003), p 35
                 Pabrai, p 197-198, 217-218
                 Hartley & Jones, p 133
                 Rada, p 9
COMPETENCY: Security: 2A, 2B, 4A, 4B, 4C

188.Right-sizing the HIPAA security standard for your organization includes all of the following except
A) self-certification compliance
B) risk analysis
C) due care to meet standards
D) select minimal standards
REFERENCE: Amatayakul, et al., p 8-14
                 Proctor, Davis, & Rosenblum (2003), p 35
                 Pabrai, p 197-198, 217-218
COMPETENCY: Security: 2A, 2B, 4A, 4B, 4C

189.Marvin has decided to meet the HIPAA security rule's integrity requirements by storing data on a magnetic disk. Is this appropriate?
A) yes
B) no
C) only if organization is an OHCA
D) only if organization is an affiliated entity
REFERENCE: Amatayakul, et al., p 60-62
                 Rada, p 37
COMPETENCY: Security: 4F, 7A, 7E, 9B

190. The sanction policy that you are writing should be based on:
1. security rules mandates for sanctions
2. past experience
3. severity of violation
4. sanctions determined by organization
   A) 1 and 2 only
   B) 1 and 3 only
   C) 2 and 3 only
   D) 3 and 4 only
REFERENCE: OCR 164.308
                Amatayakul, et al., p 44-45
                Rada, p 23
                Pabrai, p 224-225
COMPETENCY: Core: 1C, 1G
                Security: 2B, 2C, 2D, 2E, 4E

191. Which of the following is not subject to the security rule?
   A) PHI stored on a computer
   B) PHI sent by fax
   C) PHI on paper copies
   D) Both B and C
REFERENCE: Amatayakul, et al., p 1, 9-10
                Rada, p 8
                Pabrai, p 196-197, 475-477
COMPETENCY: Security: 2B, 4A, 9B

192. Which policy (policies) on passwords should be established?
   A) password should be a minimum of 8 characters
   B) passwords should use a variety of different types of characters (i.e. alphabet, numbers and symbols)
   C) passwords should not use a sequence like XYZ
   D) all of the above
REFERENCE: OCR 164.308, 164.312
                Amatayakul, et al., p 57-58, 100-102
                Rada, p 23
                Johns (2002a) 356-357
COMPETENCY: Security: 2A, 2B, 2C, 2D, 2E, 4D, 4F, 6A, 6C

193.A large covered entity that is legally one organization which conducts covered and uncovered activities and which includes health care operations is called a:
A) OHCA
B) business associate
C) affiliated entity
D) hybrid entity
REFERENCE: OCR, 164.103
              Amatayakul, et al., p 21-23
              Rada, p 63
              Pabrai, p 156-157
COMPETENCY: Security: 9A, 9B

194.Margaret is an at home coder. To protect patient privacy when she is not working, Margaret should be required to:
A) turn of her pc after hours
B) return the pc to the office at the end of each day
C) utilize access controls to prevent unauthorized access
D) remove the hard drive
REFERENCE: Rada, p 67
COMPETENCY: Security: 2A, 2B, 2C, 2D, 2E, 4A, 4C, 4D, 4E

195.Authentication is demonstrated by:
A) documentation of administrative approval
B) your role in the organization
C) unique user identification
D) none of the above
REFERENCE: OCR, 164.304, 164.312
              Amatayakul, et al., p 90-91
              Rada, p 85
COMPETENCY: Security: 4D, 4E, 4F, 6C

196.Midtown Hospital and Atlanta Physician Group are separately owned and operated. They work very closely which includes their marketing plan, quality improvement, and business office. This type of arrangement is called:
A) organized health care arrangement
B) trading partner agreement
C) standard setting organization
D) covered entity
REFERENCE: OCR, 160.103
              Amatayakul, et al., p 20-22
              Pabrai, p 157-158
COMPETENCY: Security: 8E, 9B, 9D

197. I have been asked to justify why to use DES. What should I say?
  A) it is available for use with hardware and software
  B) it is the most recent technology developed
  C) the 56 bit key is too long
  D) none of the above
REFERENCE: Nichols & Lekkas, p 196-197
               Miller & Gregory, p 172-173
COMPETENCY: Security: 6E, 7A, 7E

198. Encryption is a wonderful tool. It is infallible. Which of the following statements best addressees this comment?
  A) nothing is perfect
  B) encryption does not protect data as it is being converted
  C) that is why the security rule requires encryption
  D) none of the above
REFERENCE: Nichols & Lekkas, p 203
COMPETENCY: Security: 6E, 7A, 7E

199. Risk analysis includes all of the following components except:
  A) determining threats to your information systems
  B) comparing your policies to the HIPAA requirements
  C) calculating the probability that the threats could actually happen
  D) determining how badly the event would affect the organization
REFERENCE: OCR 164.308
               Amatayakul, et al., p 29-31
               Johns (2002a), p 340
               Pabrai, p 223-224, 477-478, 480-483
COMPETENCY: Core: 1F, 1M, 1T, 1U
               Security: 3A, 3B, 4A, 4B

200. Risk assessment easily calculates how much an event costs the hospital. Evaluate this statement.
  A) this is true
  B) risk may also be based on intangible damage caused by the event
  C) sometimes costs that can be calculated using expenses incurred to restore system, lost revenue, and impact on billing
  D) both B and C
REFERENCE: OCR 164.308
               Amatayakul, et al., p 38-40
               Johns (2002a), p 340-342
               Pabrai, p 223-224, 477-478, 480-483
COMPETENCY: Core: 1F, 1M, 1T, 1U
               Security: 3A, 3B, 4A, 4B

201. Information system operations can be halted in various ways. These means can be called:
A) natural disasters
B) human created
C) legal
D) both A and B
REFERENCE: Amatayakul, et al., p 35-36
                Johns (2002a), p 360
                Pabrai, p 202
COMPETENCY: Security: 3A, 3B, 3D

Use the table below to answer questions 202 and 203.

System	Criticality (scale 1 most critical to 3 least critical)
CPR	1
Financial information system	2
Performance indictor monitoring system	3
Encoder	3

202. We have had some damage to our data center. The four systems listed above are down. Based on the information above, I would place most of my resources to implement disaster recovery plans for the:
A) CPR
B) financial information system
C) performance indicator monitoring system
D) encoder
REFERENCE: OCR, 164.308
                Amatayakul, et al., p 30-34
                Johns (2002a), p 346-347, 360
                Pabrai, p 223-224, 477-478, 480-483
COMPETENCY: Security: 3A, 3B

203. I only have so much money to spend on contingency plans. I have decided to utilize a wide range of options including: hot site, redundant hard drive, and back-ups. Which of the systems above would you recommend using only back-ups as your contingency plan?
A) CPR
B) financial information system
C) performance indicator monitoring system
D) encoder
REFERENCE: OCR, 164.308
                Amatayakul, et al., p 108-112
                Johns (2002a), p 361
                Pabrai, p 231-233
COMPETENCY: Security: 3A, 3B

204.Which of the following is not a part of the business contingency plan?
   A) back-up plans
   B) testing plan
   C) audit trail
   D) responsibility for monitoring plan
REFERENCE: OCR 164.308
                  Amatayakul, et al., p 60
                  Johns (2002a) p 360-361
                  Pabrai, p 213, 231-233, 479
COMPETENCY: Security: 3A, 3B

205.One of the network connections for the laboratory information system just
   failed. The system is still operating. This is an example of a:
   A) fail-soft system
   B) failover system
   C) fail-safe system
   D) fault-tolerant system
REFERENCE: Miller & Gregory, p. 205
COMPETENCY: Security: 3A, 4B

206.There is a hardware failure for the radiology information system. The system
   automatically started using the mirrored database. This is an example of a:
   A) fail-soft system
   B) failover system
   C) fail-safe system
   D) fault-tolerant system
REFERENCE: Miller & Gregory, p. 205
COMPETENCY: Security: 3A, 4B

207.Which of the following findings from a review of the audit trail is most likely to
   concern you?
   A) John McNamara viewed Sarah McNamara's medical record
   B) The nurse on 3E viewed a patient's record who was not assigned to her
   C) The volunteer at the front desk looked up the room number of a patient
   D) A coder in the HIM Department looked at 100 charts over the past 2 days.
REFERENCE: HIMSS, p 366
COMPETENCY: Core: 1L
                  Security: 2A, 4E, 4F, 4G, 4I

208.You believe that some data has been altered in the medical record of a patient
   who is suing the hospital. Which of the following activities are being utilized as
   you determine what happened?
   A) enforcement of accountability
   B) investigation
   C) event reconstruction
   D) problem identification
REFERENCE: Miller & Gregory, p 231
COMPETENCY: Security: 4F, 4G, 4I, 6C, 6F, 6G, 7D, 7E

209. The hospital has lost several lawsuits lately based on documentation in the medical record. All of the cases have the same attorney. The HIM Director suspects that one of her staff is altering the records for the attorney. Which of the following activities would be utilized to prove this?
A) enforcement of accountability
B) investigation
C) event reconstruction
D) problem identification
REFERENCE: Miller & Gregory, p 231
COMPETENCY: Security: 4F, 4G, 4I, 6C, 6F, 6G, 7D, 7E

210. Differentiate between business continuity planning (BCP) and disaster recovery planning (DRP).
A) BCP includes keeping the hospital operational when the EHR is down and DRP is implemented in the event of a natural disaster in the area.
B) BCP includes keeping the hospital operational when the EHR is down and DRP includes restoring the database when the hardware problem is fixed.
C) DRP includes keeping the hospital operational when the EHR is down and BCP includes restoring the database when the hardware problem is fixed.
D) DRP includes keeping the hospital operational when the EHR is down and BCP is implemented in the event of a natural disaster in the area.
REFERENCE: Miller & Gregory, p. 247
COMPETENCY: Security: 3A, 3C, 3D

211. I am writing the business continuity plan and the data recovery plan. Which of the following would not be a requirement of both?
A) determining which of the many information systems are critical business functions
B) listing possible disasters that you may encounter
C) hiring a consultant to evaluate the plan
D) having the plans developed by experts who understand your critical business functions
REFERENCE: Miller & Gregory, p. 247
COMPETENCY: Security: 3A, 3C, 3D, 4G

212. Differentiate between a warm site and a hot site.
    A) The hot site has computer systems and current databases that can be up and ready quickly. A warm site is an empty room waiting on computers to be installed.
    B) The hot site has computer systems and current databases that can be up and ready quickly. A warm site is a room with computers, but needs software and database to be installed.
    C) The warm site has computer systems and current databases that can be up and ready quickly. A hot site is an empty room waiting on computers to be installed.
    D) The warm site has computer systems and current databases that can be up and ready quickly. A hot site is a room with computers, but needs software and database to be installed.
REFERENCES: Miller & Gregory, p. 256
COMPETENCY: Security: 3A, 3B, 3C

213. You suspect that a hacker has been into your system. Which of the following investigatory steps should be conducted first?
    A) notification of management
    B) disclosure determination
    C) identification of suspects
    D) detection and containment
REFERENCES: Miller & Gregory, p. 292
COMPETENCY: Core: 1R, 1S
            Security: 4G, 4I, 4J, 6G

214. The network security staff has just identified that a hacker has entered your EHR. The incident plan is being implemented. Which of the following would not be a part of the incident plan?
    A) a list of resources available to address the incident
    B) define the responsibility of each member of the incident response team
    C) list of the steps to be taken in the event of a hacker accessing your system
    D) define a code of ethics for network security staff
REFERENCES: Miller & Gregory, p. 293-394
COMPETENCY: Core: 1R, 1S
            Security: 4G, 4I, 4J, 6G

215.You are writing the purpose statement at the beginning of the incident
    response plan. This should address:
        1. gathering evidence for a criminal court case
        2. containing damage resulting from security breech
        3. ensuring that the facility operates normally as soon as possible
        4. gathering evidence for a civil court case
    A) 1 and 2 only
    B) 1 and 3 only
    C) 2 and 3 only
    D) 2 and 4 only
REFERENCE: Miller & Gregory, p. 294
COMPETENCY: Core: 1R, 1S
                  Security: 4G, 4I, 4J, 6G

216.Which of the following methods of cryptography is used by Internet
    communications such as determining insurance eligibility?
    A) SSL
    B) MIME
    C) public key infrastructure
    D) PGP
REFERENCE: Miller & Gregory, p. 187
COMPETENCY: Security: 6E, 7A

217.Which of the following methods of cryptography is used by email systems?
    A) SSL
    B) MIME
    C) public key infrastructure
    D) PGP
REFERENCE: Miller & Gregory, p. 186
COMPETENCY: Security: 6E, 7A

218.Which of the following methods of cryptography is used by mobile devices?
    A) SSL
    B) WTLS
    C) public key infrastructure
    D) PGP
REFERENCE: Miller & Gregory, p. 189
COMPETENCY: Security: 6E, 7A

219.In our encryption key management plan, the timeframe to change the key is
    addressed. The policy states that the key will be changed:
    A) every 30 days
    B) every 60 days
    C) weekly
    D) based on how frequently the key is used
REFERENCE: Miller & Gregory, p. 185
COMPETENCY: Security: 4B, 4D, 4E, 6E, 7A

220.The newspaper identified the new Senatorial candidate is an AIDS patient Our investigation has found that Daniel sent the email to the newspaper. Daniel says that he did not do it. His private key was attached to the email. This is an example of:
A) repudiation
B) stenography
C) ciphertext
D) non-repudiation
REFERENCE: Miller & Gregory, p. 185
COMPETENCY: Security: 4F, 6E, 6G

221.The administrator does not understand how a virtual private network can be secure when it uses the Internet. Your response is that it is because _____ is used.
A) encryption or encapsulation
B) a separate T1 line
C) a strong firewall
D) a intrusion detection system
REFERENCE: Miller & Gregory, p. 93
COMPETENCY: Security: 2C, 4G, 7A

222.I want to implement the most secure type of firewall. Which of the following types of firewalls would I choose?
A) packet-filtering
B) application-level gateway
C) circuit-level gateway
D) any of the above since they all maintain essentially the same level of security
REFERENCE: Miller & Gregory, p. 90
COMPETENCY: Security: 4G, 6F, 7A

223.I just installed an active intrusion detection system. One of my co-workers wanted to know why I chose this type of intrusion detection system. My response is that it:
A) alerts the user to potential problems
B) automatically addresses suspected breaches
C) identifies breeches based on past experiences
D) bases alarms on patterns
REFERENCES: Miller & Gregory, p 95
COMPETENCY: Security: 7A, 7B, 7E

224. The intrusion detection system that we have installed identified a breech in security like we had last week, but missed a type of breech that had never happened before. I must be using what type of system:
A) behavior based
B) active
C) passive
D) knowledge based
REFERENCES: Miller & Gregory, p 96
COMPETENCY: Security: 7A, 7B, 7E

225. My administrator says that we need to encrypt faxed data because of HIPAA security rules. My CSO says that it is not necessary. Who is right?
A) the administrator, since this is a HIPAA security requirement
B) the CSO, since faxes are not covered under the HIPAA security rule
C) neither are right, since HIPAA requires using secure phone lines
D) both are right and wrong, since PHI faxes must be encrypted, but other fax transmissions do not
REFERENCES: HIMSS, p 287
COMPETENCY: Security: 7A, 9B, 10A, 10B

226. Victoria just identified a security breech. Which of the following should she do FIRST?
A) contact the administrator
B) contact the Chief Security Officer
C) contact her supervisor
D) call the incident reporting hotline
REFERENCES: Walsh, p 16
COMPETENCY: Security: 2A, 2B, 2C, 4J

227. A security incident has been reported by the ER Director. The incident turned out to be a false alarm. Which of the following applies?
A) do not document since the incident was not confirmed
B) document the incident as it was officially reported
C) delete the incident report from the official log
D) none of the above
REFERENCES: Walsh, p 16
COMPETENCY: Security: 2A, 2B, 2C, 4J

228. A computer that was being used to store PHI is being replaced by a faster computer. The current computer is being moved to the hospital's medical library to replace an outdated computer. Which of the following should take place prior to the transfer?
A) empty the recycle bin
B) format the hard drive
C) format the hard drive a minimum of three times
D) delete the PHI
REFERENCES: Walsh, p 17
COMPETENCY: Security: 5A, 6B

229. Sarah and Daphne are talking about the new computer system. Sarah says that the use of a PIN and password means that it has two-factor authentication. Respond to this statement.
A) Sarah made an astute observation
B) Sarah is wrong, since both of password and PIN are based on "what you know"
C) Sarah is wrong, since authentication deals with digital signatures
D) Sarah is right, since it takes two entries to access the system
REFERENCES: Walsh, p 18
COMPETENCY: Security: 6A, 6C

230. Human Resources is severely backlogged and new staff cannot be hired. The administrator has received so many complaints that he called the Director. He found that a complete background check was being done on every person hired. The administrator's response should be:
A) try to streamline the process
B) outsource the background checks
C) not all of the job categories require complete background check
D) do background check on random sample
REFERENCES: HIMSS, p 37
COMPETENCY: Security: 4E, 4G

231. I have created a log of all personal computers (pcs) in the organization. This log records: the purchase date, the location of pc and any transfers and/or disposal of pcs. This log:
A) can be manual
B) can be electronic
C) should be part of the risk management plan
D) all of the above
REFERENCES: HIMSS, p 47
COMPETENCY: Security: 4G, 4H, 5A

232. Which of the following set(s) is an appropriate use of the emergency access procedure?
A) A patient is crashing. The attending physician is not in the hospital, so a physician who is available helps the patient.
B) One of the nurses is at lunch. The nurse covering for her needs patient information.
C) The coder who usually codes the emergency room charts is out sick and the charts are left on a desk in the ER admitting area.
D) A and B
REFERENCES: HIMSS, p 48
COMPETENCY: Security: 2A, 2B, 2C, 2D, 2E, 4E, 6D

233. My hospital has a computer in the lobby that allows visitors to look up the location of physician offices, the lab, the radiology department and other locations in the hospital. Which of the following statements is true?
A) This is a violation of HIPAA.
B) This is acceptable as long as the computer cannot access PHI.
C) This would be a great place to give access to the patient directory, too.
D) None of the above is acceptable.
REFERENCES: HIMSS, p 46
COMPETENCY: Security: 5C

234. The transcriptionists are getting new computers. The dietary staff will receive their old computers. Prior to the move, what must be done?
A) complete the re-install of all software
B) cancel the move, since you must destroy pcs, not transfer them
C) remove any PHI that may exist
D) destroy the hard drive
REFERENCES: HIMSS, p 47
COMPETENCY: Security: 5A, 6B

235. Appropriate methods of preparing a hard drive for reuse includes all of the following EXCEPT:
A) reformatting
B) write over existing PHI
C) degaussing
D) deleting PHI
REFERENCES: HIMSS, p 47
COMPETENCY: Security: 5A, 6B

236. I recently completed an assessment of our computer security. All of the changes required have been completed. Which of the following should I do now?
A) retain the executive summary and destroy the rest
B) retain detailed information for 6 years
C) trash the notes since the implementation has been completed
D) destroy the information after one year
REFERENCES: HIMSS, p 19
COMPETENCY: Security: 2A, 2B, 4A, 4B, 4G

237. My organization was just flagged for audit since we were reported for a security violation. I am concerned since the violation was related to a standard that was listed first, so it is therefore the most important standard. This fear is:
A) unfounded since none is more important
B) valid since the standards are listed in order of importance
C) understandable since it is coming from my nervousness over the audit
D) none of the above
REFERENCES: HIMSS, p 24
COMPETENCY: Security: 4G, 9B

238. In preparing to implement the HIPAA security rule, I am reviewing all of the following except:
A) characteristics of the organization such as the size of the facility
B) costs of implementation
C) current policies
D) infrastructure
REFERENCES: HIMSS, p 17
COMPETENCY: Core: 1G
                   Security: 2A, 2B, 4A, 4B, 4G

239. We just determined that the addressable encryption standards are not appropriate to our organization. We should:
    1. document our reasons
    2. implement an equivalent alternative
    3. notify DHHS
    4. revise policies and procedures so encryption is not mentioned
A) 1 and 2 only
B) 1 and 3 only
C) 2 and 3 only
D) 3 and 4 only
REFERENCES: HIMSS, p 18
COMPETENCY: Security: 2A, 2B, 2E, 4A, 7A

240. Evaluate this statement: My facility is located in Illinois but we must still have a plan to address hurricanes.
A) True. This is mandated by the HIPAA security rule.
B) This is not true. We only must address risks to our facility.
C) This is not a mandate, but we still should do it.
D) This is not required, but is addressable.
REFERENCES: HIMSS, p 33
COMPETENCY: Core: 1G
                   Security: 2A, 2B, 4B

241. The OSI reference model is a security standard that is specific to healthcare.
A) True.
B) False. It is used in healthcare and business.
C) False. It is used in healthcare and the government.
D) False. It is a general model used to organize standards.
REFERENCES: HIMSS, p 65
COMPETENCY: Security: 4G

242. The OSI reference model has how many levels?
A) 7
B) 10
C) 8
D) 6
REFERENCES: HIMSS, p 64
COMPETENCY: Security: 4G

243. We have just identified that an employee looked up his own medical record. Which of the following actions should be taken?
   A) notify his or her supervisor since this is a minor incident and therefore not subject to the incident response procedure
   B) follow incident response procedure
   C) terminate the employee on the spot
   D) notify OCR
REFERENCES: HIMSS, p 40
COMPETENCY: Core: 1Q, 1R
                       Security: 2A, 2C, 2D, 2E, 4E, 4G

244. The administrator wants to know why I feel the need to conduct a test of our contingency plan. What should I tell him? Conducting the test
                   1. checks to see if plan works
                   2. is required by HIPAA
                   3. trains staff so they are ready to implement
                   4. reduces the facilities liability
   A) 1 and 2 only
   B) 1 and 3 only
   C) 2 and 3 only
   D) 1 and 4 only
REFERENCES: HIMSS, p 42
COMPETENCY: Security: 2A, 2D, 2E, 4G

245. I have just completed a data criticality plan. So what?
   A) The findings can be used to determine risks.
   B) I have met HIPAA security requirements and will retain the findings for 6 years.
   C) I can assign priorities to systems and determine how I will protect them.
   D) This lets me know when a violation is critical.
REFERENCES: HIMSS, p 42
COMPETENCY: Core: 1J
                       Security: 3B

246.   The network security plan that I just developed addresses the Internet, but not leased lines.   This is
   A) a violation of the HIPAA security rule since both are required to be secured
   B) a violation of the HIPAA security rule since all means of network communication must be addressed
   C) appropriate since this is the most insecure network method
   D) appropriate since the Internet is a public network
REFERENCES: HIMSS, p 50
COMPETENCY: Security: 4B, 4G, 7A, 10B

247. Which of the following statements are true?
    1. ANSI is a governmental agency
    2. ANSI is a nonprofit organization
    3. ANSI allows interested parties to participate in standard development
    4. Compliance with ANSI standards is mandatory to U.S. businesses
  A) 1 and 3
  B) 2 and 3
  C) 2 and 4
  D) 3 and 4
REFERENCES: HIMSS, p 64
COMPETENCY: Security: 4G, 9D, 9E

248. The security standards serve two roles. They
    1. ensure confidentiality of PHI
    2. eliminate possibility of breech
    3. ensure that all covered entities use the same security methods
    4. ensure integrity of PHI
  A) 1 and 2
  B) 1 and 4
  C) 2 and 3
  D) 2 and 4
REFERENCES: HIMSS, p 65
COMPETENCY: Security: 4G, 10A, 10F

249. I am developing a plan to protect PHI from message sequencing. This includes all of the following except:
  A) replay of messages
  B) preplay of messages
  C) delay of messages
  D) deletion of messages
REFERENCES: HIMSS, p 66
COMPETENCY: Security: 4G, 7A

250. The administrator is concerned that employees will deny that they accessed PHI when questioned. He asks me how this can be solved. I tell him that repudiation is the key. Our option(s) is (are):
  A) digital signature
  B) encryption
  C) audit trail
  D) both A and B
REFERENCES: HIMSS, p 67
COMPETENCY: Security: 2D, 4G, 6C, 6E

251. I am concerned about ways that people can gain access to our system so I conduct a test to look for weaknesses. I am conducting a:
A) virus scan
B) weakness assessment
C) vulnerability assessment
D) risk assessment
REFERENCE: HIMSS, p 189
COMPETENCY: Core: 1J
                      Security: 3B

252. Margo has just gone through some computer training. One of the issues covered was how to prevent viruses from being spread. Actions that she, a user, should take include all of the following EXCEPT:
A) do not email a file to anyone else in the organization if a virus has been identified
B) do not download shareware on her computer
C) do not share diskettes between computers
D) update the virus protection on at least a daily basis
REFERENCE: HIMSS, p 137
COMPETENCY: Security: 2C, 4E, 4G, 7E

253. A security standard which prevents unauthorized users from reading data, ensures bytes from being changed because of a check digit and works well in a TCP environment. This standard is:
A) public key
B) SSL
C) RSA
D) DEA
REFERENCE: HIMSS, p 73
COMPETENCY: Security: 7A, 7E

254. Which of the following activities would most likely be reported as an incident?
A) an employee in the business office forgot her password
B) HIM department looking up patient record at 1:00 a.m.
C) ten consecutive unsuccessful attempts to log into the system
D) printing of a PHI report in risk management department
REFERENCE: HIMSS, p 369
COMPETENCY: Core: 1Q, 1R
                      Security: 2A, 2B, 2D, 2E, 4E, 4G

Answer Key for Security Questions (CHS)

1.   A   This assumes that the patient is not authorizing the request. If the patient authorized the release of information, then the minimum necessary rule does not apply.

2.   A

3.   D

4.   B

5.   B

6.   B

7.   B   The issue here is that the individual is talking about the patient in a public area. It is not the fact that the monitor is in a public areas since the screen faces away from the public.

8.   B

9.   D

10.   B

11.   D

12.   D

13.   D

14.   D

15.   A

16.   D

17.   D

18.   A

19.   B

20.   B

21.   D

Answer Key for Security Questions (CHS)

22.	B
23.	A
24.	C
25.	D
26.	D
27.	A
28.	A
29.	A
30.	B
31.	D
32.	C
33.	D
34.	C
35.	C
36.	C
37.	A
38.	B
39.	C
40.	A
41.	B
42.	D
43.	B

44.   D

45.   B

46.   D

47.   A

48.   D

49.   D The vendor can include system back-up utilities in the system, include activity reports as a standard report and provide the ability to delete passwords, but they cannot be responsible for awareness training.

50.   D

51.   B

52.   C

53.   A

54.   D

55.   D

56.   D

57.   A

58.   C

59.   A

60.   C

61.   C

62.   B

63.   D

64.   D

65.   D

Answer Key for Security Questions (CHS)

66.   B

67.   A

68.   B

69.   A

70.   C

71.   A

72.   D

73.   D

74.   C

75.   B

76.   D

77.   A

78.   C

79.   A

80.   A

81.   A

82.   B

83.   A

84.   B

85.   B

86.   A

87.   D

88.   C

89.   D

90.   C

91.   A

92.   C

93.   B

94.   C

95.   C

96.   C

97.   C

98.   D

99.   B

100. C

101. D

102. A   A contingency plan is based on the information gathered during a risk analysis and assessment.

103. D   Natural disasters, equipment failure, and human error are usually unintentional threats to security Data theft is intentional.

104. B   Because one of the greatest threats to security is the organizations employees, good personnel security must be implemented.

105. C   Systematic testing of software prior to implementing is a procedure included in technical security measures.

106. A

107. B

108. D   Would not normally expect the patient number or middle initial to be different across the process of activity of the record. These inconsistencies would be investigated to see why the difference exists.

109. C   The other items may also be documented

110. B

111. A

112. D

113. A

114. D

115. B

116. C

117. D

118. B Technical safeguards are not infallible. You could still have incidents such as an employee altering data.

119. A

120. A

121. D

122. C

123. A

124. D

125. B

126. D

127. C

128. B

129. D

Answer Key for Security Questions (CHS)

130. B

131. A

132. A

133. D

134. C

135. C

136. D

137. A

138. B

139. C

140. C

141. A

142. B

143. A

144. C

145. B

146. D

147. D

148. A

149. D

150. A

151. A

152. D

Answer Key for Security Questions (CHS)

153. B

154. D

155. B

156. C

157. C

158. A

159. B

160. A

161. C

162. D

163. B

164. D

165. A

166. C

167. A

168. A

169. C

170. A

171. D

172. B

173. B

174. C

175. C

176. A

177. A

178. A

179. D

180. B

181. D

182. B

183. B

184. A

185. D

186. C

187. D

188. D

189. A

190. D

191. D

192. D

193. D

194. C

195. C

196. A

197. A

198. B

199. B

200. D

201. D

202. A

203. D

204. C

205. D

206. B

207. A

208. C

209. B

210. B

211. C   The organization may benefit from the use of consultants to
          evaluate/develop the plan, but it is not a requirement.

212. B

213. D

214. D

215. C

216. A

217. B

218. B

219. D

220. D

Answer Key for Security Questions (CHS)

221. A

222. B

223. B

224. D

225. B

226. D

227. B

228. C

229. B

230. C

231. D

232. A

233. B

234. C

235. D

236. B

237. B

238. C

239. A

240. B

241. D

242. A

243. B

Answer Key for Security Questions (CHS)

244. B

245. C

246. B

247. B

248. B

249. D

250. D

251. C

252. D While virus software should be updated at least daily, it is not typically done by the user.

253. B

254. C

REFERENCES FOR SECURITY QUESTIONS

Abdelhak, M., Grostick, S., Hanken, M., & Jacobs E. (Eds.) (2001). *Health information: Management of a strategic resource*. Philadelphia: W.B. Saunders Company.

Abraham, P. R. (2002). HIPAA changes home health, hospice documentation practices. *Journal of AHIMA, 73*(2), 39-40.

AHIMA (2001). Help wanted: Privacy officer. *Journal of AHIMA, 72*(6), 37-39.

Amatayakul, M. (2000). Getting ready for HIPAA privacy rules. *Journal of AHIMA, 71*(4), 34-36.

Amatayakul, M. (2001a). HIPAA on the job series: Five steps to reading the HIPAA Rules. *Journal of AHIMA,* 72(8), 16A-C.

Amatayakul, M. (2001b). HIPAA on the job series: Managing individual rights requirements under HIPAA privacy. *Journal of AHIMA,* 72(6), 16A-D.

Amatayakul, M. (2001c). HIPAA on the Job: Forms and documentation for HIPAA privacy – a closer look. *Journal of AHIMA, 72*(5), 16A-D.

Amatayakul, M. (2002a). HIPAA on the job: A reasonable approach to physical security. *Journal of AHIMA, 73*(4), 16A-C.

Amatayakul, M. (2002b). Practice brief: Implementing the minimum necessary standard. *Journal of AHIMA, 73*(9), 96A-F.

Amatayakul, M. (2002c). The first line of defense against privacy complaints. *Journal of AHIMA, 73*(9), 24A-C.

Amatayakul, M. (2002d). HIPAA on the Job: United under HIPAA: A comparison of arrangements and agreements. *Journal of AHIMA, 73*(8), 24A-D.

Amatayakul, M. (2002e). Make your telecommuting program HIPAA compliant. *Journal of AHIMA, 73*(2), 16A-C.

Amatayakul, M., et al. (2004) *Handbook for HIPAA Security Implementation.* AMA Press.

Amatayakul, M., & Johns, M. L. (2002). HIPAA on the job series: Compliance in the crosshairs: Targeting your training. *Journal of AHIMA.* 73(10), 16A-F.

Amatayakul, M., & Walsh, T. (2001). HIPAA on the job series: Selecting strong passwords. *Journal of AHIMA, 72*(9), 16A-D.

REFERENCES FOR SECURITY QUESTIONS

Apple, G. J., & Brandt, M. D. (2001). Ready, set, assess: An action plan for conducting a HIPAA privacy risk assessment. *Journal of AHIMA, 72*(6), 26-32.

Beaver, K. (2003). Information security issues that healthcare management must understand. *Journal of Healthcare Information Management, 17*(1), 46-49.

Brandt, M. (2001). HIPAA security standards: Working with your information technology vendors. *AHIMA Convention Proceedings*. Retrieved January 16, 2003 from http://www.ahima.org.

Callahan-Dennis, J. (2000). Privacy and confidentiality of health information. San Francisco: Jossey-Bass.

Callahan-Dennis, J. (2001a) Leading the HIPAA privacy risk assessment. *AHIMA Convention Proceedings.* Retrieved January 16, 2003, from http://www.ahima.org.

Callahan-Dennis, J. (2001b). The new privacy officer's game plan. *Journal of AHIMA, 72(2)*, 33-37.

Cassidy, B. S. (2000). HIPAA on the job: Understanding chain of trust and business partner agreements. *Journal of AHIMA, 71*(9), 16A-C.

Cassidy, B. S. (2001). HIPAA on the job: The next challenge: Employee training on privacy, security. *Journal of AHIMA, 72*(1), 16A-C.

Choy, A., Pritts, J., & Goldman, J. (2002). E-health: What's outside the privacy rule's jurisdiction? *Journal of AHIMA, 73*(5), 34-39.

Cisco Systems (n.d.a). Data sheet: *Cisco IOS Public-Key Infrastructure: Deployment Benefits and Features*. Retrieved January 14, 2004, from http://www.cisco.com/warp/public/cc/pd/iosw/prodlit/pkids_ds.htm.

Cisco Systems (n.d.b) Security technologies. Internetworking Technology Handbook. Retrieved January 14, 2004, from http://www.cisco.com/univercd/cc/td/doc/cisintwek/ito(doc/security.htm

Comer, D. E. (1999). *Computer networks and Internets* (2nd Ed). Prentice Hall: New Jersey

Davis, J. B. (2003). *HIPAA Compliance manual: A comprehensive guide to the administrative simplification provisions for health care professionals*. Practice Management Information Corporation: Los Angeles, CA

REFERENCES FOR SECURITY QUESTIONS

Dougherty, M. (2001). Practice brief: Accounting and tracking disclosure of protected health information. *Journal of AHIMA,* 72(10), 72E-H.

Dougherty, M. (2002). It's time to finalize your privacy policies. *Journal of AHIMA 73*(10), 61-64.

Fuller, S. (1999). Implementing HIPAA security standards – are you ready? *Journal of AHIMA,* 70(9), 38-44.

Hartley, C. P., & Jones, III, E. D. (2004). *HIPAA plain & simple: A compliance guide for health care professionals.* AMA Press: Chicago, IL.

Hjort, B. (2001). AHIMA practice brief: A HIPAA privacy checklist. *Journal of AHIMA 72*(6), 64A-C.

Hjort, B. (2002). Privacy and security training. *Journal of AHIMA,* 73(4), 60A-G.
Hughes, G. (2001a). Managing exceptions to HIPAA's patient access rule. *Journal of AHIMA,* 72(9), 90-92.

HIMSS (2003). HIMSS CPRI Toolkit. Retrieved on October 5, 2004 from http://www.himss.org/asp/cpritoolkit_homepage.asp

Hughes, G. (2001b). AHIMA practice brief: Consent for the use or disclosure of individually identifiable health information. Journal of AHIMA, 72(5), 64E – F.

Hughes, G. (2002a). AHIMA practice brief: Understanding the minimum necessary standard. *Journal of AHIMA 73*(1), 56A-B.

Hughes, G. (2002b). AHIMA practice brief: Notice of information practice (updated November, 2002). Retrieved February 1, 2003, from http://www.ahima.org

Hughes, G. (2002c). AHIMA practice brief: Laws and regulations governing the disclosure of health information (Updated November, 2002). Retrieved February 1, 2003, from http://www.ahima.org

Hughes, G. (2002d). AHIMA practice brief: Understanding the privacy rule amendments *Journal of AHIMA 73*(10), 64-66.

Hughes, G. (2002e). Creating Privacy Rule Implementation Efficiency. *Journal of AHIMA,* 73(9), 97-99.

Hughes, G. (2002f). AHIMA practice brief: Preemption of the HIPAA privacy rule. *Journal of AHIMA,* 73(2), 56A-C.

REFERENCES FOR SECURITY QUESTIONS

Johns, M. L. (2002a). *Information Management for Health Professions.* Albany, NY: Delmar Publishing.

Johns, M. L. (2002b). *Health information technology: An applied approach* Chicago, IL: American Health Information Management Association.

Klein, J. (2001). Conducting a HIPAA security risk assessment. *AHIMA Convention Proceedings.* Retrieved July 31, 2002 from http://www.ahima.org.

LaTour, K. M., & Eichenwald, S. (2002). *Health information management: Concepts principles, and practice.* Chicago, IL: American Health Information Management Association.

Miller, Lawrence and Gregory, Peter. *CISSP for Dummies.* (2004). Wiley Publishing, Inc.: New York

Nichols, R. K., & Lekkas, P. C. (2002). *Wireless security: Models, threats, and solutions*. McGraw-Hill: New York.

Nicholson, R. (2002). The dilemma of psychotherapy notes and HIPAA. *Journal of AHIMA 73*(2), 38-39.

OCR
U.S. Department of Health and Human Services Office for Civil Rights (2003) *Standards for Privacy of Individually Identifiable Health Information Security Standards for the Protection of Electronic Protected Health Information General Administrative Requirements Including, Civil Money Penalties: Procedures for Investigations, Imposition of Penalties, and Hearings Regulation Text* (Unofficial Version) (45 CFR Parts 160 and 164) December 28, 2000 as amended: May 31, 2002, August 14, 2002, February 20, 2003, and April 17, 2003. Retrieved January 15, 2004, from http://www.hhs.gov/ocr/combinedregtext.pdf

Pabrai, Uday. (2003). *Getting Started with HIPAA.* Boston, MA: Premier Press

Pelletier, A., Bresee, S. A., & Hill, J. R. (2003). Strategies for complying with the HIPAA security rule. *Journal of Healthcare Information Management, 17*(3), 49-53.

Pozgar, G. D. (1999). *Legal aspects of healthcare administration (7th Ed.).* Gaithersburg, MD: Aspen Publications.

Proctor, P. E., Davis, N., & Rosenblum, B. (2003). Rightsizing HIPAA security compliance for smaller organizations. *Journal of Healthcare Information Management, 17*(3). 34-40.

REFERENCES FOR SECURITY QUESTIONS

Rada, R. (2003). *Health information security: HIPAA.*
Health Information Management Systems Society: Chicago, IL.

Roach, M. (2001). HIPAA compliance questions for business partner agreements.
Journal of AHIMA, 72(2), 45-51.

Roach, Jr., W. (1998). *Medical records and the law* (3rd edition). Boston, MA:
Jones and Bartlett Publishers.

Rhodes, H. (2001). Marketing privacy: HIPAA's new sales pitch. *AHIMA convention
proceedings.* Retrieved January 16, 2003 from http://www.ahima.org.

Rode, D. (2001). Final privacy rule puts health information in national spotlight.
Journal of AHIMA, 72(2), p 32A-C.

Rode, D. (2002). Quest for patient's trust only just begun.
Journal of AHIMA 73(10), p 16, 18.

Ruano, M. (2003). Moving toward a unified information security program.
Journal of   AHIMA, 74(1), 66, 68.

Stallings, W. (2000). *Data & Computer Communication* (6th Ed). Prentice Hall:
New Jersey.

Sullivan, T. (2002). Mind your business associate access: Six steps.
Journal of AHIMA, 73(9), 92, 94, 96.

U.S. Department of Civil Rights (2002c). *Minimum Necessary.*
Retrieved January 16 2003 from
http://www.hhs.gov/ocr/hipaa/guidelines/minimumnecessary.pdf

U. S. Department of Health and Human Services (2003) HHS Fact Sheet:
Protecting The Privacy Of Patients' Health Information (April 14, 2003)
Retrieved January 15, 2004, from
http://www.hhs.gov/news/facts/privacy.html

Wagner, L. (2002). Uniting security forces against risk.
Journal of AHIMA, 73(6), 39-42.

Walsh, T. (2004). Best practices for compliance with the final security rule.
Journal of Healthcare Information Management 17(3).